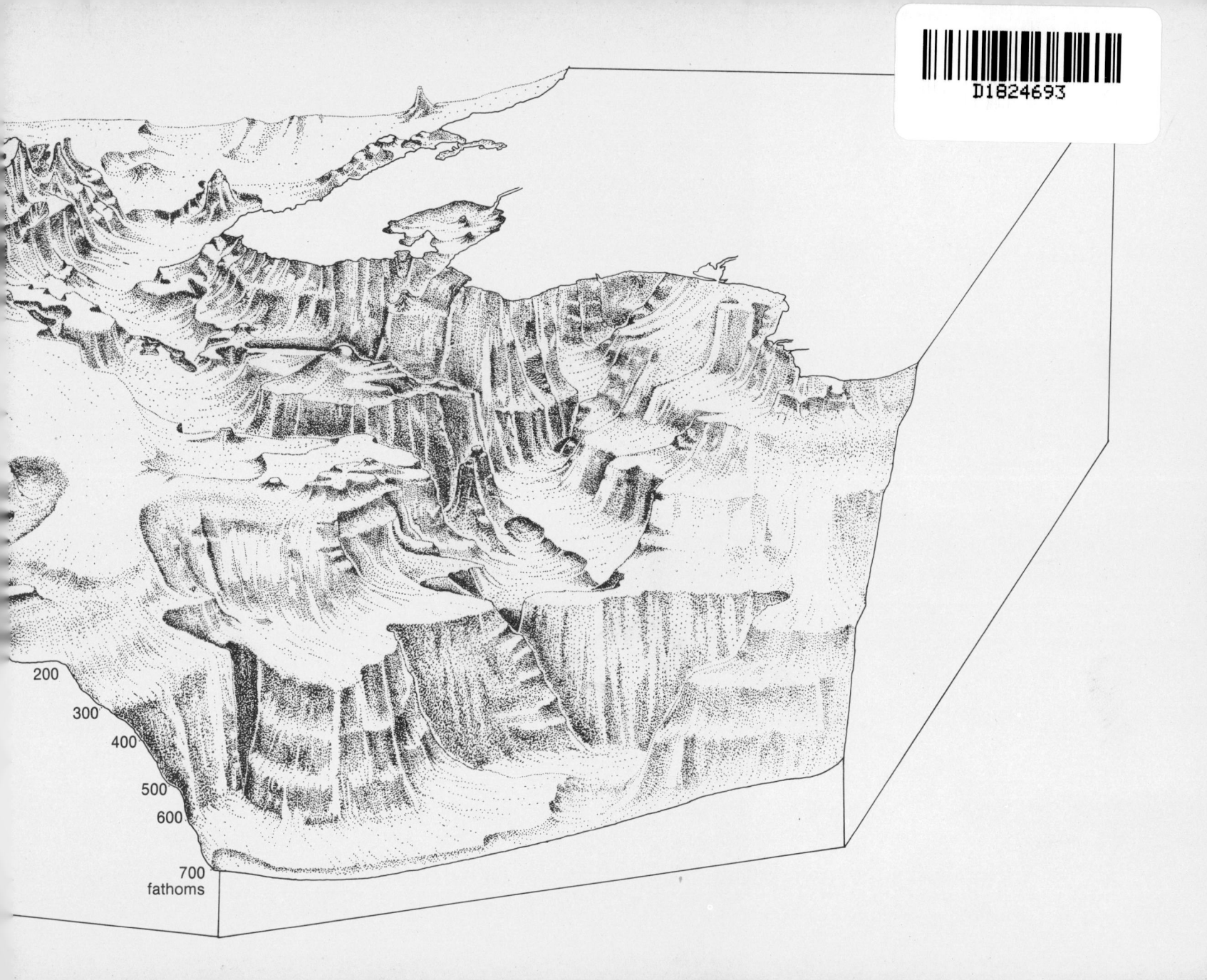

200
300
400
500
600
700
fathoms

COOK'S WILD STRAIT

THE INTERISLAND STORY

COOK'S WILD STRAIT

THE INTERISLAND STORY

David MacINTYRE and Michael FIELD with Christine QUINN

REED

First published 1983

A.H. & A.W. REED LTD
68-74 Kingsford-Smith Street, Wellington 3
also
16-18 Beresford Street, Auckland
85 Thackeray Street, Christchurch 2

ISBN 0 589 01449 8

Typeset by Computype Services Ltd, Wellington
Printed by Kyodo-Shing Loong Printing Industries
    Pte, Ltd., Singapore.

Contents

Acknowledgements

The authors would like to acknowledge the assistance and co-operation they received from the following during the preparation of this book: Alexander Turnbull Library, Dagmar Andersen, Lynne Ashenden, Peter Avery, Brian Barraclough, Geoff and Nyra Bentley, John Brown, Peter Carr, Lawrie Collins, Chris Cooney, Bill Coulter, D.M. Furness, Joe Henry, Peter Holthouse, Gail Jordan, John Knox, David Lackey, Kathy Lewis, Tim Lovell-Smith, Brian Lundy, John Mansell, Peter Maxwell, Alan McIntyre, Nigel Mouat, National Archives, New Zealand Oceanographic Institute, Ron Palmer, Graeme Peebles, Anne Robertson, Gene Saunders, Peter Taylor, Gilda Tompkins, I. McL. Wards and the Wellington Public Library.

Chapter I

Canyons and cables – the modern Cook Strait

Let us make certain that New Zealand ... is not divided by a strip of water ...

KUPE killed a great sea creature there, Abel Tasman suspected it existed but never found it and when Captain James Cook discovered the strait which today carries his name he underestimated its dangers.

Cook Strait has always provided challenges to those who have encountered it. Often it was the scene of lost battles, and even today modern technology has been unable to tame the strait — the strip of wild water has taken the life of many a sailor and traveller.

In anger, Cook Strait is ugly. The water is grey and wild, flecked by foam driven by a mean wind from the south, and drizzle and rain hides the islands from view while mighty waves crash against each other. But it can also be a strait of rare beauty. Few seascapes can match that offered on a fine, crisp and still winter's day, looking out from the North Island and over the strait towards mighty Tapuaenuku — "foot-step of the rainbow god" — the highest peak in the jagged Kaikoura mountains of the South Island.

Although Wellington, New Zealand's first planned town, was planted on the shore of the strait, Cook Strait has been an impediment to the development of New Zealand as a single nation. Alan Mulgan, in the centennial book on Wellington, *The City of the Strait*, wondered if nature had been in a malicious mood in creating the strait:

Politically [Cook Strait] might be described as a major disaster in New Zealand's history, for it made two islands out of one, and the separation by such a formidable waterway gave a clearer definition to the long-drawn-out battle of North versus South ...

... the Wellington dweller grows to appreciate Cook Strait or to accept it more or less cheerfully as a characteristic background to his high-pitched and wind-cleansed home. It may be unfriendly, but it is strong and beautiful, and it carries a large part of his fortune. Its strength may slow down the powerful steamer express that drives southward nightly to Lyttelton; its beauty is most penetrating on still clear days in spring, autumn or winter, when its rhythm tumbles lazily in a smother of foam on the rocks at Island Bay, and beyond the wide floor of deep blue are seen the snows of the Kaikouras ...

In simple terms Cook Strait is a stretch of water between the North and South Islands, linking the Tasman Sea in the west and the Pacific Ocean in the east. The western approaches are made up of a massive bay with Cape Egmont in the north and Farewell Spit 150 kilometres to the south. Into the two arms of the bay are funnelled the prevailing westerly "roaring forties" winds and the relentless Tasman Sea swell, which are concentrated at the strait's narrowest point — the 19 kilometres between Cape Terawhiti on the North Island and Perano Head (or Wellington Head as it once was) on Arapawa Island at the tip of the South Island.

Geologically speaking, Cook Strait is little

Cook Strait on its best behaviour. The ferry *Arahanga* sails towards Wellington against the awesome backdrop of the Kaikoura Ranges. The highest peak is Mount Tapuaenuku, which rises to 2,885 metres. *Ian Mackley, "Evening Post"*

more than a babe in arms. Three to five million years ago it was just an indentation in the side of a large island which roughly resembled the modern South Island. In what is today the central North Island there was a massive strait, the so-called "Manawatu Strait".

In the ebb and flow of ice-ages large parts of New Zealand emerged from the sea only to be flooded again. At one stage Cook Strait was flooded. Rapid currents passing through quickly carved a deep channel, making Cook Strait a rather more enduring feature than the Manawatu Strait (the latter eventually emerged from the sea and remained high and dry). In the last big ice-age, some 10,000 years ago, sea levels dropped markedly, leaving Cook Strait as a fiord. Although it was later flooded again, land bridges have occasionally formed since in the western approaches

to the strait. One such bridge gave South Island moas the chance to go north, starting a migration trend that continues to this day with people.

Another factor in the shaping of the area has been the movements of various blocks of countryside along fault lines. The major fault in the Cook Strait, the Wairau Fault, put the bend into an otherwise straight strait. It is also moving the Marlborough Sounds toward the North Island at the rate of 6.3 millimetres per year . . . so we will need the rail ferries for at least another three million years, unless some cataclysmic event speeds up the process.

One such event was a series of earthquakes in January 1855, the biggest of which was centred in Cook Strait and is estimated today to have been around magnitude 8 on the Richter Scale. German geologist Ferdinand von Hochstetter was in Wellington for the big shake:

A sea wave caused by it rolled from Cook Strait into Wellington Harbour. Mukamuka Point near Wellington was uplifted nine feet, while the uplift in the town itself reached only two feet and on the opposite side of Cook Strait, at the mouth of Wairau River, submergence took place. In the Awatere Valley the ground suffered powerful rents and fissures, which could be followed for a distance of 40 miles and still gaped locally several feet wide in the year 1858. Near Cape Campbell landslides occurred laying bare the white rocks so that coasting vessels reported it to be freshly fallen snow, and in Cook Strait Captain Kennedy, two days after the earthquake, saw the surface of the sea covered with dead fish.

All observed phenomena point to an epicentre out in Cook Strait, and it is an opinion generally circulated by the colonists that a submarine volcano is situated here, having a connection with these outbreaks of earthquakes. In fact, the soundings carried out by English naval officers show that in front of the entrance of Wellington harbour. . .a deep crater-like hole is found on the sea bot-

Gold, albeit in rather small quantities, has been discovered on both sides of Cook Strait. A minor gold rush saw the town of Wakamarina near Picton rise rapidly and fall just as quickly. These remains of machinery near Oteranga Bay, west of Wellington, are all that remains of another gold rush which led to the working of the Cape Terawhiti region in 1883. However, the small amount of gold taken from the quartz rock was uneconomic to mine and the enterprise soon died. *F.G. Fitzgerald, Alexander Turnbull Library*

tom, over which the sea restlessly heaves up and down.

Marlborough settler Frederick William Trolove recorded the earthquakes in his diary. His entry for 21 January 1855 reads:

About half past nine or 10 p.m. a very severe shock of earthquake took place. So sudden was it that in running out of the house we had great difficulty in keeping our balance; we staggered like drunken men.

Four days later Trolove wrote:

We have had a fearful night indeed, and we had three shocks heavier than any before, while during the whole night until day break we have been in — I might almost say — perpetual motion.

Five people died in the 1855 earthquakes — a low toll when one considers what the quake did to the landscape. Had it occurred 100 years later the toll would have been very high. The uplifting that Hochstetter noted, some two metres in the harbour area, was the making of Wellington as it exposed a platform along the western edge of the harbour.

Colonel Charles Emilius Gold made this sketch of a landslip near Wellington which was caused by the 1855 earthquake. *Alexander Turnbull Library*

is a mighty canyon, carved out by powerful currents which sweep through the strait. The Cook Strait Canyon, with its extremely steep, almost sheer, walls, reaches depths of up to 365 metres. An arm of the big Hikurangi Trench which runs down the eastern side of New Zealand, the Cook Strait Canyon features rough and rugged terrain. Oddly, some sharp, rocky outcrops reach from the depths to the surface, or almost. Fishermans Rock in mid-strait off the northern end of Arapawa Island is an example. Although wave patterns had been observed over the top of the rock several metres below the surface, it wasn't until the 1950s that the survey ship HMNZS *Lachlan* actually proved its existence. In the same series of surveys *Lachlan* eliminated from the maps "Canterbury Rock", which was found not to exist at all. Rocky outcrops, such as The Brothers, and deep holes off the South Island shore, produce dangerous eddies and violent sea conditions.

The Cook Strait Canyon is home to a variety of marine life, including itinerant blue, sperm and right whales and the largest-known invertebrate animal, the giant squid. They are occasionally swept ashore, causing problems for local residents. Old newspapers report one squid with 15-metre-long tentacles being swept up alive on Lyall Bay in the 1880s. In the 1920s a large blue whale came up on the same beach and could be smelled for kilometres.

The tides of the Tasman and the Pacific vary in both time and height, producing in Cook Strait what oceanographers call "large slopes in the sea surface". Tidal currents in the strait run up to eight knots westward and

Upon this could be built a much more reliable road link than that which had existed previously. The Kilbirnie area, first lifted out of the sea to link Miramar with the mainland some 900 years before in an earthquake spoken of in Maori legends, rose further out of the sea. The 1855 earthquake also put paid to an interesting idea for the city. A swampy area of land at the northern end of Newtown was designated as a shipping basin to be connected to Port Nicholson by canal. The earthquake cut out any such possibility, so instead of a shipping basin Wellington now has the Basin Reserve sports ground, and instead of a canal there are the broad Kent and Cambridge Terraces.

Von Hochstetter was wrong about an undersea volcano in Cook Strait. Instead there

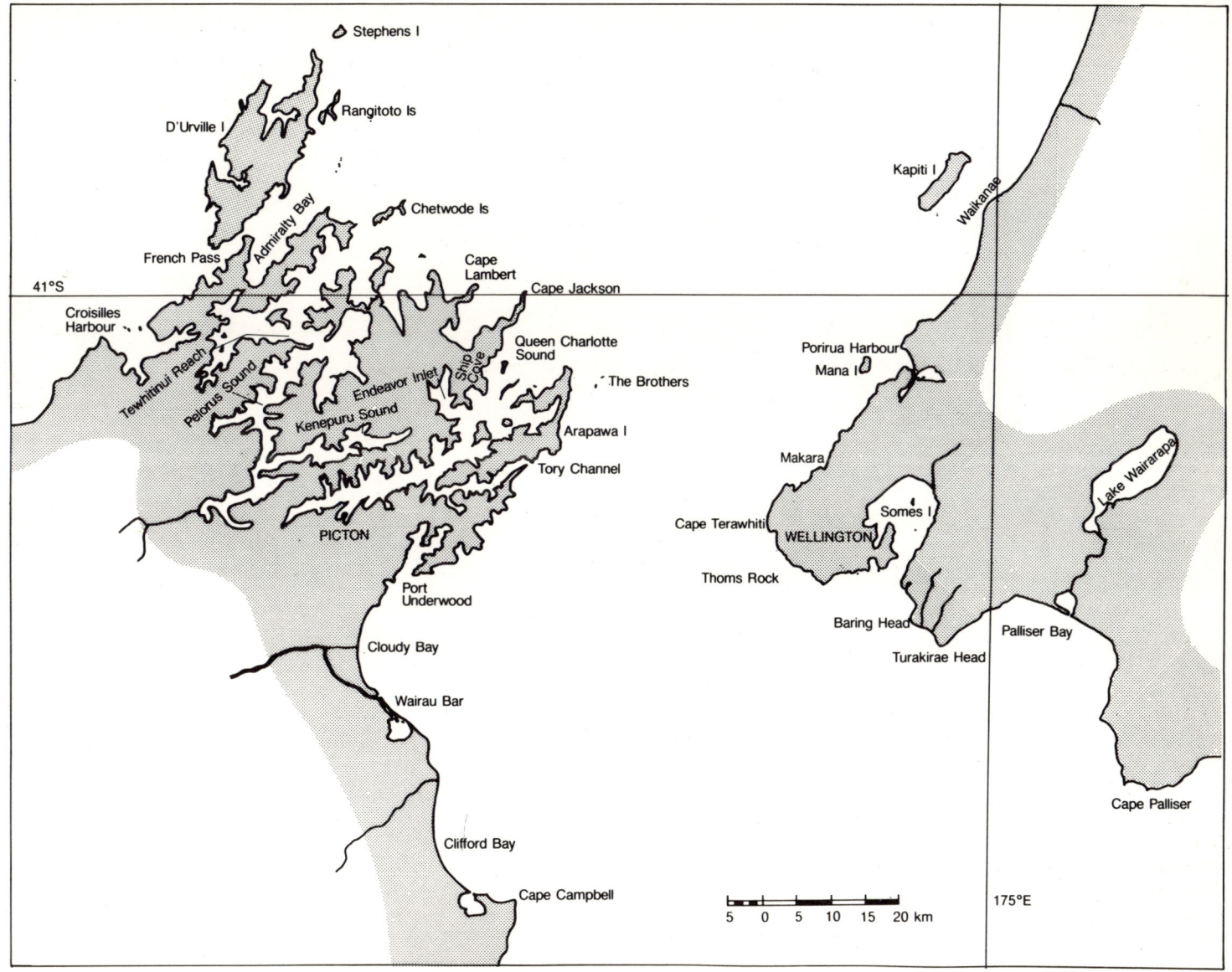

Stephens I

Rangitoto Is

D'Urville I

Admiralty Bay

Chetwode Is

French Pass

Cape Lambert

41°S

Cape Jackson

Croisilles Harbour

Tewhitinui Reach

Pelorus Sound

Endeavor Inlet

Ship Cove

Queen Charlotte Sound

Kenepuru Sound

The Brothers

Arapawa I

Tory Channel

PICTON

Port Underwood

Cloudy Bay

Wairau Bar

Clifford Bay

Cape Campbell

Kapiti I

Waikanae

Porirua Harbour

Mana I

Makara

Cape Terawhiti

WELLINGTON

Somes I

Lake Wairarapa

Thoms Rock

Baring Head

Palliser Bay

Turakirae Head

Cape Palliser

5 0 5 10 15 20 km

175°E

Cook Strait

On several occasions in the 1920s whales were washed up on to the beach at Lyall Bay. Like this one, they caused rather smelly problems for nearby residents. *S.C. Smith Collection, Alexander Turnbull Library*

four knots eastward. To make matters worse, the currents are erratic, and off the Karori Rock area they can produce dangerous rips.

Of all the hazards to seamen, the one seldom encountered in the strait is fog. The air never stays still long enough for it to settle. The explanation for this does not rest in esoteric scientific language — it is very simple. Cook Strait is the only gap in a 1,200-kilometre chain of mountains, from East Cape in the North Island to Puysegur Point in the South Island, lying smack across the path of the roaring forties. The environment of a wind-tunnel is regularly produced in the strait.

New Zealand's highest-ever wind gust — 145 knots or 268 kilometres/hour — was recorded at Oteranga Bay near the narrowest point in the strait on 10 April 1968, the day of the *Wahine* disaster. If the prevailing westerlies strike the mountain on the western side, as they do two-thirds of the time, the wind travelling through the strait is usually a north-westerly; but if the winds strike the mountain ranges from the south-west the effect in the Cook Strait region can be a quick switch from a modest north-westerly to a nasty southerly. Coming on often as a line squall, the southerly is felt in Wellington as a gusty, unpleasant and occasionally violent wind, accompanied by a sharp drop in temperature. At sea the onset of a southerly can be felt with tremendous ferocity and is often accompanied by big swells, particularly around Karori Rock. The wind, often the main feature of any Auckland-based criticism of the capital, has, according to weathermen, beneficial effects. They believe the continual stirrings of the air protect the city from extremes of temperature, and seldom is the area afflicted with fogs, thunderstorms, hail or snow. Wellington's weather is mild and congenial . . . and that's official.

Despite the dangers, Cook Strait has been on a regular shipping route almost from the beginning of European contact — both for ships heading in and out of Wellington and for ships using the prevailing winds on the New South Wales-to-England route. When Europeans were sufficiently settled to think about items like lighthouses, their attention was focused first on Wellington and the strait. Governor William Hobson, who visited Wellington in 1841, raised the matter in a report to London:

> As to the capabilities of the port, I am of opinion that few places can surpass it, but the entrance is rather difficult to distinguish, and appears very dangerous to a stranger. A more general knowledge of the coast and a lighthouse at one of the heads will obviate these difficulties.

But like so many civil servants with other, more pressing matters to worry about, he did nothing in particular to solve the problem. Artist Charles Heaphy, a regular visitor to early Wellington, once complained of the

Italian fishermen pose around cases of motor spirit *circa* 1910 in Island Bay. *S.C. Smith Collection, Alexander Turnbull Library*

inconvenience experienced in the city "from the want of lights and beacons, for the guidance of strangers into the harbour".

Modest efforts were made to correct the situation. A crudely constructed wooden pyramid was erected at Pencarrow to guide ships in daylight, but it was soon blown over. A lighthouse — and the term must be used in its broadest context on this occasion — was erected at Pencarrow in 1849. It consisted of a simple lean-to hut with a bay window where each night the light-keeper, one Mr

G.W. Bennett, placed a lantern. Conditions were grim, as an unnamed correspondent noted at the time:

> The interior of this building, a lighthouse and dwelling combined, was accessible to wind and rain on all sides, and in heavy gales it rocked and shook so much as to frighten the keeper and his family out of it, who in that case took refuge in a sort of cave or cabin which he had scooped out of the side of the hill, over which he had fixed

An impression of the Pencarrow "lighthouse", drawn in 1923 by the Wellington city librarian. *Alexander Turnbull Library*

a rude thatched roof and in which he had built a rude stone chimney. This cabin was his house of refuge and his cooking place.

One night in 1852 the barque *Maria* mistook the Karori Stream mouth for the harbour entrance and went ashore on the wild coast, killing 29 people. The lack of a reasonable light on the coast was held responsible, so Governor George Grey approved a proper lighthouse. A protracted debate then followed over how it was to be paid for and where it would go. So it was not until 1 January 1859 that the cast-iron lighthouse at Pencarrow went into operation. The £6,422 and fourpence that it cost was raised by the Wellington Provincial Government

The lonely Brothers, topped by a lighthouse. *Alexander Turnbull Library*

over the opposition of the central Government.

In charge of the new kerosene light was the widow Mrs Bennett. Her husband had died when he was tipped out of a dinghy one day as he was rowing across Wellington harbour. The new light, visible on a clear night for 39 kilometres, was supposed to exhibit a revolving light with eclipses at intervals of two minutes to distinguish its light from numerous bush fires which occurred. But the machinery did not function well and it was left as a fixed light, laying the foundation for further problems.

The second lighthouse was installed in 1865 on Mana Island because it had a good landing and an easy building site. Like Pencarrow, it had a fixed light, and the two lights were easily confused. In 1872 the barque *City of Newcastle* went aground near Tory Channel with the loss of two lives, and two years later the *Cyrus* went ashore between Lyall Bay and Sinclair Head with a loss of five people.

When the Government recognised the problem, the steamer *Luna*, with two experts aboard, was sent to explore the strait for a better site. They picked The Brothers, a rocky group of islets off Arapawa Island. Local sailors say tidal surges against the rocks act like gigantic rapids, and a huge surge makes it virtually impossible for a sailing vessel to come in to the rocks. Lighthouse artificer John Mill and his team spent a year on the exposed and bleak rocks, often totally isolated from the rest of the world by the weather. On the night of 24 September 1877 The Brothers light was switched on and Mana light switched off. Eventually the iron

The lighthouse tender *Enterprise* noses carefully into the Karori Rock light tower near Wellington, while one of the servicing team waits at the bow for a chance to leap ashore. *"Evening Post"*

New Zealand's first lighthouse, situated at Pencarrow. *Alexander Turnbull Library*

Mana tower was taken up to Cape Egmont and put into service there. The Brothers was New Zealand's only "rock station", meaning women were not allowed to live on the station.

Between 1870 and 1877 further lighthouses were erected at Cape Campbell, Stephens Island and Cape Palliser, sharply reducing the number of shipping accidents. But the campaign for safer navigation was not complete, as the *Penguin* disaster of 1909 illustrated only too well. Seventy-five people died when the steamer ran ashore at Tongue Point on the wild and remote south-western tip of the North Island. The blame was partly laid on the lack of a light in the area. A strong campaign resulted in which shipping masters, led by Captain Walter Manning, called for a light there. The *Evening Post* leapt in with both feet:

> Tom's Rock and other rocks are pitless fangs of ocean near Tongue Point. They have torn the sides and bitten the ribs of several ships. The tale of horrors done by them in the misty night will not end until the treacherous Tongue is tipped with light.

The Government wanted a manned lighthouse on the mainland at Cape Terawhiti, while mariners preferred a light on Tongue Point. The compromise was an acetylene automatic light on Karori Rock.

Pencarrow light was switched off for good in June 1934. Experience had shown it was in the wrong place, so a new lighthouse was built at nearby Baring Head on land donated by a local farmer, Mr Eric Riddiford. Pencarrow is now equipped with a foghorn and serves as a day marker, just as the old un-stable wooden pyramid did. But despite the equipment at Pencarrow and the light at Baring Head, the area still sees its share of shipwrecks. As recently as 1981 a large new cargo ship, the *Pacific Charger*, went aground right below the Baring Head light.

The other manmade feature of Cook Strait isn't visible above sea level and its continued existence is tenuous at best. Like amateur stitching, the telegraphic, telephone and electric power submarine cables tie the North and South Islands together.

In the 1850s telegraph lines were laid between various centres in both islands, and as the network expanded consideration was given to linking the two islands. In 1863 Postmaster-General Wood suggested a submarine cable from Auckland to the South Island. Ambitious even by modern standards, he was hoping to avoid having the skirmishing between Maoris and Europeans affect the telegraph. The following year Julius Vogel announced approval for a more modest cable — across Cook Strait.

As usual with these issues, rows followed over the best way of doing things — especially over the choice of route. It was finally decided that the first cable would run from Lyall Bay in the north to Whites Bay near Blenheim in the south. The London firm of W.T. Henley won the contract to provide the cable at the cost of £48 per nautical mile. It was composed of seven fine copper wires, each insulated with a compound of gutta-percha (rubber) and covered with tarred jute. Galvanised wiring was wrapped around this, giving the cable a diameter of just under 2 centimetres. A total of 85 kilometres of cable was made.

A fully rigged iron China clipper sailing ship, *Weymouth*, brought the cable out along with Henley's representative, Mr Edward Donovan. At 11.30 p.m. on 27 July 1866, beneath a full moon, the cable-laying operation began when one end was run ashore at Lyall Bay. *Weymouth* was towed by the steam ship *Taranaki*. The paddle steamer and colonial gunboat *Sturt* acted as tender, while HMS *Esk* provided 25 bluejackets for manual labour. The following morning the convoy was moving at a clip that proved too fast. When a knot developed in the cable, crewmen were not able to act quickly enough to stop it hitting the elaborate cable-laying machinery on the deck. When the knot hit,

The staff, and some of the family, photographed at the Whites Bay telegraph station at the southern terminal of the Cook Strait cable at the turn of the century. *Alexander Turnbull Library*

The telegraphic cable-laying ship *Recorder* in Wellington in 1926, prior to taking out another Cook Strait cable. *Evening Post*

Cable laying in 1926 in Lyall Bay, where *Janie Seddon* (left) and the scow *Kohi* came in close to the shore where the main laying vessel *Recorder* could not sail. *"Evening Post"*

the machinery virtually exploded and the cable snapped. The *Weymouth* had to return to port for repairs, leaving 11 kilometres of cable on the seabed.

A month later the team was back in action. As far as the public was aware, the operation went smoothly until *Weymouth* was approaching Whites Bay. Then it was realised they did not have enough cable. Another delay resulted while ships returned to salvage the cable abandoned earlier. Officially, the reason for the cable being too short was that it had been kept too taut when laid and the current had swept it into a large semi-circular arc. That may have been true, although the fact that *Weymouth* had one night got lost and ended up near Tory Channel had not helped matters either. Although this mistake meant a considerable loop in the cable, the Government kept it a secret.

The first cable cost £29,864 and was declared by a British engineer to be the best cable ever to have left England. Yet in 29 years of service it broke down eight times. It had been run over some sheer cliffs on the side of the Cook Strait Canyon, leading to continuous friction. In 1895 when it broke down in four different places it was finally abandoned.

Other telegraphic cables were laid over the following 20 years, and in 1926 the first telephone cable was put down. Like that chosen for the original cable, the route proved bad. At one point over a distance of 274 metres the seabed dropped from a depth of 97 metres to 365 metres, and the cable was found to be resting on the top of a rock in the middle of the dip with cable sagging on either side. Not even England's finest could withstand pressures of that kind.

As with the telegraphic system, New Zealand developed two electrical-transmission networks. Development of hydro resources from 1886 was based solely on the requirements of each island, and as populations were small this was no particular problem. But by the 1950s it became apparent that the North Island's hydro power supply was not going to meet needs. The North Island had far greater requirements, but the South Island had far more abundant hydro resources.

Credit for first suggesting a submarine electric cable goes to the New Zealand Electricity Department's chief engineer, Mr M.G. Latta, who initiated research in 1950. In 1957 a joint committee came up with the idea to run 540 megawatts from the planned Benmore power station, on the edge of the South Island's MacKenzie country, north on a 644-kilometre-long link to Haywards, a large sub-station north of Wellington. Both islands ran an alternating current system, but it was felt that a direct current system had a number of economic and technical advantages.

Fighting Bay was chosen as the submarine cable's South Island terminal. On the outer coast of Port Underwood, it was so named because South Island paramount chief Hone Tuhawaiki had defeated Te Rauparaha there. The northern terminal was to be Oteranga Bay, where a submarine telegraph cable came ashore from Cloudy Bay.

Opposition to the electricity cable was based on problems that had occurred with the existing cables, and the sheer logistics of getting a large ship close in to such rocky shores were thought overwhelming. There was also concern that any repair work on the cable would be unduly time-consuming because it would take so long to find a suitable ship. Others felt the North Island would

Photinia in Cook Strait on a calm day laying a cable for the transmission of electricity across the strait. *Electricity Division*

become overly dependent on a long, single electricity circuit. One of the more interesting objections spoke of enemy sabotage and a group of consulting English engineers had to address themselves to the problem in a report to Government:

> One criticism of the scheme is that the supply from South to North Island could be cut off as a result of enemy action, especially near the cable terminations where skin divers could approach under water and plant bombs directly on the cables . . .

An attack on the submarine cables is, of course, only one of many possible methods of attempted interference with power supplies in times of hostility, and it is certain that many safeguards and special precautions would be introduced if war were threatened or declared. Guards would no doubt be provided for terminal points and stations, patrols for principal supply routes by land and sea, and scientific devices for detecting enemy approach by air and sea.

This was a polite way of telling people that national development objectives could not suffer because of the long shot that New Zealand might go to war.

In the debate over whether to go ahead with the scheme, the then leader of the opposition, Mr (later Sir) Keith Holyoake, came out for it in patriotic terms. "Let us make certain that New Zealand is just New Zealand and not divided by a strip of water and a lot of prejudice."

By 1961 the green light was given for a cable consisting of three lines 1,000 metres apart running on the seabed at a maximum depth of 243.2 metres, from Oteranga Bay to Fighting Bay. It was thought that the problems with currents that had hampered telegraphic cables would be avoided because the electric cable would be so much heavier.

British Insulated Callender's Cables Ltd, which won the cable-laying tender, found no existing cable ship could handle the 12-centimetre-thick cable which weighed in at 34 kilograms/metre. Nor was it economic to build a special ship, so B.I.C.C. modified a brand-new grain carrier, the 10,000-ton *Photinia*. In its large hold-space the cable could be coiled.

For laying each of the three lines, 18 hours of calm weather and seas were required, six hours at each bay and six hours to cross the strait. Once in New Zealand *Photinia* and the crew rehearsed the operation. On 12 November 1964, in perfect weather, the first line was laid and the link was made at 10.30 p.m. on 13 November. Nothing untoward occurred in laying the second line, but the third and final line caused so many problems that B.I.C.C. eventually lost money on the whole contract. When 20 kilometres out from the North Island on 11 December, the *Photinia* was unexpectedly caught in a swift current. There was a momentary loss of control in the tension of the line and the cable twisted. Testing later showed that the cable could not stand the required voltage. *Photinia* was forced to use explosives to break the line and lift it back on board in order to make a new join.

On April Fool's Day 1965 the South Island was officially linked with the North Island grid. The connection was one of the major submarine cable installations in the world. A gas-filled duct in the centre means that should the cable be punctured, the pressure of the gas, being greater than that of water, will seal the leak until the damage can be found and repaired. Each cable consists of a conductor of 5.16-centimetre square copper strands around the duct filled with nitrogen. Up to 600,000 kilowatts can be transmitted with two cables in service (the third always acts as spare), and if only one is used it is still possible to transmit 300,000 kilowatts using the earth as a return. Since 1976 the cable has been capable of transmitting electricity both ways.

"A great British first," was how B.I.C.C. chairman, Sir William McFadzean, described the cable. "I will stick my neck out and say there is not another company in the world which could have done it."

The cable has been reliable, although the joint in number three, where the twist had been, failed once. *Photinia* came back in August 1977 and, in 35-knot winds with a four-metre swell, she lifted the cable for repairs. One night during the operation a mooring line parted. According to *Photinia's* skipper, Hugh Selkirk:

> It was pitch dark with a strong wind and a spring tide and four-knot current. When the first line carried away three others quickly followed, and the ship swung out on the line towards the forward moorings. We could not use the main engine in case we got wires fouled around the screw, and it took us some time to slip the other lines. It was a difficult situation.

Photinia, an ugly ship by many standards, won a warm place in the hearts of Wellingtonians, but August 1977 was the last time the ship sailed the strait. The British magazine *Sea Breezes* reported in 1978 that *Photinia* was sailing Lake Michigan that year on the grain trade when she was blown on to mud-flats off a Milwaukee suburb. The crew was rescued by helicopter, but the ship was abandoned.

By way of final introduction to Cook Strait, it is perhaps amusing to note that shepherds, who consider Cook Strait as the only place in New Zealand where they cannot run a sheep dog, have named their interisland competition trophy the "Cook Strait Cup".

Chapter II

Discovery

And notwithstanding the strength of the tides ... there is no great danger in passing it.

Ka titi au, ka tito au, ka tito au,
Kia Kupe te Tangata,
Nana i tope te whenua,
Tu ke a Kapiti,
Tu ke Mana,
Tu ke Arapawa,
Ko nga tohu tena,
A taku tupuna,
A Kupe . . .

I will sing, I will sing of my ancestor Kupe!
He it was who severed the land.
So that Kapiti, Mana and Arapawa
Were divided off and stood apart.

*A Maori chant quoted by Sir Peter Buck in
"The Coming of the Maori"*

ONE day the legendary Kupe and his men went fishing off-shore from their mythical homeland, Hawaiki; but while they spent all day out, not a single fish was caught. It was a mystery as the bait had been stolen from the hooks, but no tug was ever felt on the lines. When the same thing occurred the next day Kupe suspected supernatural forces. He consulted a priest who gave him a charm, which revealed the next day that a school of small octopuses were stealing the bait. They were encouraged by a large octopus off in the distance, which was a pet of Muturangi, a man with whom Kupe did not see eye to eye. Kupe confronted him, demanding that the octopus be killed, but Muturangi refused and it was left to Kupe and his men to do the job.

Getting rid of the small octopuses was easy, but the great creature remained in the distance and whenever Kupe and his men approached, it moved out to sea. After preparing for a long voyage, Kupe, his wife, and five children and a crew of 60 manned the canoe *Matahorua*. Accompanied by the canoe of Ngake, they set out in pursuit. After a long chase the two canoes arrived off Te Ika a Maui, which we know today as the North Island, and finally caught up with Muturangi's pet in Cook Strait. Kupe and Ngake trapped the octopus between the canoes and thrust spears into its side. In great pain the animal grabbed at Kupe's canoe, nearly sinking it. Kupe saved the occupants by hauling calabashes (waterholders) over the side, which the octopus took to be human heads. As it grasped for them, Kupe struck the octopus with his adze, killing it.

That story, or versions of it, has been taught in schools for several decades, along with the Great Fleet tradition which tells of Kupe's return to his homeland and a return to the new land with his people. Kupe and the fleet probably never existed, although the question of how New Zealand, and the rest of Polynesia, was settled is the subject of much academic debate. At one extreme Polynesia's population spread is explained as the product of accidental voyages — fishermen being blown offcourse. At the other end of the debate is the suggestion of great seamanship and voyages of discovery by Polynesian sailors. The answer probably rests somewhere in the middle.

Whatever the method the Maoris used to come to New Zealand, the Cook Strait area saw settlement soon after the newcomers arrived. In terms of human survival, New Zealand was hardly a land of milk and honey. The only real flesh to eat was that of the flightless moa. And as the early Maoris killed them off in the North Island, the settlers were forced to follow the surviving bird population southward, meeting Cook Strait.

15

Modern evidence shows the sea was not a major barrier to the Maori and at Wairau Bar on the South Island's Cloudy Bay archaeologists have found one of the most famous burial sites in Polynesia. Dating from between A.D.1100 and A.D. 1350, the material found matches well with what is known of the cultures of the Marquesas and Society Islands at much the same period. Covering an area of about 8 hectares, Wairau Bar, better known in New Zealand's history for a battle between Te Rauparaha and European land speculators, is a sand bar at the mouth of the Wairau River. There high-ranking Maori leaders were buried with moa-egg water bottles, necklaces made from shark or whale teeth, harpoons, adzes and stone fishing hooks.

Wairau represents the earliest evidence of occupation in the Cook Strait area, but for many years Europeans believed those buried there were representatives of a warlike group, who destroyed another tribe living in New Zealand. Notable early contributors to Maori history, such as Elsdon Best, were convinced that there was a distinct race living in the country prior to the Maori. This group was given a variety of names, but today is most commonly referred to as the Moriori. They were held to be a peace-loving, agricultural people of probable Melanesian origin. They were also said to have had straight hair, a most un-Melanesian feature. The "Hawaikans" or Maoris discovered them here when they arrived in their fleet, and so set about to wipe them out. Eventually the Moriori were driven to a last refuge — D'Urville Island according to some; Arapawa according to others.

T. Lindsay Buick in *Old Marlborough* published in 1900 wrote of the Maori people:

They were conquerors, or they were nothing, and the spirit of conquest which brought them ended in a policy of expulsion; the weak and inoffensive Moriori were driven out, and then covetousness and tribal pride added to the hideous anarchy, for after they had exhausted the aborigines they sought new adventures in plundering each other, and when tired of plunder they fought for precedence.

The whole story sounds like a farce in Stephen Gerard's *Strait of Adventure*, published in 1938, in which he claimed there was evidence of pre-Maori habitation on D'Urville Island. He wrote:

The Moriori is more than a legend, for the crude pits of his habitation still scar the Marlborough hills. A feeble fighter, he was driven back and back by the first Polynesians, the Waitaha, children of Tamatea. At last the only Moriori stronghold, was on D'Urville Island, and all round them enemies. It was no longer safe for them to fish in the sounds or hunt in the mainland woods. Their end was only a matter of months. So one day, launching their slight canoes and storing them with a few roots and a basket of fish and a gourd or two of water, they turned their backs on the islands of their birth, where their forefathers had dwelt for more than 300 years, and pushed out on to the unfriendly waters. The Waitahas saw them go, six canoes, heading eastward, for the bleak and lonely islands of the Chathams, where they lingered till this present century.

How Mr Gerard deduced all this was not explained.

In fact, the notion of mainland Moriori has long been dismissed as a myth, and it is now generally accepted that the Chatham Islands Moriori were decendants of New Zealand Maori people who may have drifted from New Zealand on a double canoe and found they were unable to return.

By way of speculation one could conceive of a group of Maori people making a Cook Strait crossing in rough weather and getting blown off course until they came upon the Chatham Islands. The Maoris recognised the dangers of the strait and declared it a tapu sea although, as an early European traveller noted, the way they handled that tapu was not very conducive to good seamanship:

They coasted along until they came to the narrowest part of the strait when every man but the steersman covered his eyes. They obliged the Englishman to do the same, and to sit down in the bottom of the boat. In this singular position they paddled across ... The natives remained blindfolded and speechless until the canoes came within a quarter of a mile of the land, when at a signal from the steersman, they resumed their normal condition amidst demonstrations of great joy.

It is little wonder that one or two canoes drifted well off course now and again.

Elsdon Best in his 1919 classic, *The Land of Tara and they who settled it*, says the tapu was based on a sacred shoal in the middle of the strait, which was said to have been guarded by a small bird, komako-huariki. In a somewhat more embracing version of the tale of Lot's wife, it was held that first-time Cook Strait travellers could look neither right nor left, or behind. Eyes were hidden behind karaka leaves and pregnant women were covered up completely. Stern and prow carvings on the canoe were also covered. Stealing a glance caused the canoe, no doubt to the considerable annoyance of fellow passengers, to be held by a supernatural power in mid-strait for a day and a night. Only if a tohunga (priest) happened to be in the canoe could the spell be broken.

For one Hine Poupou that tapu was only a minor problem when she was stood up by her husband. D'Urville Island legend has it that she accompanied her husband and brother-in-law on a social visit to Kapiti Island. That night while Hine slept the two men slipped away and paddled back to D'Urville where it was announced that Hine was dead. Over on Kapiti it was plainly apparent that not only was Hine alive, she was also extremely angry. Nobody seemed willing to row her back to her home, so Hine waited for the right tide before she plunged into the sea and began swimming home. Her first stop was The Brothers, although in an early appearance of male chauvinism the feat was under-rated by speculation that the semi-spirit dolphin Tahurangi had helped her. While swimming from The Brothers to D'Urville Hine noticed a big school of sharks near Sentinel Rock.

Once home she secretly called on her father, who wanted instant revenge when he heard what the two men had done. Hine went

for finer retaliations. One version of the legend says she had the two men sent out fishing and then called in the taniwha (monster) to drown them. Another tells how the men were sent fishing at a previously unknown fishing ground – the place where Hine saw the sharks. Either way, the marriage ended up on the rocks.

Maori people seemed to be settled in fairly well around the strait area when Abel Janszoon Tasman's two ships, the *Heemskerck* and *Zeehaen*, showed up in 1642. History has never treated the Dutchman well. He is often mistakenly blamed for naming what he found after a dreary Dutch plain and he seems to have totally misunderstood his discovery. He thought New Zealand to be the western coastline of a vast continent that stretched to South America. But for simple bad luck, in the form of foul Cook Strait weather, he may have disproved that theory 120 years before Captain James Cook.

Tasman first saw New Zealand in December 1642, dropping anchor in Golden Bay on 18 December where he had a somewhat ill-conceived and disenchanting meeting with local Maoris which ended with four of his crew dead. He sailed on and on 20 December 1642 Tasman's journal states:

On 20th d° in the morning Saw here land lying around about [he was near the Manawatu River mouth] as that [we] had sailed fully 30 miles into a bight, we had previously thought the land where we had been at anchor to be an island not doubting [we] Shall find from there a passage into the open South Sea, but this

turned out to our hearts' pain very much otherwise.

Four days later the two ships were anchored off the west side of D'Urville Island.

On 24th d° still hard unsettled weather the wind still north west with storm; in the morning had a calm interval had the white flag flown, and received the officers of the Zeehaen on our ship and have proposed to them since the flood comes from the south east; so that there might indeed be a passage, whether it would not be best as soon as weather and wind will permit, to inquire into the same; and see whether one cannot get fresh water there . . .

While "still dark out at Sea" the ships crews celebrated the first Christmas in New Zealand.

Tasman was finally able to leave the area two days later, but as he sailed north a drizzle obscured the view southward. They never saw the strait, although in drawing up the first maps the pilot, Visscher, who had sold the idea of the voyage to the Governor of the colony of Batavia in the first place, left a gap on the map at the point where modern maps now mark Cook Strait.

The gap gained scientific credentials from a self-educated Yorkshireman, Captain James Cook, who arrived off the New Zealand coast in 1769. Later when Cook approached the strait from the west he did not initially see it and instead sailed into Queen Charlotte Sound and Ship Cove which was to be his southern base for subsequent voyages. Several days after arriving, on 23 January 1770, Cook and a party, which included biologist Joseph Banks, went exploring the sound. What Cook saw was noted in his journal:

> Climbed up the Top of one of the Hills, but when I came there I was hindered from seeing the inlet by higher hills, which I could not come at for impenetrable woods, but I was abundantly recompensed for the trouble I had in ascending the Hill, for from it I saw what I took to be the Eastern Sea, and a Strait or passage from it into the Western Sea; a little to the Eastward of the Entrance of the inlet in which we now lay with the Ship.

Cook returned to the rest of the party, which had remained at the base of the hill. Banks described the captain's return:

> The captn went to the top of a hill and in about an hour returned in high spirits, having seen the Eastern sea and satisfied himself of the existence of a straight communicating with it.

It was Banks who insisted on naming the find after the *Endeavour's* captain. Three days after the first hill climb Cook, Banks and Dr Daniel Solander climbed another of the towering hills that crowd Queen Charlotte Sound. Cook's journal:

> Upon our landing we assended a very high hill; from which we had a full View of the passage I had before discovered, and the land on the opposite shore, which appeared to be about four leagues from us; but as it was hazy near the Horizon we could not see far to the SE. However, I had now seen enough of this passage to convince me that there was the Greatest probability in the World of it running into

the Eastern Sea, as the distance of that Sea from this place cannot exceed 20 leagues even to where we were. Upon this I resolved after putting to Sea to search this passage with the ship.

It was not simply a strait that Cook had found. It was proof that Te Ika a Maui was an island, the North Island, and that the southern continent, so firmly believed in by chair-bound "experts" in Europe, did not exist.

At a ceremony to name Queen Charlotte Sound Cook spoke through the Tahitian Tupia to an old Maori.

> . . . we asked the old man about the Strait or Pasage into the Eastern Sea, and he very plainly told us there was a passage, and as I had some conjectures that the lands of the SW of the Strait (which we are now at) was an Island and not a Continent, we questioned the Old Man about it, who said it consisted of two Wannus, that is two lands or Islands that might be circumnavigated in a few days, even in four. This man spoke of three lands, the two above mentioned which he called Tovy-poinammu [Te Wai Pounamu – the South Island], which Signifies green talk or Stone, such as they make their Tools or ornaments, etc, and for the third he pointed to the land on the East side of the Strait; this, he said, was a large land, and that it would take up a great many Moons to sail around; this he called Aeheino Mouwe [Te Ika a Maui – the North Island], a name many others before had called it by. That part which borders on Strait he called Teiria Whitte.

Actually, there was no place called Terawhiti. The old man was simply telling Cook that there was land to the east of where they were standing.

On 3 February the *Endeavour* left from Ship Cove with its captain keen to sail through the strait he had seen. His ambition nearly came to grief on The Brothers rocks when the tide swept the tiny vessel close to danger. The ship's longboat was put out and seamen tried to tow the *Endeavour* to safety. Fortunately, the tide changed at the right moment and Captain Cook was free to sail into Cook Strait:

> The narrowest part of the Strait we have passed lies between Cape Koomaroo [Koamaru] on Tovy-poinammu and Cape Teerewhitte on Aeheino Mouwe; the distance from one to the other I judged to be between four and five leagues. And notwithstanding the strength of the tides, now that is known, there is no great danger in passing it; in the doing of which I am of opinion that the NE shore is the safest to keep on, for upon that side there appear no danger, whereas on the other shore there are not only the Islands and Rocks lying off Cape Koomaroo for I discover'd from the hill which I had the second view of the Strait, a Reef of Rocks stretching from these Islands six or seven miles to the southward, and lay about two or three Miles off from the Shore.

On that first voyage the great harbour we know today as Wellington was not seen. Aboard *Resolution* on his second voyage, Cook was sailing through the strait from the Pacific to Ship Cove in November 1773 when he noticed something:

> As we approached the [North Island], we discovered on the east side of Cape Tee-rawhitte, a new inlet I had never observed before. Being tired with beating against the NW winds, I resolved to put into this place, if I found it practicable, or to anchor in the bay which lies before it. The flood being in our favour, after making a stretch off, we fetched under the Cape and stretched into the bay along by the western shore, having from thirty-five to twelve fathoms, the bottom everywhere was good anchorage.

Cook was frustrated in his attempt to get in the harbour when the tide went against him, and it wasn't until 1826 that Captain James Herd on the *Rosanna* sailed in and found a place where, as he put it, "all the navies of Europe might ride in perfect security".

Cook had been in the strait on that second voyage in an effort to meet the other half of the expedition — *Adventure* under the command of Captain Tobias Furneaux. When Cook made it to Ship Cove the *Adventure* had not arrived. After waiting several weeks the *Resolution* sailed, and a few days later, on 30 November 1773, Furneaux arrived at Ship Cove to find that Cook had been and gone. By 17 December he was ready to set sail for England, but before doing so he sent ashore the first mate, Jack Rowe, and nine men to pick medicinal herbs. When they did not return, second lieutenant James Burney lead a search party to find them. At a nearby bay he found rollock parts from Rowe's cutter and some shoes. Burney wrote of further discoveries on that grim day:

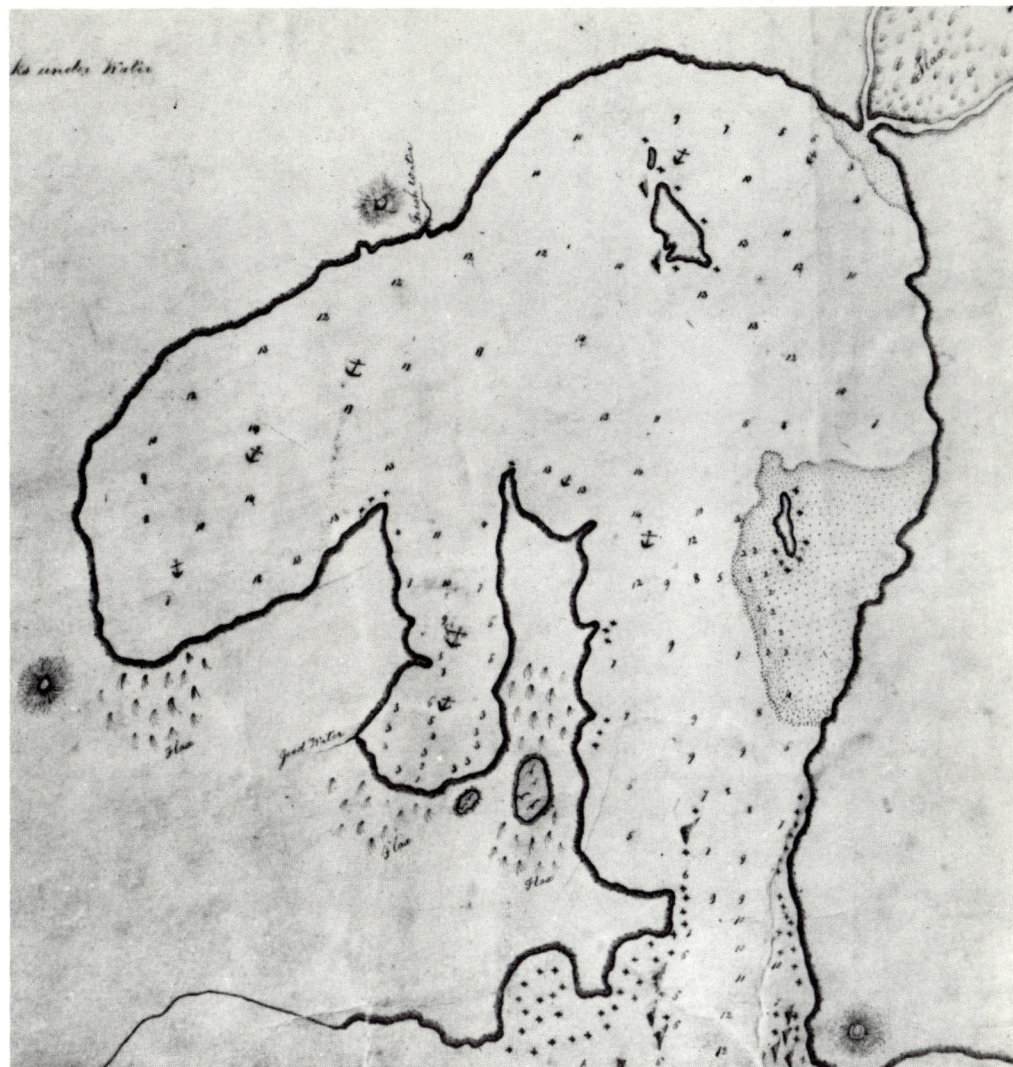

A place where "all the navies of Europe might ride in perfect security" — Captain James Herd's map of Wellington harbour. *Alexander Turnbull Library*

A piece of flesh was found by one of our people which at first we thought to be some of the salt meat belonging to the cutter's men, but, upon examination, we supposed was dog flesh. A most horrid and undeniable proof soon cleared up our doubts, and convinced us we were among no other than cannibals; for advancing further on the beach, we saw about twenty baskets tied up and a dog eating a piece of boiled flesh, which upon examination, we suspected to be human.

Further on, a hand with the initials T.H. tattooed on it was found. One Thomas Hill had been a crewman. Burney realised they had found the killing ground.

. . . the most horrible scene was presented to our view; for there lay the hearts, heads and lungs of several of our people, with hands and limbs in a mangled condition.

Furneaux, writing in his log after interviewing members of the search party, filled in the additional detail:

They found the Relicks of several and the intrails of five men lying on the beach and in the Canoes they found several baskets of human flesh and five odd shoes new, as our people had been served Shoes a day or two before; they brought on board several hands, two of which we knew, one belonged to Thomas Hill being marked on the Back T.H. another Mr Rowe who had a wound on his fore finger not quite whole, and the Head, which was supposed was the head of my servant by the forhead he being a Negro.

What could be found of the men was collected and placed in a hammock and, with usual Naval ceremony, the remains were buried at sea. Then the *Adventure* sailed without even taking revenge or even trying to find out why the incident had taken place. Cook and a Tahitian, Omai, on the third voyage of discovery, learnt the reasons later. It turned out that Rowe and his men had been bartering with a group of Maoris when one produced a stone axe and offered to exchange it for bread. A sailor took the axe, and when he offered neither bread nor the axe back the Maori went down to the water's edge and began to help himself from the boat. Furneaux's servant saw that latter part of the event and assumed the Maori was looting from the cutter, so he struck him with a piece of wood. The Maori cried out in pain and his fellows, believing him dead, attacked the sailors. Cook was inclined to blame the incident on the sailors.

After Cook the next explorer to visit the area was the Russian Faddeyevich von Bellingshausen and his two ships *Mirnyy* and *Vostok*. He used Cook's charts to sail into Queen Charlotte Sound in May 1820. As far as the strait was concerned, Bellingshausen's sole achievement in the area was the doubtful one of being blown backwards through it. The translated version of his log reads:

We were already off Cape Terra Vitta and rejoicing in a successful passage when suddenly, towards evening, the wind shifted to the south with mist and rain and then so strengthened that we were forced to beat about in the strait with top sails close-reefed.

Bellingshausen did note what looked like a big harbour at the end of the North Island, and it is perhaps fortunate for the citizens of the capital that he was, like Cook, frustrated in an attempt to sail into it. The Russian had the habit of handing out extraordinary names to places — such as "Prince Golenitschev-Kutuzov-Smolenski Island" to Makemo Island, a tiny atoll in the Tuamotu Archipelago.

In 1827 the vessel *Astrolabe* arrived. Under the command of Admiral Jules Sabastien Cesar Dumont D'Urville, the man who found the Venus de Milo, the ship initially spent time in New Zealand fighting the winds of Tasman Bay. Eventually D'Urville found himself off the coast of the island which today bears his name. There he noticed a pass which appeared to offer a quick route into Admiralty Bay, which D'Urville knew of from Cook's charts. In what came to be considered a masterly bit of seamanship, D'Urville decided to sail through the pass instead of taking the longer trip around the island.

The first attempt was made on 24 January 1827. *Astrolabe* was in full sail and only a cable (180 metres) away from entering the pass when the tidal rip rose "like a seething sheet and water rushed into the basin and formed whirlpools of incredible violence". The vessel was carried towards the rocky shore, and it was only when a long-boat was put in the water to tow and an anchor dropped that disaster was averted.

Astrolabe remained in Current Basin south-west of the pass for four more days. While waiting for the right conditions, D'Urville studied the pass from the shore and

"It is nothing — we are over it." *Astrolabe* clears French Pass in a dramatic moment in early New Zealand exploration. *Alexander Turnbull Library*

French Pass at the turn of the century — a regular feature on the Wellington-Nelson ferry route.
Halse Collection, Alexander Turnbull Library

had soundings taken, all of which confirmed his view that a ship could sail through it. Then the right day came — a steady west-south-westerly was blowing and the tide was slack. The naturalists, artists and surveyors were put ashore and an attempt was made to sail through the pass. D'Urville wrote in his log:

At last, on January 28th, a favourable day arrived. So as not to omit any precautions, at 4.30 a.m. I climbed the ridge over-looking the south-east point. It was not easy owing to the steepness and impene-trable fern. In looking towards the graceful fabric, riding at anchor below me, that had so long been our home, I could not help reflecting that by my order she might be exposed to be lost on the rocks at my feet and her crew, even if saved, reduced to a miserable existence on an inhospitable shore.

All went well in the attempt until *Astrolabe* reached the most dangerous point in the pass:

For some minutes we steered very well but at the moment we entered the pass the wind failed and the impetuous current caused us to swerve to port. In vain I instantly put the helm up and furled all sail in an attempt almost to touch the coast on the right. The corvette was mastered by the currents and bodily carried on the rocks at the end of the reef. She touched slightly; then again; there was an ominous

This view of French Pass, looking up from the southern end, was engraved from a map by Dumont D'Urville. *Alexander Turnbull Library*

cracking of timbers, a prolonged shaking, and a sensible pause in the movement of the ship as she heeled strongly to starboard. The crew involuntarily raised a cry of alarm. "It is nothing — we are over it," I cried. The current dragged the corvette, the wind freshened; the *Astrolabe* heeled over as if it was about to sink, then rising gracefully she sailed — with the fragments of her false keel floating behind her — into the calm and peaceful waters of Admiralty Bay.

A happy crew wanted the island named after the man who had performed such a masterly piece of seamanship. He agreed as long as the island's Maori name was used once it was discovered. He wanted the only permanent name to recognise his people, thus he named the object of his efforts "French Pass". D'Urville Island's Maori name was discovered later, but was never used. Perhaps it is just as well for it could have been doubly confusing — it was known to the Maori people as "Rangitoto ki te Tonga".

D'Urville's two voyages to New Zealand now form important aspects of our history, and the incident of French Pass is now part of folklore. The colourful D'Urville, his wife and child, died 14 years after the French Pass passage when the train they were travelling on crashed near Paris and caught fire.

Chapter III

Turmoil and lawlessness – the days of settlement

It's rough here, but the longer you stay the better you'll like it.

WELLINGTON, the city of the strait, may not have become what it is today had not a 30-year-old man taken a mercenary interest in a wealthy young girl. That man, Edward Gibbon Wakefield, was born in London in 1796, the eldest son of a land agent. School life for him had been no great success and, as a young adult, his minor position in the diplomatic service held no promise either. At the age of 20 he eloped with a wealthy 16-year-old, but four years later she died, leaving him with a son, Edward Jerningham Wakefield, and a daughter.

As a 30-year-old widower, Wakefield, then an attaché in Paris, decided his future lay with the House of Commons. As he lacked sufficient money for this, he set out to get some through the marriage bed. The object of an arranged marriage was one Ellen Turner, the only child of a wealthy man and heiress to her well-off uncle. To most people the two main obstacles in this match would have appeared insurmountable: Ellen and

Edward Gibbon Wakefield in 1823.
Alexander Turnbull Library

Edward had never met, and she was only 15. But such problems meant nothing to Edward.

Wakefield and his brother, 23-year-old William, knew Ellen's mother was often ill, so one night they had a servant take a letter to the principal of the boarding school where Ellen lived. Signed "John Ainsworth, M.D.", it said Mrs Turner had been "seized by a sudden and dangerous attack of paralysis". It also said the servant should immediately take the girl to her mother, but without telling her of the reason for the late-night trip "so as not to alarm her".

The principal believed all, and within a short time Ellen was *en route*, although not to her mother, but to a London meeting with a man named "Captain Wilson".

The dashing captain, none other than Edward, told the girl that her father was near financial ruin, but that if she married him immediately members of his [Edward's] family could come to the rescue. At some stage Ellen said yes, although later the precise nature of the question was never clearly established.

England had tough marriage laws, but fortunately for Wakefield and many other English couples these laws did not apply in Scotland. The canny Scots catered for the quick-marriage business at a place called Gretna Green near the border, and it was there that old David Laing conducted a rough and ready, but perfectly legal, marriage service. Mr and Mrs Wakefield spent their marriage night at a hotel in Penrith each sleeping in a single room.

Meanwhile, William was meant to be working out matters with Ellen's father, but he had trouble finding him. The father first suspected foul play when the school's principal reported to Mr Turner that his daughter appeared to have been kidnapped. Then, in the odd ways of the times, the marriage was formally announced in London newspapers.

After the marriage Edward and Ellen went to France and while in Calais, Edward sent a letter to Mr Turner assuring him of his daughter's happiness. A lawyer and two of Ellen's uncles were promptly sent off to France by Mr Turner, charged with finding out whether the marriage had been consummated. If it had, the best possible face was to be assumed. However, Edward cut off that route.

"I have a daughter," he sternly told his father-in-law's delegation, "and if any man were to take her off in the same manner [as Wakefield had] I believe I should put a bullet through his head. I assure you upon my honour that Miss Turner is the same Miss Turner she was when I took her away."

With that Ellen was returned to her family.

William, meantime, had eloped as well, although his match was not inspired by money. His love-partner was Emily Shelley-Sidney, cousin of the poet Percy Bysshe Shelley. They had been married in Paris, but William immediately returned to England to surrender voluntarily to justice for his role in what had by then become a major scandal — the kidnapping of little more than a child. William was to never see his wife as she died while he was in prison. She left him a daughter, Emily Charlotte, who was later to marry Edward Stafford who became one of the early premiers of New Zealand.

Edward also returned and joined his brother under arrest in Lancaster Castle (144 years later in 1981 the same place was the scene of the trial of a gang of New Zealanders known internationally for their involvement in the "Mr Asia" drugs and murder ring). The trial of the Wakefields produced much wild press speculation centred on why Edward had not slept with the young girl. The Wakefields were found guilty of kidnapping and were sent to jail for three years. Publicly shamed and seemingly ruined, Newgate Jail was to turn Edward into a man of genuine greatness and lead to the establishment of New Zealand's capital city.

Young Ellen, her first marriage annulled by Act of Parliament, married later but died giving birth to her first child.

In jail Wakefield wrote two books. One of them, *The Punishment of Death*, attacked the use of the death penalty for a range of some 200 crimes and was to play a large part in having the number cut back. *A Letter from Sydney*, his second book, was seen as both radical and ridiculous by some, but became

important in subsequent colonial developments. Even Karl Marx referred to Edward Wakefield. Wakefield was opposed to the fashion of giving land grants in the colonies to almost anyone. He felt land should be sold to selected settlers and the proceeds used to finance labour from England.

Once out of jail Wakefield founded the Colonisation Society to press his ideas for a colony he proposed in South Australia. As he became enmeshed with the detail of negotiation with the Government, Wakefield's daughter died in Portugal. By the time he was over that, the South Australian idea had foundered.

In May 1837 Wakefield and a growing band of influential supporters formed the "New Zealand Association" to press for the establishment of a Wakefield-style colony there. The missionary societies, particularly powerful at the time, were strongly opposed to Wakefield, as was the London *Times*. Not quite the newspaper it is today, it took a dim view of the idea and expressed sympathy for the Maoris, whom they saw as "prey to all sorts of vultures, unprincipled Jews, French usurpers, fugitive convicts, licentious crews, fraudulent bargainers, peddling grog sellers, Durham land-companies, and what not".

The association had two groups of members. One was the prospective settlers, and the other was the backers, who apparently stood to gain little financially.

When the association failed to gain a royal charter it was floated in August 1838 as a joint-stock "New Zealand Colonisation Company". By May of the following year the company had a ship, the *Tory*, which was to sail to New Zealand for the buying of land for the company. Business was to be conducted by the principal agent on board, William Wakefield.

After his release William had travelled around Europe before entering the British Auxiliary Force in Spain. As a lieutenant-colonel he was so successful at arms that the grateful Queen Isabella created him a Knight in the Order of San Fernando. After his adventures he rejoined his brother in the New Zealand Company. It wasn't the first company by that name. Ten years earlier a group of wealthy financiers had assigned the ship *Rosanna* and the cutter *Lambton* to New Zealand with 60 tradesmen aboard, charging them with the duty of establishing agricultural communities in Thames and Hokianga. *Rosanna*, under Captain Herd, was the first European vessel to sail into Wellington Harbour, but despite this promising start the men aboard lost their nerve for remote settlement and headed off to Sydney.

Tory left Plymouth on 12 May 1839 to plant a settlement on the other side of the world in a country where there was no Government and where the company had no land to call its own. Among those on board was Charles Heaphy, later to be the only man awarded the Victoria Cross in the Maori-European wars, and the scientist Dr Ernst Dieffenbach. The first European to scale Mount Egmont and to note seeping hydrocarbons along the Taranaki coast, he is best known for his book *Travels in New Zealand*, one of the most important records today of early New Zealand. Edward Jerningham Wakefield was on *Tory* as well, and the book he wrote of the trip, *Adventure in New Zealand*, is also important, but it is

The New Zealand Colonisation Company ship *Tory* in Queen Charlotte Sound — a lithograph after a painting by Charles Heaphy in 1839. *Alexander Turnbull Library*

This pencil sketch of Tory Channel was drawn in 1839 by Charles Heaphy. *Alexander Turnbull Library*

generally better known for what really amounts to racism. His father, Edward, did not come on that pioneering first voyage.

Three months after leaving England, on 16 August 1839 *Tory* anchored in Ship Cove, Marlborough Sounds. Shortly after, agent William Wakefield met Dicky Barrett who ran the whaling station at nearby Te Awaiti, and together they explored Pelorus Sound looking for potential areas of settlement. They saw little hope for the area so *Tory*, with Barrett aboard as a guide, sailed for Wellington, arriving off Petone Beach on 20 September.

Charles Heaphy wrote of what they saw: The harbour resembles an inland lake rather than an arm of the sea and in beauty certainly far surpasses our English lakes. As we worked up to the anchorage, the nobel expanse of water, surrounded by a country of the most picturesque character, formed a scene of indescribable beauty . . .

An estimated 500 Maoris lived around the harbour in a number of small settlements. Honiana Te Puni of Petone and Te Wharepouri of Ngauranga came on board *Tory* as it arrived in the harbour.

"One of mature years named Te Puni, advanced with much dignity of manner to greet Barrett as an old friend," Edward Jerningham wrote in his book. "The old man was as famous for his wisdom in council as for his former deeds of war. Te Puni inquired as to the motive of our visit, and on hearing we wished to buy the place expressed the most marked satisfaction."

Among the Europeans only Barrett could speak Maori and it appeared he could speak only a bastardised form known as whalers' Maori. This crude language led to later speculation that the Wellington Maori people really did not get a clear idea what it was those aboard the *Tory* wanted. Some Wellington Maoris were opposed to the sale of land, but Te Puni seemed happy and agreed to sign a deed for the sale on 27 September. In return for selling Wellington, the New Zealand Company paid the local Maoris a variety of goods including 100 scarlet blankets, 100 muskets, tobacco, tomahawks, fish-hooks, bullet-moulds, shirts, 60 red nightcaps, 200 pencils, one dozen umbrellas, one gross of Jews harps, one dozen sticks of

"... one of mature years ..." — Honiana Te Puni, one of the local chiefs who sold Wellington to the New Zealand Company, portrayed by Charles Heaphy in 1845. *Alexander Turnbull Library*

sealing wax and a variety of both useful and useless items. In today's value the goods would be worth around $8,000 — very little for the site of a future capital city. However, Te Puni may have had much more pragmatic reasons for selling out. His small band of people were out of favour with Te Raupa-raha on the west coast and the Ngati-Kahungunu in the Wairarapa. Sandwiched between the two, Te Puni may have seen in the pakeha protection for his people. Equally, he may have had no idea of the significance of what he had done.

On 22 January the following year the first New Zealand Company emigrant ship, *Au-rora*, arrived in Wellington harbour bearing those whose task it was to create a city out of the bushed Hutt valley. The plan for the city had been drawn up in London and consisted of a rectangle with forts at the corners, and a "Covent Garden" and "President's Palace". After early floods the settlers found that the nearby Port Nicholson area appeared a better place to live, so the plans were simply transposed, unsuccessfully many would say today, to the new location.

Port Nicholson was New Zealand's first colony, and between 1839 and 1843 the company despatched 57 ships and 8,600 emigrants to Wellington.

One of the migrants was Henry Woulden, who arrived in January 1841. He wrote of the experience in a letter to his family left behind:

We had a fair wind when went up Cook Straits but jest as we wass about entrying the harber, the winds sprung up, which it blew us out to sea gain and we thought we should be all lost; 8 times we wass served

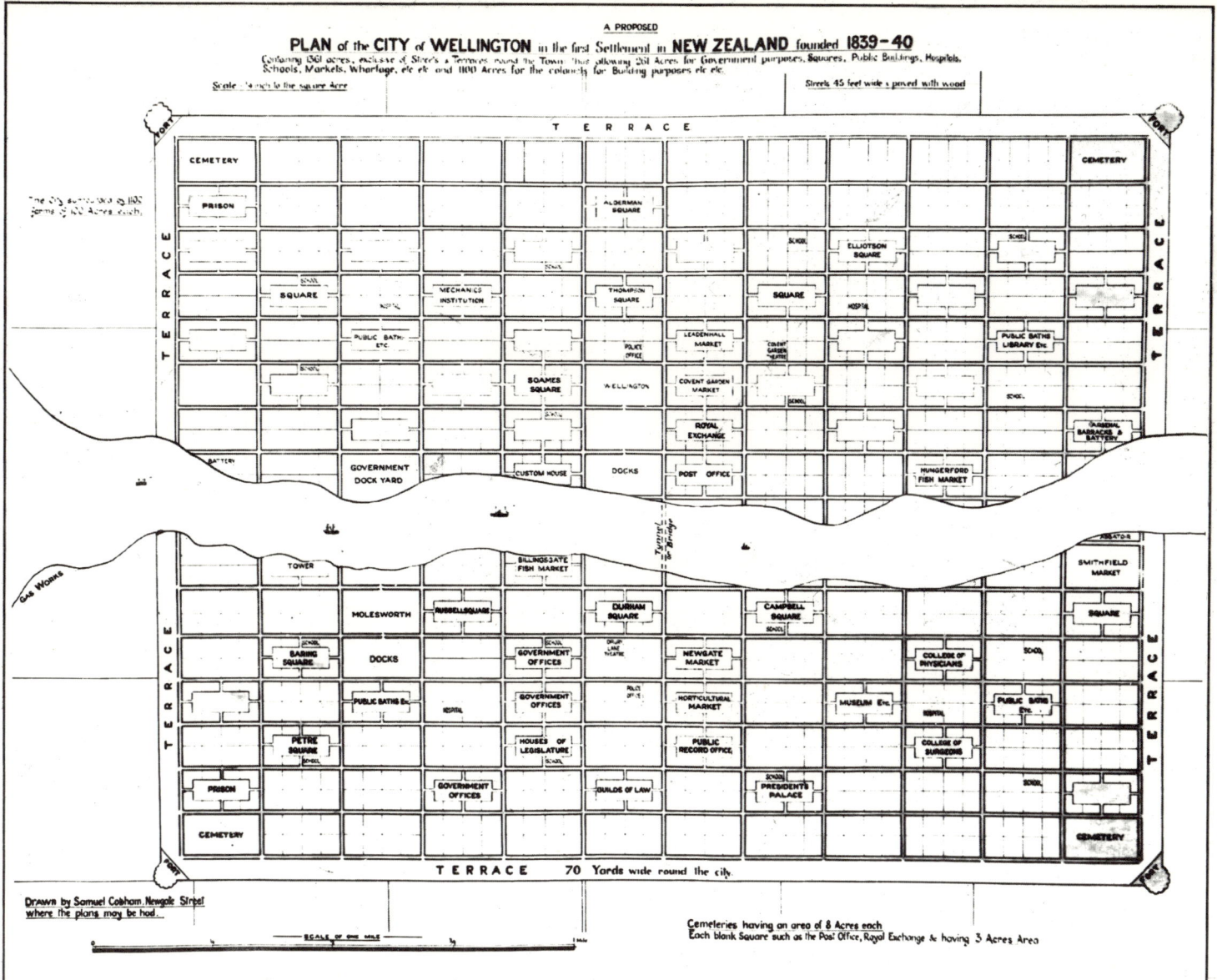

A PROPOSED

PLAN of the CITY of WELLINGTON in the first Settlement in NEW ZEALAND founded 1839-40

Containing 1361 acres, exclusive of Streets & Terraces round the Town thus allowing 261 Acres for Government purposes, Squares, Public Buildings, Hospitals, Schools, Markets, Wharfage, etc etc and 1100 Acres for the colony for Building purposes etc etc.

Scale 1/4 inch to the square Acre

Streets 45 feet wide paved with wood

Drawn by Samuel Cobham, Newgate Street where the plans may be had.

Cemeteries having an area of 8 Acres each
Each blank Square such as the Post Office, Royal Exchange & having 3 Acres Area

One Samuel Cobham who drew this plan for the New Zealand Company clearly had no notion of either Port Nicholson or the Hutt Valley when he sketched out his ideas for the new settlement. The only evidence of the plan today is Wellington's business alley, The Terrace. *Alexander Turnbull Library*

William Fox sketched this "Bird's Eye view of Waitoi' in 1848. The beginnings of what we know today as Picton can be seen at the water's edge. *Alexander Turnbull Library*

that way, 9 time we got in and a moist beautiful harber it is; for it is surrounded with mountain and we have plenty of fresh water close to my Hutt which runs down from the mountains; we wera Trubbled very much with flies and grasshopers for they eat up everything as i plant out; it is very hot in the day time and cold nights; the winds blow very strong . . .

The Treaty of Waitangi signed in 1840 gave the Crown exclusive land rights, placing the New Zealand Company in a difficult position with its settlers over the ultimate right to the land on which they had settled. The burden of dealing with this situation fell to William Wakefield. In March 1847 he was attacked in one of the town's early newspapers, the *Wellington Independent*, on the question of land. This led to a celebrated duel between the editor, Isaac Featherston, and William in Te Aro. Featherston fired the first shot and missed. William, who with his extensive military background was probably a good shot, fired his pistol into the air, saying he could not shoot a man who had seven

daughters.

Wellington became the capital in 1865, although not without some trouble. Government records and officials moved down from Auckland on board the steam ship *White Swan*, but the vessel was wrecked at Castlepoint. The civil servants were rescued, but the documents were lost.

Picton, one of the oldest boroughs in New Zealand, was another New Zealand Company enterprise. Captain William Stein on *William IV* found the site in 1832, then a Ti Ati Awa pa. The Maoris called it Waitohi and Captain Stein called it Hornes Bay after the company that owned the ship. In following years the place underwent a bewildering number of name changes until, in 1848, the company purchased the site for £100 in gold.

One John McDonald was among its first settlers. Known for the line, "It's rough here, but the longer you stay the better you'll like it", McDonald married a Te Ati Awa woman, and together in a rough hut on the beach front they established a substantial family.

Picton's early development was encouraged by a short-lived gold rush at Wakamarina. Although £200,000 worth of gold was recovered, the workings proved uneconomic. A Picton boarding-house owner found a better way of making money. He was long suspected of running an illegal whisky still on nearby Allport Island, but despite numerous searches it was never found. Only when the man died was the still discovered — hidden in the chimney of his boarding house.

Nearby Blenheim owes it origins to James Wynen, a man whose wife had been brutally murdered at nearby Port Underwood. In

The township of Picton at the turn of the century. *Alexander Turnbull Library*

1855 he built a store to serve small ships which sailed up the Opawa River, taking goods to farm settlers in the area. Although the area was swampy, other people set up near Wynen and the resulting settlement came to be known as The Beaver, or Beavertown, because of the wet look of the place. Wynen later built a celebrated "gin palace", a larger trading store made from gin packing cases.

With the establishment of provincial councils, Marlborough's two settlements, Picton and Blenheim, came close to civil war over the subject of which town should be the provincial capital. When the council opened shop in May 1860 it was in Picton, but in the subsequent five years the council debates involved little else than the subject of the capital's location. The last great debate on this topic took place in 1865. Arthur Beauchamp of Picton filibustered for 11 hours, but failed to prevent Blenheim stealing the honours by sheer force of numbers. So everything was loaded onto carts and taken

down the road to new offices in Blenheim — and that included Picton's town clock and sundial. When Picton's outraged citizens looked set to break out into open warfare, Blenheim returned the two items.

Things eventually settled down, and by 1872 work was under way on putting through a railway line from Picton to Blenheim. But work had barely started when the 160 navvies went on New Zealand's first rail strike, demanding, as their slogan said, "Eight hours work, eight hours pay, eight bob a day". They won their case.

Coal was discovered in Shakespeare Bay

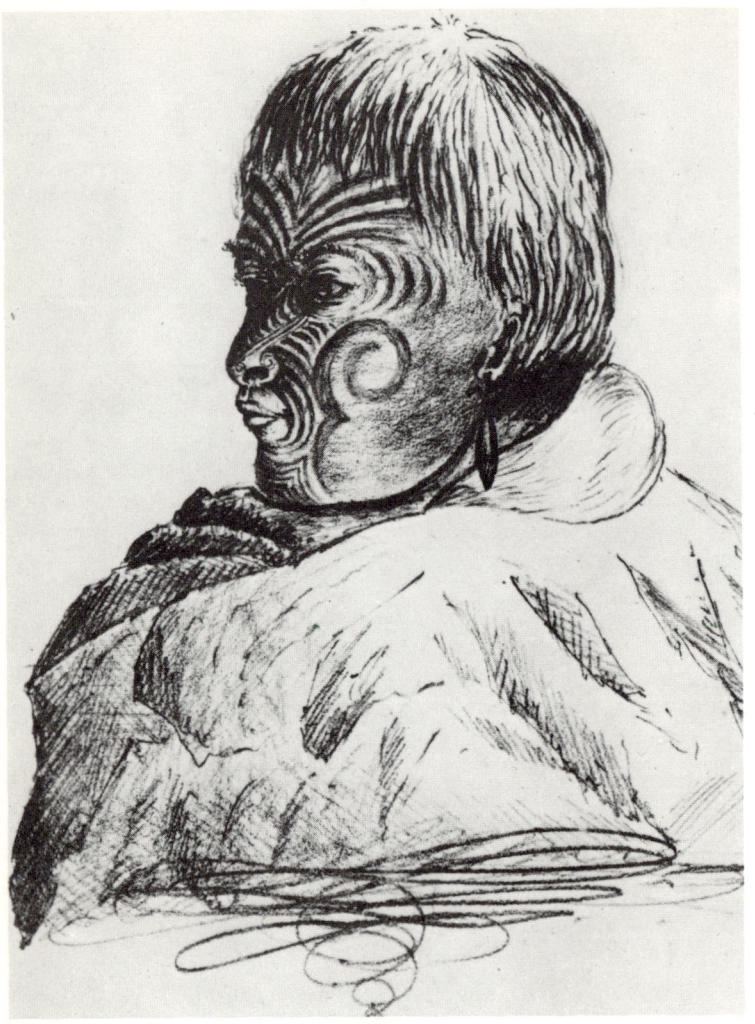

An 1839 drawing of Te Rauparaha by Charles Heaphy. Known as a great chieftain, Te Rauparaha dominated the Cook Strait area both before and after European settlement. *Alexander Turnbull Library*

A memorial to the Europeans who died in the Wairau massacre on 17 June 1843. *Alexander Turnbull Library* near Picton. A 1919 Government handbook saw a great future as a result:

> In view of the probability of Picton becoming a naval base in the near future the advantage of having a coal mine in the Sound is recognised and it is hoped that the dreams of long ago will soon be realised.

But like the gold, the coal was uneconomic to mine.

An account of European settlement in the Cook Strait area ignores one rather important fact: long before Europeans arrived the Maori people were already very well settled. And in the Maori side of the story one name stands out — Te Rauparaha, the outstanding leader of the Ngati Toa.

He was born at Kawhia on the coast north of Taranaki in 1768, two years before Captain Cook arrived on the New Zealand coast. His tribe, it appears, had problems with those round about, and by the time Te Rauparaha was 50 years old and a warrior leader of his people the situation became so tense that migration southward appeared the only solution. Te Rauparaha had travelled widely before the move and he knew the Cook Strait area. His eyes fixed on Kapiti, an island at the western entrance to the strait which had the advantage of being a natural fortress. It was also attracting Europeans, through whom Te Rauparaha saw possibilities for trading.

Of course, it is difficult to capture a fortress, a problem Te Rauparaha knew only too well. Kapiti was held by the Te Ati Awa, who saw Te Rauparaha arrive opposite Kapiti on the mainland. They also saw the warrior make preparations for an attack on a tribe to the north, and when they saw him leave they relaxed their guard. That proved fatal, for a small group stayed behind, led by Te Rauparaha's uncle, paramount chief Te Pehi Kupe. They rowed unnoticed out to Kapiti. W.T.L. Travers in *The Stirring Times of Te Rauparaha*, published in 1872, took up the story:

> Thrown off their guard by the knowledge of Te Rauparaha's absence with the bulk of the warriors, they had neglected their ordinary precautions against surprise, and were easily defeated, many being slain, although the greater number escaped in their canoes to the main land, and found refuge in the forests and swamps of the Manawatu.

With Kapiti as a base, Te Rauparaha and the Ngati Toa came to dominate the region. His attacks on the South Island were many and widespread, from Queen Charlotte Sound to D'Urville Island, and down to Akaroa and Kaiapoi. It was all grim stuff involving much revenge and cannibalism, and in the process Te Rauparaha came to be seen as a dark force in the European version of events.

The Wairau affray or massacre or affair as it is also known was the major Cook Strait incident involving Te Rauparaha. The Wairau Valley, a fertile and pleasant place around Cloudy Bay, was among Te Rauparaha's early South Island conquests. The origins of the later trouble began when a whaler, John Blenkinsopp of the *Caroline* had Te Rauparaha sign a document which the chief believed gave the whaler rights to wood and water in return for a cannon. Te Rauparaha later found out that he had instead sold the Wairau Valley to the whaler in return for what turned out to be a spiked cannon.

When the New Zealand Company later came upon the scene they purchased a copy of the Blenkinsopp deed for £300, believing it gave them the right to the land. It is uncertain whether they knew the background to the sale, but Edward Jerningham Wakefield makes it clear that the attitude towards Te Rauparaha was such that they would probably have acted in the same manner had they known. He wrote in *Adventures in New Zealand*:

> The great chieftain, the man able to lead others, and habituated to wield authority, was clear at first sight; but the savage ferocity of the tiger, who would not scruple to use any means for the attainment of that power, the destructive ambition of a selfish despot, was plainly discernible on a near view . . . . Innumerable accounts have been related to me of Te Rauparaha's unbound treachery. No sacrifice of honour or feeling seems to have been too great for him, if conducive of his own aggrandizement or security. . . .

In 1841 yet another Wakefield showed up — brother Captain Arthur Wakefield. Recently retired from the Royal Navy, he had come to New Zealand to assist the family in the migration business. The company was feeling pushed for land, and Captain Wakefield was determined to settle Wairau despite numerous warnings about the outcome.

Chief Surveyor Frederick Tuckett and a

After the whalers and the sealers, came the fishermen, and among the earliest attracted to Cook Strait were Italian migrants. These Italians were based in Makara in the late 19th Century.
J.N. Taylor Collection, Alexander Turnbull Library

team were pegging out an area when Te Rauparaha and his men arrived. They were firm and non-violent. The surveyors were put in their boats and told to go and a single grass lean-to hut was pulled down. Captain Wakefield was outraged and in the company of Police Magistrate Henry Thomson he set out from Nelson to arrest Te Rauparaha and his powerful nephew Te Rangihaeata. At Wairau neither man submitted and, while a heated discussion was taking place, a musket went off — to this day we do not know whether this happened by accident. Nine Europeans died in the fighting that followed and an unknown number of Maoris. As Captain Wakefield and the group retreated, they decided to surrender to avoid further bloodshed. The 13 survivors of the initial round of fighting, including Captain Wakefield, were then killed by Te Rangihaeata, who used his mere to crash in their skulls.

His action was seen later as revenge for the murder of Rangiawha Kuika, wife of James Wynen who later founded Blenheim. In 1839 the couple and their child had been living in Port Underwood where word spread that he was a man of considerable wealth. It was known that he kept a satchel of bright new coins under his bed, although their value was not known. One Dick Cook set out to steal the money and while Wynen was away he went to the house. With a tomahawk he murdered Rangiawha and the child, watched from a distance by his wife. The house was ransacked, but the satchel was found to contain only useless tokens. When word of the deed became known, the local Maori people were for summary justice, but their chief, Rawiri

Kingi Puaha, and the Methodist minister, Reverend Samuel Ironsides, wanted Cook to be sent to Wellington for British justice. Cook's wife could not be made to give evidence against her husband, but other circumstantial evidence seemed strong. He had been seen walking around after the murder with the tomahawk and blood-stained clothes and, the court was told, he had a bad reputation for violence. Nevertheless the jury acquitted him. Reverend Ironsides noted later:

I could not resist the conviction that greater care and diligence should have been manifested in preparation for the trial. It was only a Maori girl; of course I might have been mistaken, but such was my conviction at that time.

At Wairau the British paid for their faulty justice and their greed for Maori land.

After the incident at Wairau, Te Rauparaha, by then a grand old man of 73, was seized by the British and held under arrest in Auckland. He was released shortly after with an admission by the Government that Wakefield had been wrong to try to take the land. The chief was eventually paid £4,600 for it.

In 1848 the warship *Calliope* landed Te Rauparaha back at Otaki beach after his arrest in Auckland. Thomas Beven, an early colonist who saw the scene, later wrote of it:

A British man-of-war hove in sight and anchored off the mouth of the Otaki river, boats were lowered therefrom, soldiers and marines, in gorgeous uniforms filled them, and as they neared the shore Te Rauparaha stood proudly amongst them, attired in an admiral's uniform and carrying a sword. He was accompanied by Governor Grey and the commander of the warship. Maoris lined the shores and gave their chief a right royal welcome home. The very earth trembled with the stamping of thousands of dusky warriors feet.

Te Rauparaha died aged 81 in November 1849. He was to be buried at Otaki, but while the tangi was in progress, Te Rangihaeata and others took the body to a cave on the sacred island of Kapiti and buried it there. One European saw where the body was laid but in common with all involved he kept the cave's location a secret.

Today the great chief of the Cook Strait area still rests on Kapiti.

Chapter IV

The rise and fall of destructive Cook Strait whaling

The shore-whalers . . . have felled the tree to obtain the fruit.

MARINE scientists believe there are now less than 1,000 right or southern black whales left in the oceans of the world. The gentle creatures used to arrive off the New Zealand coast in their hundreds to give birth to calves. For a brief period in the 19th Century the habit was often fatal.

Whaling, so often romanticised in our history, was New Zealand's oldest industry. Unfortunately, it is difficult to conceive of a more ruinous one.

Captain James Cook noted in his journal that Cook Strait attracted many whales. Only 12 years after his death the first whaling ship in New Zealand waters, *William and Ann* under Captain William Bunker, called at Doubtless Bay in the course of a sperm-whaling voyage. Large-scale pelagic (open-sea) whaling made its base in the Bay of Islands shortly after, but it was not until 1827 that one Joseph Guard went into the whaling business in the Cook Strait.

Born in London in 1792, at the age of 21 Guard found himself before a Middlesex court on a breaking-and-entering charge. He was found guilty and as punishment was transported to Australia. After serving seven years as a prisoner, Guard was freed in 1829 and became an apprentice on a sailing vessel that traded as a sealer in the South Pacific. Later he went into business on his own account with a small 66-ton schooner, *Waterloo*, and was attracted to New Zealand by the profits to be made from sealing.

Those who wrote of him described him as a gigantic person with a flowing black beard. His strength was legendary, and one tale has it that during a shipboard dispute with two crewmen he picked them up, one in each hand, and tossed them overboard.

Jackie, as he was known, traded with the Maori people for some years until, in 1827, he encountered a strong storm in Cook Strait which nearly wrecked his boat on the rocks of the Marlborough coast. By an extraordinary stroke of good luck he was blown through the entrance of the Tory Channel. Once in the quiet waters, Guard was quick to appreciate the potential of the area as a whaling station.

One of the passengers on that voyage was a 13-year-old girl, Elizabeth ("Betty") Parker, whose parents in Sydney had, for some unexplained reason, felt a sea voyage would improve the girl's health. But given the events which were to fill her life later, she evidently had the strength of several oxen. She must also have had feminine charms, for two years later she was to marry Guard and become the first European woman to settle in the South Island.

Guard set up a whaling station in a bay just inside the Tory Channel entrance at a place the Maoris called Te Awaiti (the name was soon rendered "Tar White" by the whalers). By all accounts, Guard's first few years hunting whales were tough. The whaler's diet consisted, naturally enough, of whale meat and wild turnip tops. Guard was able to kill the whale only for bone as he had neither the men nor the equipment initially to boil the flesh down for oil. His first export of whale oil from Te Awaiti was landed in Sydney on 3

February 1830 and consisted of a solitary 2 tuns, a tun equalling 1,145 litres. The export shipment included 1,185 seal skins.

The young Mrs Guard lived at Te Awaiti with her husband in what quickly became known as a hell-hole. The difference from the beauty spot she first saw in 1827 must have been stark. Yet in the middle of the stinking horror of a whaling station populated by men most people considered sub-human, Jackie Guard had introduced the first rose to Marlborough Sound — the delicate plant called "Maiden's Blush".

Nine years after setting up in Te Awaiti, Guard moved his station to nearby Port Underwood in Cloudy Bay (where, to this day, the family still runs a farm on what is believed to be the oldest freehold European property in New Zealand). He moved to keep in contact with the growing number of vessels in the area, which, on account of the narrow Tory Channel entrance, would not call at Te Awaiti.

Moving into the Tory Channel station after Guard was Dicky Barrett, another colourful character of the times. Born in 1807 in Great Britain, he had been a mate on a trading schooner operating between Sydney and Ngamotu near the site of modern New Plymouth. In 1829 the vessel was unloading at Ngamotu when a cask of port slipped from its sling and plunged through the vessel, sinking it. Instead of finding passage to Australia in another vessel, Barrett stayed on and married a local girl and quickly became absorbed in the affairs of her tribe. His involvement grew to the extent that he helped the Te Ati Awa defend Ngamotu from attack by Waikato tribes in 1832. Although they

A sketch by an unknown artist shows the positions of crewmen in a typical whaleboat on the New Zealand coast. *Alexander Turnbull Library*

won the first round of fighting, the tribe and Barrett saw that their continued future lay to the south. Barrett moved with them as they headed to the Cook Strait area to attempt settlement.

"Dressed in a white jacket, blue dungaree trousers and round straw hat," as Barrett was described in a contemporary report, "he seemed perfectly round all over; while his jovial ruddy face, twinkling eyes and good-humoured smile, could not fail to excite pleasure in all beholders."

The Cook Strait area, particularly Cloudy Bay, also attracted whalers from all around the world, most notably from New England in the United States. April 1836, for example, saw 18 whaling vessels at anchor in Port Underwood.

The whalers, a rough and ill-paid bunch of men, left little in the way of the written word to describe how they saw life. Ships' logs usually contained only brief descriptions of the weather and the number of whales seen and caught.

Some odd incidents, such as the story of the *Louisa*, have survived to be recorded by Robert McNab whose book, *The Old Whaling Days*, published in 1913, has proved a historical New Zealand classic. According to McNab, the *Louisa* an American whaler, was noticed one day anchored off Mana Island. There was nothing much wrong with the ship, but it had absolutely no crew. McNab wrote:

It appears that there had been a merrymaking on board another Colonial whaler and all hands had imbibed too much, with the result that, on return to *Louisa*, the boat was upset and the chief officer and the whole of the crew drowned.

The caption on this photograph taken in 1910 read: "It is almost impossible to realise the magnitude of these animals, but compare the height of the man standing alongside the thing. He is six foot high and that is a baby whale." *Alexander Turnbull Library*

Growing interest in Cook Strait led to whaling bases being set up in Tory Channel, Cloudy Bay, Kapiti and Mana Islands and Porirua. Captain Green of the *Mediterranean Picket* pointed out the problems of such widespread interest:

When the spout of a whale would casually come within scope of vision from the look-out point, no less than seventy to eighty boats would put off in pursuit. One out of six (on an average) of those seen and pursued in the offing, was fastened to, the monsters generally on the approach of such a multitude of boats, became terrified and effected their escape, by wading their way, with all the fleetness they are capable of, beyond the bounds of vision.

There were odd hazards as well. In 1837 lightning struck the main top-gallant masthead of the whaling boat *Isabella* and ran down the topmast, striking the steward who was on deck. He was badly burnt down the left side from neck to toe ("completely cooked" was how less-delicate crewmates described it) and died a few days later.

When souls more fluent with the pen arrived upon the scene, whaling operations were in full swing. The Reverend John Bumby visited Tory Channel in 1839 to see if there was any need for a mission station. He found that the "untutored barbarians", the Maoris, were less opposed to missionary operations than the so-called civilised Europeans:

There may be about fifty Europeans connected with the whaling establishment of this place; some of whom present specimens of human nature in the worst state. Dwelling in the region of the valley of the shadow of death they practice every species of iniquity without restraint and without concealment. The very sense of decency and propriety seems to be extinct. The very soil is polluted. The very atmosphere is tainted.

One Te Awaiti character, Jimmy Jackson, was given to quoting frequently from the Bible, but he swore that "Sunday will never come to the bay". His other source of quotations was *Gutherie's Geography*, and he frequently made admiring comments about Napoleon Bonaparte.

The writer James Crawford also visited the area, but didn't think much of the scene that met his eyes. There were bones everywhere,

Two whale-chasing crews go through their paces for the benefit of the camera in the mid 1890s. In the background is part of the Te Awaiti settlement. *Alexander Turnbull Library*

blubber was stacked awaiting boiling down, thick oil was lying about the place, the men were unshaven and there was a stench of whales, dirt and rum:

> One of the horrors of a whaling station was the smell of arrack rum, which infected the air to a great distance. It was simply the most detestable liquid that I have ever met with, and although I tasted it, I could go no further, it must have been poisonous; and as it was the liquor with which the whaling stations were generally supplied, many deaths must have resulted from the use of it.

Whalers were not very well paid, but employers ensured they stayed on by allowing them to run up big debts by providing them with plenty of rum. In this hard-drinking society some men gained infamous reputations for simply never being sober. For all that, the whalers, often runaway sailors or former New South Wales convicts, frequently did leave jobs without the formality of notice, as the New Zealand Company naturalist Dr Ernst Dieffenbach observed when he visited the area on *Tory*:

> The jealousy existing between the several employers, the system of decoying each other's men by every means in their power, the character of the population itself, the universal use of adulterated and poisoned spirits, have created a state of society in which it is only to be wondered that, in the absence of all restraint and law, outrages on each other's property and person are not of a more frequent occurrence.

He saw Cloudy Bay as "the Golgotha of the whale", although as a scientist he found Te Awaiti interesting:

> A curious spectacle presented itself on the beach, which was covered with remains of whales — skulls, vertebrae, huge shoulder-blades and fins: and blubber, in

pieces a square foot in size, was still boiling in large pots; the fire was fed with those pieces of blubber, after the oil had been boiled out of them. There was much stench from the whale-oil, but this was disregarded, so great was the interest I felt in the whole process.

The view that things were grim at whaling stations was widely held, as this contemporary account showed:

Kororakeka and the Bay of Islands have been celebrated for the immorality of their populations; but they are a paradise compared to Cloudy Bay, where crimes of every discription flourish as in their native soil. If there be a Pandemonium on earth, it must be constituted by the settlement of a number of whaling gangs in the midst of a native population. The Europeans are, as a matter of course, vicious and abandoned; but they have made the natives of Cloudy Bay equally so.

The commander of HMS *Pelorus*, Lieutenant Chetwode, who visited the area in 1838, felt whalers were a disreputable and lawless set, "distrusting each other, and telling innumerable falsehoods to support their villainy".

Diefenbach did not seem to agree with the view that the whalers were having a bad effect on local Maoris:

I was astonished, and at the same time gratified, to find that the character of the natives had been so little affected by this state of things. I have not seen one instance of drunkenness amongst them, common as the vice is amongst the Eu-

ropeans; although mixing with the latter in the boats, they did not join in their revelries, which are contrary to their tastes and inclinations, and which do not begin until evening, after the return of the boats.

One product of the whalers' contact with the Maori people was the growth of "whalers' Maori", a kind of pidgin Maori language. The South Island chief Hone Tuhawaiki became known as "Bloody Jack" because he picked up the adjective from whalers and used it frequently. It seems likely that Dicky Barrett conducted the negotiations for the sale of Wellington in whalers' Maori, a totally inadequate form of communication.

It is easy to be critical of 19th-century whalers as they were outcasts from society, often former convicts, badly paid and consigned to the end of the world to work in dreadful conditions. A former whaler, who did not give his name, put together a good defence for his kind in an article in the *Wanganui Herald* in 1874:

The whaling industry had drawn together characters of the worst type — outcasts of society, men whose lives and liberties had been forfeited in other places. They lived almost outside the pale of civilisation, an eventful, dangerous and reckless kind of existence, indulging in debaucheries and all manner of sensualism during the intervals between the seasons, and wasted their hard-earned money in gambling and excesses of all kinds. There was necessarily a hardening of susceptibilities, even among those who might otherwise have striven for better things; and there was a total disregard of the rights of others, and

frequently, of the sacredness of human life. Nevertheless, although in a majority of instances might was the only acknowledged right, and it was thoroughly tested on the "convincing ground" — a space specially set aside in each occupied bay — a strong disposition towards honour obtained. Tyranny and injustice were repressed by being discountenanced, and the perpetrator of a mean or cowardly action was quickly made to feel that he had offended against the understood laws of the settlement and the disgust and scorn of men who had fallen to the depths of infamy was very pungent and very real.

Of course, temptations were numerous. Rum was plentiful and cheap; many of the native women were lewd and lecherous in their manners and conversations, and the life led by the whalers as a whole rendered them indifferent to all beyond the gratification of the passing moment. But it must not be imagined that indiscriminate intercourse was permitted by the laws of self-constituted legislature. Where a native woman was recognised as being the sole property of one man, with whom she lived — as many did — a lifetime of affection, and to whom she yielded ready obedience, her virtue was as safe from the rude and reckless community among whom she resided as that of any lady of to-day.

Whalers were not all bad, if Tommy Evans' station on the island of Tokumapuna near Kapiti was anything to go by.

"The discipline of a man-of-war pervaded the whole establishment," McNab wrote.

"The crew were in a rough uniform; boats, gear and apparatus were kept spotlessly clean and carefully attended to, and when on shore separate accommodation was provided for the headsman and the boatsteers, and for the crew."

Dividends were earned from the discipline. In 1839 Evans' six boats took 250 tuns of whale oil, while the combined total of the 19 other boats on Kapiti was 216 tuns.

Another strong leader was Joseph Thoms, also known as "Geordie Bolts" (why, nobody knew), who ran whaling stations at Te Awaiti, Cloudy Bay and Porirua. The young Edward Jerningham Wakefield described Thoms as a man of "small stature and repulsive features", adding that he had been deformed as a consequence of a run-in with a whale. But James Crawford made no mention of Thoms' deformity when he wrote of the whaler:

Thoms was a noted disciplinarian. No one dared to disobey his orders. If any one ventured to dispute with him, he would tie him up and hold him prisoner. He was a short stout man with a trunk like a barrel and a bullet head, standing firm on his legs and looking everyone straight in the face. Men of the same type may be seen on Deal Beach and at other parts of the south-east of England. He had a strong and lusty voice, and was on the whole a good sort of fellow.

Joseph Thoms has the distinction of having his name on the Treaty of Waitangi, being a witness to the signatures of a number of local chiefs.

The whale oil and bone was exported from Cook Strait to Sydney and Tasmania, initially causing problems of tariff control in the Australian colonies which had lost little time in setting up bureaucracies of their own. It was while on a trans-Tasman trading voyage that Jackie and Elizabeth Guard became involved in a startling drama. With their two children, a son aged two-and-a-half years and a daughter six months, the family was returning from Sydney on the vessel *Harriet*, 240 tons, when it was wrecked on the Taranaki coast on 29 April 1834. The crew and the Guard family all managed to clamber safely ashore, but that was only the beginning of their troubles. They made camp on shore, but on the third day 30 or 40 Maoris came to plunder the wreck. They made threatening gestures to the huddled group on the shore who were poorly equipped with a few muskets. A couple of days later several hundred Maoris showed up and attacked the Europeans who defended themselves for a time. On 10 May the final attack came.

"About eight o'clock on the morning of the 10th they again made their appearance in a body, under arms," Jackie Guard said later, "and they struck one of the crew on the head with a tomahawk, and then cut him right in two; another, named Thomas White, they cut down and cut his legs off the joints of the knees and hips, . . .'"

At one stage Elizabeth and the children were seized, and she was struck on the head with a tomahawk, but was saved from a fatal injury when the blow crashed into her whalebone comb. Once out of ammunition, the group surrendered and was taken to a nearby pa where they were stripped naked.

"They several times offered us some of our

Portraits of early New Zealand whalers are few and far between — the men simply did not have the time for such refinement. But in this photograph of Joseph Thoms, Junior, one can see some of the character inherited from his famous father. The young Thoms was only the second white child born at Te Awaiti. *Alexander Turnbull Library*

own people's flesh to eat, which they had brought from the wreck in baskets."

After some days, Guard and five men were allowed to sail away in a small ship's boat that was recovered from the wreck. Nine other surviving men and Elizabeth and the children were kept as hostages.

Sailing south to the whaling station, the men in the small boat arrived safely and

Joseph Thoms' whaling station at Porirua. *Alexander Turnbull Library*

Guard was able to sail on to Sydney to seek help.

He returned to the Taranaki coast on 14 September on board HMS *Alligator*, but although he could see his wife on the beach, rough seas prevented them being reunited. It was not until 5 October that the survivors were rescued. Elizabeth Guard lived for many years after the incident, in spite of having 11 pieces of whale bone worked out of her head wound later.

Another well-known whaler-settler was James Heberley, who as a runaway youth had gone to sea and seen much of the world including the infamous Bay of Islands. His diary was reprinted in part in the 1933 book by C.A. MacDonald, *Pages from the Past*. In it he recounted how he found himself on board the *Waterloo* heading for Te Awaiti:

> The schooner belonged to John Guard, who told me that he ran a shore-whaling party and that all hands lived ashore and had a royal time, as there were plenty of houses at Te Awaiti and any amount of native women to do the work, so that, apart from whaling, all we had to do was to go out in our boats and catch fish, put them in a bag, and throw them ashore for the women to clean and cook against our coming back ashore.

Heberley ruefully noted that it had been April Fool's Day 1830 when he had set sail. Conditions of Te Awaiti proved somewhat different from what he had heard — apart from anything else he had to build his own house upon arrival. Armed with an axe he headed into the bush to do so:

> Here I was horrified to come across a great number of dead bodies, and I lost no time in leaving the place. I told an Irishman named Logan what I had seen, but he merely laughed, and said that was nothing, as there were even more in the bush the next day.

A few days later I found that he was right, for in the next bay I saw perhaps fifty or sixty bodies on the ground, as well as a number of heads and arms, and joints cut from other bodies. Some of the joints had been cooked and there was something that looked like a small child spitted on a stick, where it had been roasting in front of a fire which had died out.

The circumstances were not explained, but later writing makes it clear that the ebb and flow of Te Rauparaha's wars were frequently sweeping across the place.

Instead of building a house, Heberley settled into a Maori food hut, which led to his nickname. One morning a woman called out, "Ai tangata whata haremai mou te kai" . . . . Man of the food house, come to breakfast. This caused amusement and led to Heberley being called "tangata whata", which in whalers' Maori eventually came out as "worser". Worser Bay in Wellington carries the name still.

Heberley's writing shows that whalers were not entirely savages and were capable of affection.

> That summer [1830-31] at Port Underwood I took a wife. She was not a slave and I bought her for a blanket — that is, it was customary to give their friends something. I took her back to Te Awaiti and she has been a good helpmate to me, and has reared a large family. We were married as soon as the missionary came among us at the end of 1840.

Heberley lived to the ripe age of 90, perhaps proving that the rum wasn't all rot-gut. Joseph Thoms' great-grandson, Joe Bolton of Porirua who is an authority on the subject of earlier whalers, claims Heberley one day dressed up in his best suit and went for a walk

Members of the Te Awaiti whaling community in the mid 1890s pose for a photograph around the rotting remains of a whale head. Many of the Europeans in the photograph are members of the Thoms family. The steamer in the background is the mailboat *Torea. Alexander Turnbull Library*

along the Picton waterfront. Bolton's grandmother shortly after saw the old fellow's top-hat bobbing on the harbour. When others came it was found that the old man was standing bolt upright beneath the hat, clutching his walking stick. He was dead. They were never able to get the stick out of his hand, so he was buried with it.

Marriages, of sorts, between local women and whalers were common. Dr Dieffenbach

was impressed with the product of that kind of union:

> [The children] have finely-cast countenances, and their features remind us little of the admixture of a coloured race; the skin is not so dark as that of the inhabitants of the south of France; they generally inherit from the mother the large and fine eyes and the dark glossy hair; there are, how-

ever, many individuals with flaxen hair and blue eyes.

Elizabeth Guard did not remain the only European woman in the area for long. Sarah, the Irish-Canadian wife of the whaler Captain Daniel Dougherty, was set down in 1838 in Cutters Bay with her two daughters. Some distance from the Guards, she was alone for a lot of the time. One settler was so shocked at this that he presented her with a Russian wolfhound for protection.

Twenty-five-year-old Sarah was later a victim of a whaler's duplicity. He had his eye, not on her, but on her husband's stand of muskets. As she would not part with them, the whaler one night lit a fire on top of a nearby hill and paid two Maoris to run around it, giving the impression from Sarah's house of many tribesmen. The whaler came rushing in to say an attack was imminent and he needed the muskets for defence. Sarah, clearly frightened, handed them over quickly to the whaler who went off into the night with them. Only as the fire slowly died out did Sarah realise she had been tricked.

Although the whalers are considered to have played a major role in European settlement in New Zealand, economic whaling was possible for only a comparatively short period. The main problem was of its own making — it was a very destructive business. In 1839, only two years after Guard's shore station was established, Dr Dieffenbach could see that the industry was doomed:

> The shore-whalers, in hunting the animal in the season when it visits the shallow waters of the coast to bring forth the young, and suckle it in security, have

felled the tree to obtain the fruit, and have thus taken the most certain means of destroying an otherwise profitable and important trade.

It was the southern right whale which suffered worst. Being a slow animal, it had been hunted around the world since ancient times. Dr Dieffenbach considered that southern right whales were considerably smaller than their northern counterparts. In the south, right whale females grew to about 14 metres and males to 30 metres. The whales taken in Cook Strait were almost exclusively female as they had come into New Zealand waters to calve. That made them easy targets, as the whalers learned to kill the calf first and then take the mother, who would always stay with the dying calf.

Right whales were also known as black whales because of their skin colour. The oil from the right, known in the trade as "black oil", was not as valuable as sperm whale oil, but rights had a higher ratio of oil to bulk while at the same time they provided baleen, the horny and fibrous mouth bone usually described as "whale bone" in a range of consumer items. When whalers first began killing rights in the Cook Strait they could expect a yield of 14 tuns of oil per creature. But as they killed off the bigger animals yields dropped, to the extent that in 1839 the average yield was 9 tuns, and four years later it was down to 5 tuns. Dr Dieffenbach wrote:

> I must observe . . . that . . . shore-whaling which I have described is very detrimental to the whale fishery in general, and the number of whales has decreased from year to year. The female whale ap-

proaches the land merely for the purpose of bringing forth and rearing her young. Later in the year, when the calf has attained a certain size, the cows leave the immediate neighbourhood of the coast, and return to the "whaling ground", where the males share with them the dangers resulting from the pursuit of man. Would it not, therefore, be advisable by legislative enactments, to put an end to the whale fishery from the coasts, and restrict it to a certain distance from the shore, where it would have to be pursued in ships? To kill the calves in order to capture the mother, or to kill the latter in the times of gestation, is an unprofitable and cruel proceeding; but it carries with it its own punishment. In a few years this trade, of which, from the geographical position of the "whaling-ground", New Zealand might have continued to be the centre, will be annihilated.

When Dr Dieffenbach's warning was published in 1843 it was too late.

The shore stations operated on the principle of sending out small boats to harpoon the whale. Built for quick manoeuvring, both ends of the boat were bow-shaped to help oarsmen when they were forced to row backwards quickly when the whales lashed out. Each crew was in the charge of the "headman", whose duties included administering the final kill with a lance. The actual closing-in on the whale was directed by the "boatsteer", who held and threw the harpoon.

The killing of whales took place several kilometres from the shore, and the towing-in

Te Awaiti in its heyday at the turn of this century. *Free Lance Collection, Alexander Turnbull Library*

was a tedious business. Tides and winds frequently made it more difficult and in rough seas the whale had to be anchored so that crews could come back at a later time to pick it up. This method was far from perfect, but technology had not developed to the point where there were adequate methods of preventing a dead whale from sinking.

Maori crews hunted whales as well, but they would not tow them in. Instead they sold the kill on an "as-is where-is" basis for around £20. Back at the shore station the whale was "cut in", meaning the blubber was stripped off, and "tried out" or rendered

down in large cauldrons. For the shore parties the seasonal nature of the work meant that many of the men were not dependent on whaling and many turned their hand to small-scale farming in the off-season.

The first missionary to live at a Cook Strait whaling station was the Reverend Samuel Ironsides, together with his good lady who arrived in Port Underwood in December 1840. After settling the question of a mission house (a hastily converted cookhouse) he quickly carried out social reform by marrying five whalers to the local girls with whom they had been living.

Reverend Ironsides settled eventually in Ngakuta Bay. In the three years he stayed in the area he built up a circuit of 30 whaling stations and Maori villages. His biggest physical achievement was the building of a church at Port Underwood, which, at the time, was the biggest church in the country. Articles by him in the *New Zealand Methodist* show that he did not think highly of the whalers:

I will not sully these pages with particulars of the low, debasing code of morals prevalent among these shore parties.

Suffice it that, among other things, the services of Maori women were hired, very frequently for the fishing season, by payments such as half a keg of tobacco or rum etc. Some of the chiefs were living on the proceeds of this immorality . . .

The narratives of their [the whalers] drunken, wretched orgies, given me at times by competent witnesses, reveal a most disgraceful state of things. There was no law; everyone appeared to do that which was right in his own eyes.

Reverend Ironside's high moment undoubtedly occurred on 5 August 1842 when he married 40 couples, who until that time had "been living together on the principle of free love". Mrs Ironsides provided the wedding rings — brass curtain rings. In his time there, Reverend Ironsides baptised 613 adults, 165 infants and married 171 couples. The whaling industry was already in sharp decline when the Wairau incident involving Te Rauparaha occurred, but the tension that followed prompted the Reverend to close his mission.

Between 1830 and 1850 the indiscriminate killing described by Dr Dieffenbach practically wiped out the right whale population, and today they are still extremely rare. As he predicted, the whaling industry went into a rapid tail-spin after the peak years of 1843 and 1845. The climaxes had followed a big build-up in American, French, English and Australian whaling vessels in Cloudy Bay and shore stations involving around 500 men along Cook Strait. But aside from the high rate of killing, the industry declined because the boom in railway building in the United

Nineteen-year-old Gilbert Perano in 1963 with the harpoon gun mounted on the bow of one of the family whale chasers. *"Evening Post"*

States saw a big demand for labour there, while the American Civil War put paid to the American whaling fleet. The 1849 Californian gold rush, followed by the 1851 Australian gold strike, also pulled men away from the shore stations. The real turning point came in 1859 when Colonel E.L. Drake sank his celebrated Titusville well in the United States, which produced oil capable of being refined into kerosene.

The last destructive episode in the New Zealand whaling industry occurred in the first half of this century, from virtually the same place Jacky Guard had set up the first station.

In 1875 one Guiseppe Giovanni Agostino Perano left Italy to head for America and a job in the printing trade. He was not successful and instead found himself a job as a crewman on a ship heading out to Port

Chalmers. There he settled as a fisherman, moving north at the turn of the century to fish for pilchard out of Picton. These herrings were extremely common in the area, and earlier this century hundreds of thousands of them had beached themselves on the Picton foreshore, leading to oil pollution which threatened the health of the locals. While in Picton, Perano ran four boats and averaged a daily haul of 1.5 tonnes.

In 1911 his son, Joe senior, opened the old whaling station at Yellerton Bay, intending to pick off the few right whales that still went through the strait as well as the more common humpback whales. The station opened only in the winter months to catch the migrating whales, and for Perano and those that worked with him the rest of the year was spent in farming.

The Perano family's whaling venture used launches, which were a considerable advance on the old row boats, and together with a recently developed explosive harpoon the Peranos were able to make much higher catches. At its peak they took 226 humpbacks in a season.

Killing was a complicated and dangerous operation. The harpoon had three slightly curved slender barbs, while an explosive grenade, home-made and rough, was mounted on the harpoon and fired by a detonator from the chaser. The explosion did not usually kill the whale, but left it stunned. That operation was followed up by the chaser coming alongside to pump air into the whale. The final blow was made with a long lance with a hollow cast-iron head packed with gelignite, which was touched off near the thorax.

The Perano family sometimes used their whale chasers for social events. On this occasion in 1962 they had come out to see the new rail ferry *Aramoana* make its first commercial crossing of the strait. *"Evening Post"*

Whales were spotted from a lookout called "Angels' Rest", 100 metres above the head of Tory Channel. With the development of radio, the lookout directed the chasers towards the whales.

The dreadful business of killing whales from Tory Channel declined as the species they hunted were moved relentlessly on to the endangered list. But the dramatic decline in whale population in the area was not entirely the result of the Perano's whaling activity. The year before the station closed up an eight-ship Russian whaling fleet was operating just beyond territorial waters off Kaikoura.

"They could catch in a day what we would get in a month or more," Gilbert Perano told the newspapers. "The sight on television last night of the Russians with 12 whales was not a happy one to us. I can tell you the telephone wires between here and Wellington have been pretty hot all night."

But it was a fact that the Peranos were not particular about what they killed. Their biggest catches were two mighty, and now extremely rare, blue whales. Gilbert, the son of the station's founder, kept an 11-centimetre-long perfectly formed embryo from one of the blue whales they caught. A 30-metre-long blue whale they took in 1947 was

A blue whale weighing 50 tonnes is hauled up the ramp at the Tory Channel whaling station. *Free Lance Collection, Alexander Turnbull Library*

The Peranos' high-speed whale chasers out in Cook Strait. *Hinge Collection, Alexander Turnbull Library*

finally killed by seven explosive harpoons after an hour of toil.

In that year the electric harpoon, which Gilbert described as a "wonderful boon", came into service. Connected by a thick cable to the chaser, it gave the whales a lethal shock.

"It all seems so strange. The whale just rolled over without a struggle."

Belated environmental sensitivity began to show, as a 1949 Blenheim press report indicates:

> Even though Tory Channel whalers now require only 11 kills to equal the 1947 record of 111, the chaser crews who intercepted a big humpback in Cook Strait yesterday afternoon allowed it to proceed unharmed. The reason was that it was found to be accompanied by a calf and not even the possibility of a new record was considered sufficient excuse to harpoon the mother.

They probably got the whale the following year.

The problems facing the Peranos were set out in a Department of External Affairs paper on the regulation of whaling published in August 1959. It said University of Sydney research had shown that there was a significant measure of autonomy in the migration routes followed by herds of humpbacks:

> Thus while the various herds may mix together both in the Antarctic feeding waters and in the tropical breeding waters, they do segregate into herds which retain their identity from year to year for the

purpose of migrating between the feeding and breeding grounds. Any over-fishing by a shore station is therefore likely to rebound on that station rather than on other stations or on pelagic expeditions.

The paper sounded a warning that had been implied by Dr Dieffenbach over a century before:

> It is clear that the International Whaling Commission has reached the crisis that has been predicted for some time and unless some satisfactory international regime is established there is a distinct danger that in time whales will be exterminated in southern waters. This would destroy an existing New Zealand industry and a great world asset.

As humpback numbers declined, attention was turned to sperm whales. This whale, the largest animal with teeth, is a very different prospect to the right whale. If *Moby Dick* is to be believed, the fast whales are also dangerous. Sperm whaling was practised off the New Zealand coast by pelagic sailing ships, but it never formed a significant part of the catch made by shore stations.

For a time the Peranos, into their last whaling days, were helped out by the Royal New Zealand Air Force, which flew spotting missions for them in the course of an official Marine Department survey, but letters-to-the-editor columns were beginning to show indications of public disgust at the business.

On 4 January 1965 Gilbert Perano announced the closure of the Tory Channel Whaling Company.

"We can't see any future in it for at least

Humpbacks followed set migration routes northward during the New Zealand winter

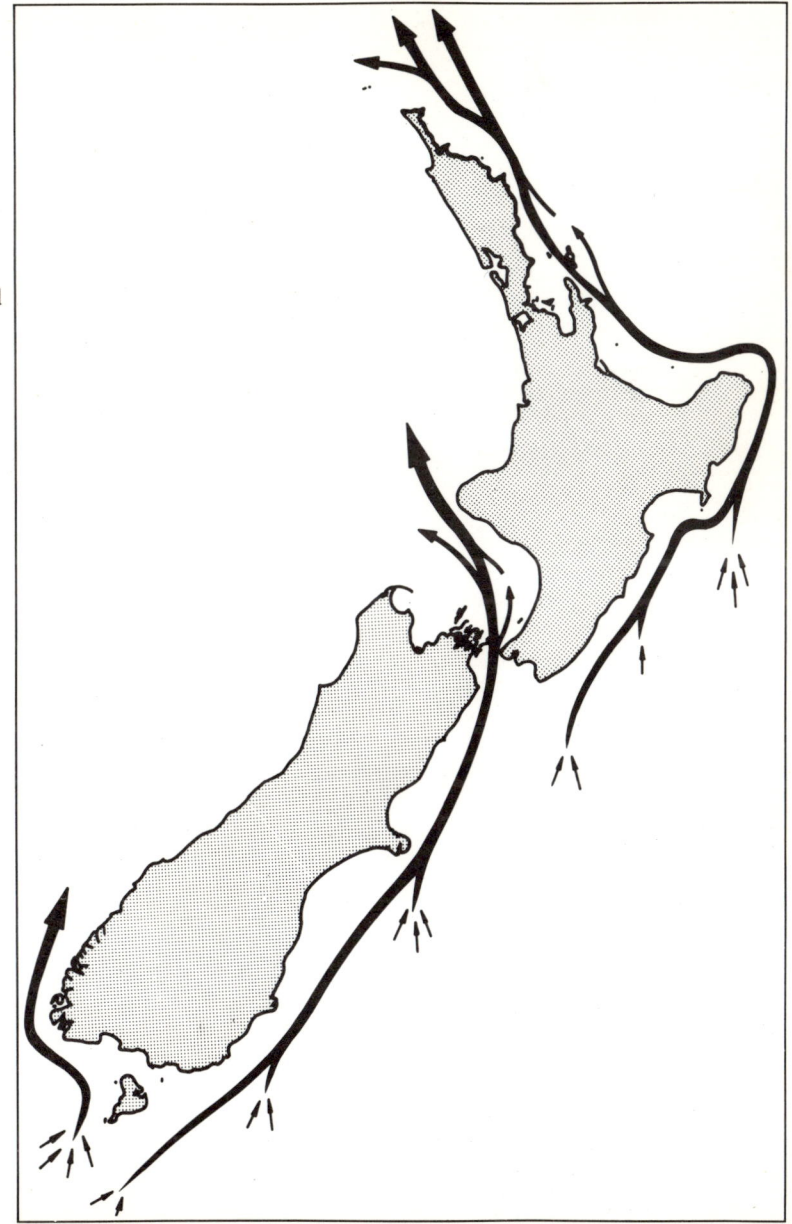

All that is left of the Tory Channel whaling station at (Te Awaiti). *Peter Avery*

two years," he told *The Dominion*. "If we could break even it would be all right, but we cannot even do that."

Three months later £250,000 worth of equipment at Tory Channel lay useless, with little chance of it being used for any other purpose. When it was in operation the plant had employed 35 shore hands.

"We have lost a lot of money over our venture into sperm whaling and the whole place is now looking like a ghost town. It doesn't seem natural after all these years and we just can't accustom ourselves to it."

Eventually the oil tanks at the whaling station were floated down to Picton where they are now used to store tallow at the local freezing works.

Today it is rare to see a whale in Cook Strait, and unless the numbers recover, which seems unlikely, we probably never will see whales there in any significant numbers again.

Chapter V

The story of Pelorus Jack

. . . he would cuddle up lovingly against the side . . . .

ONE disillusioning aspect of adulthood is the way in which sweet childhood tales die on the altar of fact; yet the story of Pelorus Jack has stood the test of time. Much of what was told us as young New Zealanders is true: it passes the tests cynical adults impose.

Pelorus Jack (it may have been Jill, but that aspect was never very clear) was a species of dolphin not common in New Zealand. The Risso dolphin or *Grampus griseus* was distinguished from other dolphins by the lack of a beak.

Pelorus Jack may have been an infant with a straying herd of dolphins when he lost his mother in the Cook Strait. This, and the rareness of the species in New Zealand, may have accounted for his odd behaviour. Lonely and out of contact with his fellows, it seems Pelorus Jack sought affection from the lumbering ships he always accompanied in a stretch of water near D'Urville Island, on the route taken by the Wellington-Nelson ferries.

Pelorus Jack, happily unaware of the international interest he created in his 20 years of accompanying ships, was believed by some to be the ghost of a sailor swept overboard from Durmont D'Urville's ship *Astrolabe*. That story had its origins with an Anchor Shipping Line executive, J. Henry Cock, who wrote an article in the *Weekly News* in 1908 in which he told of talking with an old Maori woman on D'Urville Island. Cock said the woman, "Korinete", possessed a silver medallion attached to a much-worn silver chain and bearing on one side a saint's figure and on the other a heart with the name "Colinette" on it.

"This is the only souvenir remaining of my French ancestor," the woman told Cock.

She also spoke of a dream she regularly had in which she saw a sailing ship struggling through French Pass. Two men were swept ashore and, while one made it safely, the other drowned. Then a large and strange fish appeared.

Cock linked the dream with the *Astrolabe*.

The distinctive Risso's dolphin, without a beak. *Alexander Turnbull Library*

"Pelorus Jack". *Alexander Turnbull Library*

Cover fish Pelorus Jack on a Christmas edition of the *Illustrated London News. De Maus Collection, Alexander Turnbull Library*

Two years later, when he was in France, he claims to have checked out official records and the log of the *Astrolabe*. It said the ship made an accidental voyage through the pass on 16 May 1827 and, while doing so, second officer Pierre Legassic and able seaman Jacques Tregoulet were swept overboard and lost. Cock recalled that Korinete had told him her father had named the fish of her dreams "Jacques". He tracked down the home town of the two sailors and met a Legassic family member who recalled that a strange letter had turned up many years ago from a long-lost family member. At the borough council offices the old letter was found. Cock said it was a sort of parchment pamphlet, formed of five folios and sewn together with flax. We have only Cock's version of what was in the letter; nobody else has seen it since!

Point Colinette,
near D'Urville's Island, 1829.

I grow feeble, and my desire is of late strong to send news of myself to my country. I therefore give this letter to my wife's brother, Turi, charging him to keep it until the opportunity comes to send it away by some vessel that the good God will sooner or later cause to call here. When more than two years ago I fell overboard from the *Astrolabe*, my brave countryman, Jacques Tregoulet, sprang to help me, and held me up until we both were dashed upon the rocky shore, he only to float away senseless into death, and I to be nursed back to life by the kindly natives who found me. Now, a strange thing happened. Each morning there appeared at the rocky point where I was washed ashore a curious fish about fifteen feet in length, pallid in colour, and which caused some consternation amongst the natives from its regular daily visit, and by the fixed way in which it regarded them as they approached the beach. So soon as I could walk, they entreated me to accompany them to the Point, where, upon seeing me, the fish disported itself with manifest joy, and upon my chancing to make an exclamation of surprise in the Breton tongue, it projected its head from the water,

and gazed steadily at me. My exile has perhaps given me strange fancies, but I feel sure that the spirit of Tregoulet has taken possession of this fish, which follows our canoes when we go fishing, and still comes daily to me for food and recognition. Though I have a wife and child, the fish, named by me Jacques, and by the Maoris Atuawiwi (Frenchman's ghost), comes nearer to my heart than all . . .

This extraordinary letter, made of rat skins, was alleged to have been taken out from New Zealand by an American whaler.

Cock saw more evidence for his theory in the word "Atuawiwi", pointing out that the Maoris had called *Astrolabe* sailors "wi wi" because the Europeans were given to saying "Oui, oui". From all this Cock extracted a possible reason for Pelorus Jack's habit of riding ships' bow waves:

In vain hithertoo has he pursued ship after ship in the hope of encountering a priest who shall say the holy words of exorcism and benediction needed shrive [absolve] this restless spirit. Doubtless, too, Legassic's friendly shade hovers near awaiting Tregoulet's release, when together they will in spirit revisit their beloved Brittany.

Perchance the time is not far distant when some Breton priest may journey through the Passe des Francois, and speaking to Pelorus Jacques in his native tongue, shall grant to him the peace of which he is now ever in quest.

The story has a good ring to it, but it is short on fact. The *Astrolabe's* deliberate, not ac-

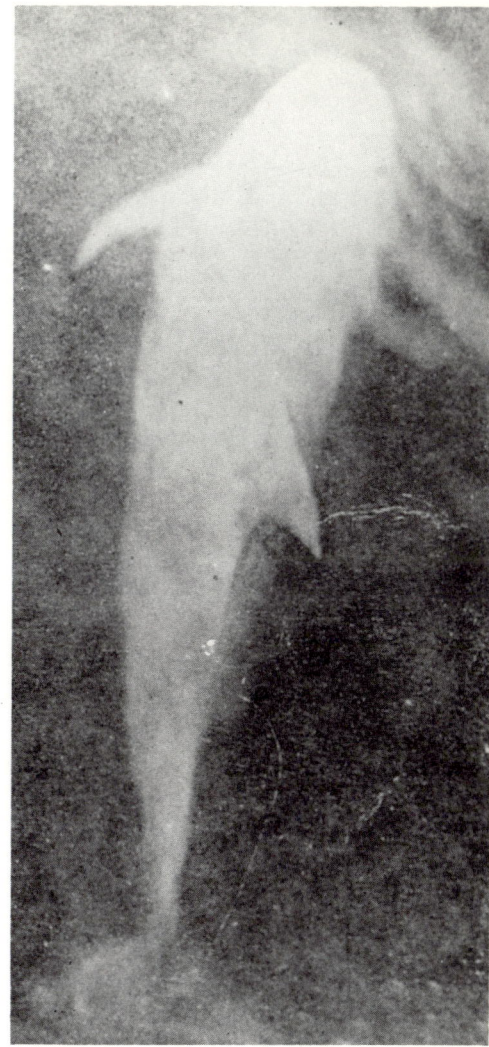

Few good photographs were ever taken of Pelorus Jack. This one was published on a postcard.
John Dickie Collection, Alexander Turnbull Library

cidental, voyage through French Pass was actually made in January, not May, a detail one would expect to be correct in a ship's log. Additionally, none of the known records of the voyage refer to a sailor by the name used by Cock, nor is there any mention of loss of crew, apart from a desertion in Tonga.

The ghost story did the rounds for a while until James Cowan, one of New Zealand's most prolific early writers, published in 1911 an interview with an old tohunga, Kipa Hemi Whiro of the Marlborough Sounds township of Okoha. Kipa described the ghost story as fearful lies. Cowan quoted him:

E tama! My taniwha "Kaikai-a-waro" is no ordinary fish. He is the embodiment of our tribal mana; a very great mana-tapu. He is many generations old. In ancient times every Maori chief had his particular family atua or god — some were birds, some were great fish, such as whales; some were stones.

Pelorus Jack was his atua. Kipa also told a story about a slave of Te Rauparaha, an old man called Irai. After the Wairau affray, Te Rauparaha's canoe ran into a storm and came close to sinking. After much material was thrown overboard in an effort to save the canoe, old Irai was tossed into the sea. But Irai was more than a slave. Before his capture he had been a chief, and stored away in his head were magic incantations, one of which he used to call up his ancestral sea god, a dolphin.

Kipa said:
As the old man, so lonely in that howling sea, swam slowly on, his face turned to the distant hills, something touched his body from behind. He turned his head and there swam his taniwha — the long greyish dolphin with the powerful shark-like tail, the sea god of whom he had so often heard, but whom he had never seen.

The creature gently sank, and rising beneath Irai, it caught him upon its back; it bore him up safely and with ease, and it swam along with him towards the far-off shore.

According to the tale old Irai was eventually deposited safely at Pencarrow Head, and in his last days among his people he was known as "Irai-eke-Taniwha", the rider of the sea god.

Moving away from myth, even if only slightly, the man who claimed credit for naming Pelorus Jack was an Anchor Line ship's purser, John William Massey. Writing in the Christchurch *Press* in 1929 he said he made a regular practice of going to the fo'c'sle of ships as they entered Pelorus Sound.

"I continually noticed that this large fish always appeared suddenly, about a mile inside the entrance and escorted us at the stem of the steamer."

But Massey's claim does not ring true; Anchor Line ships did not enter Pelorus Sound and, despite the name, there was never any evidence that the dolphin did either.

Exactly when people became aware of Pelorus Jack is not known. Some recalled years later seeing the dolphin as early as 1870, but there are no written references to a single dolphin escorting ships much prior to 1890. Because dolphins can live around 20 years, and as 1912 seems to have been the year Pelorus Jack died, the earlier sightings seem unlikely.

It was really only in the period around the turn of the century that Pelorus Jack became internationally known for his habit of meeting the regular steamer on the Wellington-Nelson service. Ships were always escorted over an 8-kilometre stretch between Collinet Point on the mainland side of French Pass and the Chetwode Islands. Despite the almost universally held belief that Pelorus Jack used to pilot vessels through French Pass, this was not the case. All the regular ships' masters reported Pelorus Jack's trips in the same area, although in both directions. None of the expert observers saw Pelorus Jack in French Pass, an area that would have been dangerous for a dolphin.

It is said that around 1904 somebody attempted to shoot Pelorus Jack. The story has its origins with the same Mr Massey who claimed to have named the fish:

I remember an incident once when the fish was famous and passengers and crew would be on the lookout for him. Some riflemen were on board and one of them suddenly appeared on the forecastle head with a rifle loaded to shoot Pelorus Jack. He got the hottest time of his life from the captain, officers and ship's hands. He retreated to his cabin and did not appear until arrival.

Others said the incident took place on the ill-fated *Penguin* and, consequently Pelorus Jack stayed clear of the vessel. But because we know Massey had his facts wrong about

Pelorus Sound, the kind of mistake one does not expect from a seaman, one is inclined to wonder about the truth of the story of the rifleman.

Several correspondents to the *Evening Post* referred to Pelorus Jack's relationship with the *Penguin*. Signed "Grandma", one person noted:

> As a child I lived in Nelson and can clearly remember seeing the Maguire children off from Nelson on the SS *Penguin* that night the ship hit Tom's Rock, and to this day I believe that was the only time Pelorus Jack didn't precede the ship from the French Pass.

This letter prompted another from "G J M":
> I came from Greymouth by ship in January 1909, and it was said that SS *Penguin* was the only ship not being escorted through the Pass by Pelorus Jack as he was hit by the ship's rudder some time previously.

The shooting story gained further status in 1931 when a writer, George Finn, referred to Pelorus Jack as "perfectly inoffensive, and was certainly interesting [and] yet on one occasion a silly fool of a passenger thought he would try his shooting skill by having a shot at Jack with a rifle, fortunately with no evil result".

Finn claimed the incident led to moves by the head of the Tourist Department, T.E. Donne, to have Pelorus Jack protected. Mr Donne did indeed write a letter about the dolphin to the Marine Department around 1908 — that fact is recorded in a registry at the National Archives in Wellington. But the

Pelorus Jack riding a bow wave.
Alexander Turnbull Library

letters themselves were destroyed in a 1951 fire.

The Government meteorologist, Reverend D.C. Bates, took a particular interest in Pelorus Jack. The Government, when it decided to declare Pelorus Jack protected, needed formal identification of the dolphin, which was given by Reverend Bates. With that, an Order-in-Council was published under the Governor Lord Plunket's name in the *New Zealand Gazette* on 26 September 1904. Under the Sea Fisheries Act 1894 it was declared that for five years from the date of gazetting, "it shall not be lawful for any person to take the fish or mammal of the species commonly known as Risso's dolphin (*Grampus griseus*) in the waters of Cook Strait, or of the bays, sounds and estuaries adjacent thereto".

Breaking the regulation would have meant a fine of not less than £5 and not more than £100.

With the order, mistaken by the world's media as an Act of Parliament, Pelorus Jack's international fame reached higher levels. There was hardly a newspaper in the world that did not run stories on the dolphin. The *Illustrated London News* ran a sketch of Pelorus Jack on the cover of its Christmas issue in 1910. Still, many people who had not seen the dolphin disbelieved the story, as did the writer Frank Bullen until he found himself on a ferry watching Pelorus Jack:

The ship was going 14½ knots, yet that grampus maintained his position by her side with the utmost of ease, only the slightest quiver of his tail being noticeable. Occasionally he changed his position from starboard to port, pausing for a few moments right ahead of the swiftly-moving ship; then dropping astern a few feet, he would cuddle up lovingly against the side, as if he enjoyed feeling her chafe against his body.

The speed of Pelorus Jack, commented on by many, was probably a result of the dolphin riding the invisible pressure wave formed below the surface by the forward motion of the ship.

So well-known did Pelorus Jack become that an Englishman was once able to post a letter to a friend in Marlborough Sounds addressed simply, "Mr A Stuart, care Pelorus Jack".

The Dean of Calcutta, Bishop Welldon, wrote in an Indian newspaper that his most memorable Christmas had been on a Cook Strait ferry watching Pelorus Jack.

In 1911 the dolphin gave a warning of what was to come: he went missing for a while. A French Pass settler sent a telegram to the Marine Department saying he had discovered the body of a dolphin which he believed to be Pelorus Jack. The news flashed around the world and newspaper columns were filled with sad stories. But like early reports of the death of Mark Twain, who had been among those to see Pelorus Jack, the news was premature. A short time after the French Pass discovery, passenger and crew on the *Pateena* reported that Pelorus Jack was back on his beat.

But the good news was short-lived. Later the next year Pelorus Jack did disappear and was never seen again. When it became apparent he had gone for good people deliberated on possible reasons. It was suggested that the dolpin had been hit by one of the double screws of the *Arahura* after being used to the single-screw *Mapourika*. But that did not seem likely as Pelorus Jack escorted ships at the bow, and, besides, he had travelled with twin-screw ships before.

Captain Vickerman of the Anchor Company felt strongly that Pelorus Jack's disappearance was connected to the passage through the strait of four whaling ships from Norway. He claimed to have seen them anchored off the entrance to Pelorus Sound in April 1912, around the time of the last sighting of Pelorus Jack.

The above explanations are plausible, but it seemed to have occurred to no-one that perhaps Pelorus Jack had died of old age. Many people had commented towards the end that the dolphin "looked old" and, after all, he had been doing escort duty for 20 years.

But in one sense Pelorus Jack did not die: the delightful creature long ago entered our folklore as an immortal.

Chapter VI

Steamer express services on the Wellington-Lyttelton run

NEW Zealanders today, particularly the young, think of a sea crossing of Cook Strait only in terms of the rail ferry voyages between Wellington and Picton. That is the only form of sea-passenger link that is available now, after a century of transportation progress has seen the wheel of shipping fortunes turn almost full circle. We started off with few regular shipping routes between Wellington and the South Island, and now we have only the one passenger link.

Between these periods, however, there was an era of intense activity in coastal shipping, now sadly fallen into nostalgia, which saw the Wellington-Lyttelton run as the real "blue ribbon" shipping route between the islands. Until the advent of rail ferry and airways competition, the 320-kilometre (174 sea miles) sea route played a major part in the economic life of New Zealand — in fact, to such an extent that the *Dominion*, Wellington's morning daily, estimated in May 1936 that outside the cities and towns "no main highway in the Dominion carries as many persons per annum as are transported over the Wellington-Lyttelton sea route.

When the ancillary interisland services, those between Wellington and Picton and Wellington and Nelson, are taken into account, this comparison becomes still more striking".

The Wellington-Lyttelton run is about more than statistics, however. It embodies people's memories of the ships they sailed in and the events that occurred on their voyages. So much went into the development of the service that in 1934 the Union Steam Ship Company finally gave it the title "steamer express service" — a title, by the way, which had been adopted by New Zealanders long before the Union Company made it official.

Interisland shipping services around the time of the growth of European settlements were a hotch-potch of small sailing craft, ketches and schooners, supplemented later by the first small steamers. These tended to be of the one-owner-one-ship variety, sailing anywhere cargoes were on offer (the Richardson line of Napier claims to be the oldest shipping company in New Zealand, placing its formation date in 1859).

At this time, 1,000-ton steamers were rare, and a speed of 10 knots (18.5 kilometres/hour) was comparatively high. To give an indication of what those figures mean in relation to the vessels of today, the Wellington Harbour Board tugs *Toia* and *Kupe* both have a gross register tonnage of 304 (a measure of volume, not weight), and the current Cook Strait rail ferries have a service speed of 17 knots (31.5 kilometres/hour).

The establishment of shipping companies, such as the Nelson-based Anchor line in 1862 (as Nathaniel Edwards and Co.) and the then Dunedin-based Union Company in 1875, meant the growth of regular coastal services, but until purely Wellington-Lyttelton services began in the 1890s the two centres were connected mainly by vessels on through voyages.

A passenger would board an Australia-bound ship and disembark at Wellington when the vessel made an *en-route* stop. Normally, there would have been four or five sailings a week between the ports, but it was not until 1889 and the holding of the New Zealand and South Seas Exhibition at Dun-

The clipper-bowed and sleek-lined *Rotomahana,* pioneer of daily sailings between Wellington and Lyttelton. *Union Steam Ship Company*

edin that the Wellington-Lyttelton route emerged in its own right.

Then, it was in the form of the 930-ton *Takapuna,* making a weekly direct run together with a weekly Lyttelton-Wellington-New Plymouth-Onehunga voyage. This was a short-lived affair, with *Takapuna's* direct service being dropped before the end of the exhibition and the passenger trade resuming with through vessels until April 1895, when *Penguin* (749 tons) began a weekly Wellington-Lyttelton run. Trade obviously was not excessive at that stage, because *Penguin* was also required for a weekly trip between Wellington, Picton and Nelson.

Later *Penguin* was the first ship to run exclusively on the Wellington-Lyttelton trip, starting in November 1896 and making three return voyages each week. Later still, she would go onto the Wellington-Nelson run until her tragic shipwrecking in February 1909, which is described in detail in Chapter XI.

By this time, changes were coming thick and fast as freight and passenger trade began to mushroom on the New Zealand coast. The Union Company removed *Penguin* from the Lyttelton run in 1897, bringing in first *Rotorua* (926 tons), then the bigger *Te Anau* (1,652 tons). *Te Anau* still plays a role on the New Zealand coast: in 1924 she was dismantled and towed to Wanganui where she was sunk to act as a breakwater.

But the memorable landmark of 1897 for the Union Company was the introduction in November of the 1,727-ton, clipper-bowed *Rotomahana.* Nicknamed "The Greyhound of the Pacific", *Rotomahana's* graceful lines gave the impression of a speedy ship. She was about the same size as *Tamahine,* which many New Zealanders still remember, and, although designed for the trans-Tasman run, she made a huge contribution to the

The carved figurehead that adorned the bows of the *Rotomahana. Union Steam Ship Company*

made the passage from Wellington to Lyttelton in about 12 hours, carrying up to 400 passengers. When required she could raise the pace, and in October 1901, after being fitted with new boilers, she completed the trip in 10 hours 43 minutes at an average of 16 knots (29.5 kilometres/hour). This was a record which stood for four years (it is now held by the first *Rangatira*, which produced an eight-hour eight-minute run in April 1939 — a startling average of 21.4 knots, or 39.5 kilometres/hour).

No account of *Rotomahana* could be complete without a reference to Captain Walter Manning. He was continuously in command of Cook Strait steamers for 36 years, starting with *Waihi* on the Wellington-Blenheim run in 1882. He was master of *Rotomahana* from February 1898 until October 1903 and he remained on other vessels in the Wellington-Lyttelton service until his retirement in 1918. Captain Manning is credited with the title "father of the steamer express service" because of his long involvement. Even his passing, in 1929, reflected his love of the Cook Strait crossing. His ashes were thrown from the decks of the first *Wahine* into the sea, 16 kilometres off Cape Campbell.

December 1899 saw the introduction of *Mapourika* (1,203 tons) to assist *Rotomahana* on the Wellington-Lyttelton trade. She was replaced a year later by the 2,003-ton *Tarawera*, and for some years this and other vessels provided a back-up to *Rotomahana* for summer-holiday traffic. The *Mararoa* and *Pateena* were principle relief vessels during this time. The 2,466-ton *Mararoa* started a special daily service with *Rotomahana* in

1904, which became a permanent feature in October the following year.

It is probably difficult for people today to envisage the romance or the feeling of pride in these ships which existed at the time. But perhaps this story illustrates the feeling of the era: on 27 June 1907 *Rotomahana* had to take quick averting action to avoid sailing too close to the Pencarrow shore. It was later discovered that an engineer, on his own initiative, had opened up the engines because he did not like seeing a slower vessel, the *Zealandia*, leading *Rotomahana* out through the Wellington Heads.

Undoubtedly, travellers had a love for those early steamers. They had a character of their own, sometimes ending a voyage with white funnels after heavy seas had sent salt spray crashing onto the hot metal where the water evaporated to leave salt deposit.

Romantic these ships may have been, but they could certainly make life a misery for the passengers. Most people would endure a rough crossing in the saloon, sitting back on a leather settee. The saloon might be oppressively overheated by steam radiators, or swept by a blast of cold air as stewards made their way in and out. The more fortunate or wealthy passengers might have booked into a Pullman berth for privacy, but even there they would not be much more comfortable than the saloon passengers.

As the biggest ship yet seen on the run, *Mararoa* represented a great advance in size and passenger comfort. With *Rotomahana*, she offered passengers a passage of about 12 or 13 hours and reasonable certainty of making train connections on either island. It was some time, however, before the Railways

development of the interisland trade. She had another claim to fame, in that she was reputed to be the first merchant ship in the world to be built of mild steel.

Rotomahana became a great favourite with the travelling public. Her handsome clipper bow carried a bowsprit and a figurehead. Propelled by a single screw, she

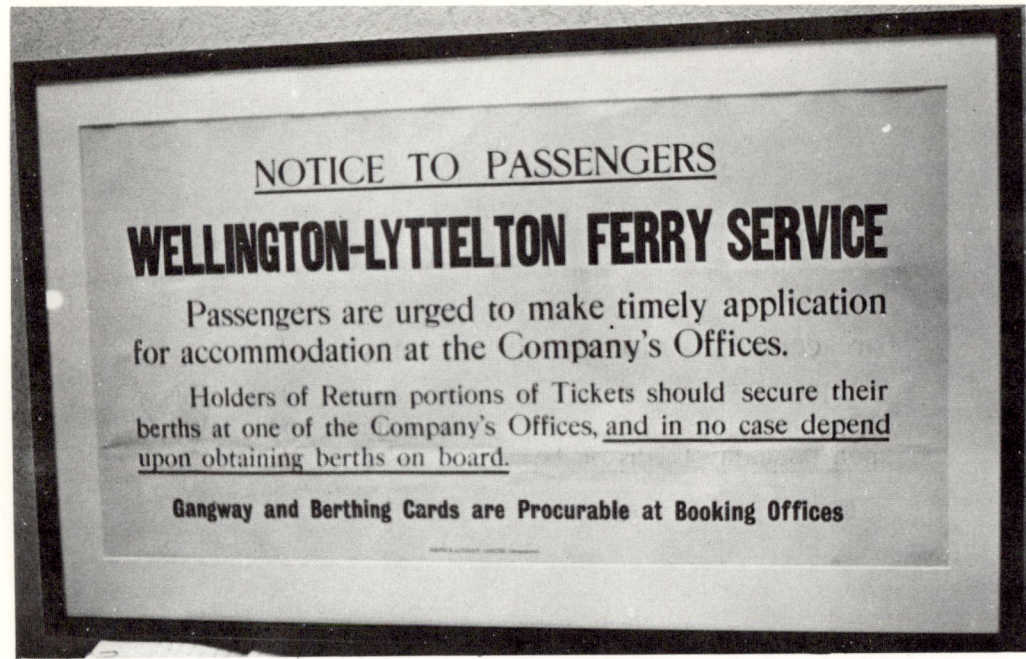

NOTICE TO PASSENGERS

WELLINGTON-LYTTELTON FERRY SERVICE

Passengers are urged to make timely application
for accommodation at the Company's Offices.

Holders of Return portions of Tickets should secure their
berths at one of the Company's Offices, and in no case depend
upon obtaining berths on board.

Gangway and Berthing Cards are Procurable at Booking Offices

An information notice from the days when Wellington-Lyttelton passengers could expect to have their own sleeping berths on board the ferry. *David MacIntyre*

Department could be induced to extend tracks to the ship-side at Lyttelton to allow passengers, baggage and mail to be transferred with the minimum of inconvenience. *Mararoa* stayed on the run until 1913, when she was replaced by *Wahine*, but she reappeared for the duration of World War I when *Wahine* was requisitioned by the Admiralty for overseas service.

In the meantime, the Union Company had taken a big step forward by replacing *Rotomahana* with the turbine-driven steam ship *Maori II* in November 1907. The 3,399-ton *Maori* was the first vessel designed and built specially for the inter-island run. Built by Wm. Denny Bros. of Dumbarton, Scotland, she was propelled by triple screws driven by direct-coupled turbines of 6,500 horsepower (4,800 kilowatts). She was one of the fastest ships of her class in the world, reaching 20.5 knots (38 kilometres/hour) on her trials, and she had the novel feature of a bow rudder to assist berthing at Wellington and Lyttelton. Her arrival was greeted with rumours that she was top-heavy and liable to capsize — rumours which soon disappeared when she

got to grips with the interisland passage.

It is worth digressing here to recall *Maori's* bizarre baptism to the shipping world. When she was launched by Dennys, she slid straight across the Leven River and stuck her stern into the opposite bank. Then, on her first day of trials, the tow ropes to the tugs parted, leaving *Maori* — complete with an official party of VIPs on board — stuck on Dumbarton Rock with the tide falling. She was refloated the next day and docked for repairs, but then she ran into another mishap during speed trials. The master of another vessel, *Kintyre*, did not realise *Maori* was capable of over 20 knots and tried to cross in front of her bows. The *Maori* struck *Kintyre* amidships, sinking her within three minutes with the loss of her chief engineer. Finally, on her voyage from the Clyde to New Zealand, *Maori* became stuck on a mudbank for 15 minutes, fortunately in thick fog, so no-one saw her dilemma.

Despite her inauspicious beginnings, the *Maori* was popular with her crew and with passengers. Captain Malcolm Livingstone, who brought her out to New Zealand, said at a press conference that she was a beautiful ship, adding: "Even the firemen have a separate dining room, and the only thing they could possible want now would be a steward with silver buttons to wait on them."

Maori went on to service the Wellington-Lyttelton run for 24 years, before becoming the relieving ship in 1931. Her success, and increasing trade, prompted the Union Company to design a bigger and faster ship for the run.

This was the 4,436-ton *Wahine I*, 110 metres in length, driven by triple screws and also built by Dennys. She had a speed of up to 22 knots (40.7 kilometres/hour) and for some years ranked among the fastest merchant ships in the world. When she started her career in July 1913 the timetables of the steamer run were speeded up and co-ordinated with those of through rail services, allowing mail posted at 5 p.m. or 6 p.m. in Wellington to be delivered in Christchurch the following day. *Wahine* and *Maori* left Wellington nightly at 7.45 p.m., Lyttelton shortly after 8 p.m., and the ships berthed at either end at 7 a.m. with almost unfailing regularity.

The partnership was broken in July 1915 when *Wahine*, requisitioned by the Admiralty, went to the Mediterranean to serve as a

The twin-funnelled *Wahine* I, painted in "neutral" colours when taking Japanese internees to Australia during World War II. *Union Steam Ship Company*

The first *Wahine* in the more familiar livery of the Union Company. *Union Steam Ship Company*

The first *Rangatira*, which joined the Union Company fleet in 1931 and remained until she was sold for scrap in 1967. *Union Steam Ship Company*

despatch-carrying ship between Malta and Mudros during the Gallipoli campaign. Subsequently, she sailed for England and was converted into a minelayer, being commissioned as HMS *Wahine* for service in the North Sea. She took part in 76 operations, laying 11,378 mines.

During the war, the Wellington-Lyttelton service was maintained by *Maori* in conjunction with *Mararoa*. One wartime voyage by the relieving vessel *Pateena* was distinguished by the birth of a child on board. Mrs M.A. Eggleton gave birth to a boy, Thomas,

with a stewardess acting as midwife. The birth was duly recorded in the ship's log.

The *Wahine* was reconditioned as a passenger ship at the end of the war and re-entered the interisland service in February 1920. Shortly afterwards, both she and *Maori* were fitted out to burn oil instead of coal.

By this time Union Company people were beginning to look at designs for an even bigger vessel, and in 1931 she arrived. This was the 6,152-ton *Rangatira I* built by Vickers Armstrong of Barrow-in-Furness, with nearly double the gross tonnage of

Maori. Turbo-electric powered, she was 120 metres long and had berthing accommodation for about 850 passengers. *Rangatira* teamed up with the *Wahine*, leaving *Maori* as the relief ship.

Rangatira arrived in Wellington at 7 a.m. on 4 November 1931 to a wharf that had been lengthened 12 metres specially for the ship's requirements. On board was a new innovation — lifeboats were driven by propellers, which were worked by hand levers. The ship's appearance was appreciated, one description reading: "The smoking room and the second-class dining saloon are both finished in bird's-eye maple and all the cabins are enamelled in white."

One of the inaugural passengers, Mr A.M. Burns, the chairman of directors of the New Zealand Press Association, felt moved to say: "There is no doubt that the steamer would be an incentive to increase interisland communications, and would undoubtedly strengthen links of commerce and personal cordiality between north and south."

In October 1933 the *Evening Post* reported a Melbourne businessman, Mr H.H. Kohn, to have said that the words "ferry service", describing the Wellington-Lyttelton run were liable to discourage tourism. His view was that the run should be known as an "express service". The following year the Union Company finally assigned to it the official title of "steamer express service".

The *Rangatira* and *Wahine* ran to a reliable and regular timetable, with the famous partnership of Captain "Scotty" Cameron and Captain Basil Irwin in command. Mrs Dagmar Andersen, of Highbury, Wellington, remembers Captain Cameron from earlier days. As Dagmar Dickie she used to work at her father's bookstall on Queen's Wharf with her identical twin sister, Dorrie. Between 1911 and 1915 Captain Cameron was a familiar figure on the Wellington wharf, known as an up-and-coming master, whose commands included *Pateena* and *Arahura*. He apparently had a good friendship with the then Wellington harbourmaster, Captain Henry Johnson, who retired in 1915. Mrs Andersen remembers Captain Cameron like this:

Captain Cameron used to get his *Auck-*

More like an old-world club or an office building interior than that of a ship — the internal staircase in the long-serving *Tamahine*. Union Steam Ship Company

land Weekly from us every Wednesday after he had paid his respects to Captain Johnson. It wasn't often that us two twins served in the shop at the same time, so many people thought there was only one of us. On this occasion, we were both standing at the counter when Captain Cameron came in. We bowed and said "good afternoon", but Captain Cameron stopped and backed out the door. That night, going down to the ferry, he stopped at father's bookstall and said, "You know, I didn't have one more drink than I usually have with Captain Johnson, but I was seeing double. I wasn't going to let Miss Dickie see me in that state". It was then that father told him there were two of us, as like as peas in a pod.

The Dickie bookstalls had an interesting history of their own, as they became regular meeting places for sailors. The Dickie family imported newspapers from the Shetland Isles, which gave lists of the ships bearing Shetlanders to New Zealand. When these papers came in once a month Scots would eagerly seek them to find out if any relatives or friends would be on board the ships that were due in port.

In 1936 both *Rangatira* and *Wahine* were involved in dramas. In February *Rangatira* crashed onto rocks near Tom's Rock. Thinking he was entering Wellington harbour, Captain Cameron had mistaken Sinclair Head for Cape Turakirae further to the east. After the grounding he backed the vessel off the rocks and the 1,000-plus passengers were fitted out with lifebelts. Captain Cameron performed an amazing feat by bringing the ship into Wellington stern first. With tugs standing by, the vessel berthed at Clyde Quay, with her bow resting on the mud bottom.

The marine court of inquiry exonerated Captain Cameron, but some critics — including the Seamen's Union — were not satisfied with this decision. The Minister of Marine, Mr Peter Walsh, ordered another inquiry, and this found that Captain Cameron had indeed made an error of judgement and that visibility was so bad that more caution was required than was displayed. Captain Cameron's master's certificate was not affected, but the Union Company transferred him to a cargo vessel.

In June of the same year *Wahine's* bows ploughed into Pipitea Wharf in thick fog. Captain Irwin's certificate also escaped endorsement by the subsequent inquiry, although it was found he made an error of judgement both in steering his course and in approaching the wharf in fog at an excessive speed. Captain Irwin later commanded *Rangatira* and was in command when that vessel had an unlucky mishap in April 1938. Irwin had ordered the anchor to be dropped in Wellington harbour to stop his ship being blown by a gale, but the anchor fouled the moorings of HMS *Achilles*, berthed at Clyde Quay Wharf. *Rangatira's* stern swung round and collided with the bows of *Achilles*.

By this time, the Union Company was looking at newer tonnage and in 1939 announced that a sister ship for the *Rangatira* was to be built.

But the outbreak of war put a stop to this plan. Instead, *Rangatira* and *Wahine* carried the service through the war years, with both being commandeered on occasions for troop movements.

On those occasions *Tamahine* would be brought over from the Picton run to help out, but her propensity to roll was not welcomed by passengers during the rough weather. Captain Alan McIntyre of Wellington, then second officer on *Tamahine*, gave an example:

We would leave Wellington at 8 a.m. for a daylight run, arriving at Lyttelton any time between 8 p.m. and 3 a.m. We had a big contingent from the South Island, being sent home for their final leave before going into action. Well, the "Tam" rolled and rolled, and 90 percent of these guys were seasick. They all had little lunch boxes supplied by a caterer, and by the time we got to Lyttelton the boxes were strewn around the decks. Those poor boys were flat out, flaked out on the deck and couldn't move. They couldn't have cared less about their lunches then.

For the ferries the war years were incident-free, apart from one or two exceptions. On 28 December 1940 *Rangatira* ran aground off Banks Peninsula. The 750 passengers were transferred to lifeboats and later picked up by the Union Company freighter *Waimarino*. *Rangatira* was refloated soon after and was docked for repairs. On this and other occasions during the war, *Maori* acted as relief vessel.

Another incident involving *Rangatira* was reported by Captain Irwin, who said that two ratings had reported seeing a torpedo pass close to the ship's stern. This was during a run to Wellington when the ship was approaching Pencarrow. Captain Irwin believed that the submarine, presumably Japanese, had been foiled because the ship was making up lost time and was moving at 20 knots (37 kilometres/hour) rather than the normal 17 knots (31.5 kilometres/hour). The other major wartime incident involved *Wahine*, when she rammed and sank the minesweeper *South Sea* off Point Halswell on 19 December 1943. There were no casualties and *Wahine* was able to complete her trip to Lyttelton.

When the war ended the Union Company was quick off the mark, taking advantage of the cancellation of an Admiralty order to lodge a shipbuilding contract with Vickers Armstrong of Barrow. This was for the 6,911-ton *Hinemoa*, which began a service in

The *Hinemoa,* which spent 20 years in the service before being sold to Tasmanian interests in 1967. *Union Steam Ship Company*

The *Maori*, one of the last ships to serve on the Wellington-Lyttelton run. *Union Steam Ship Company*

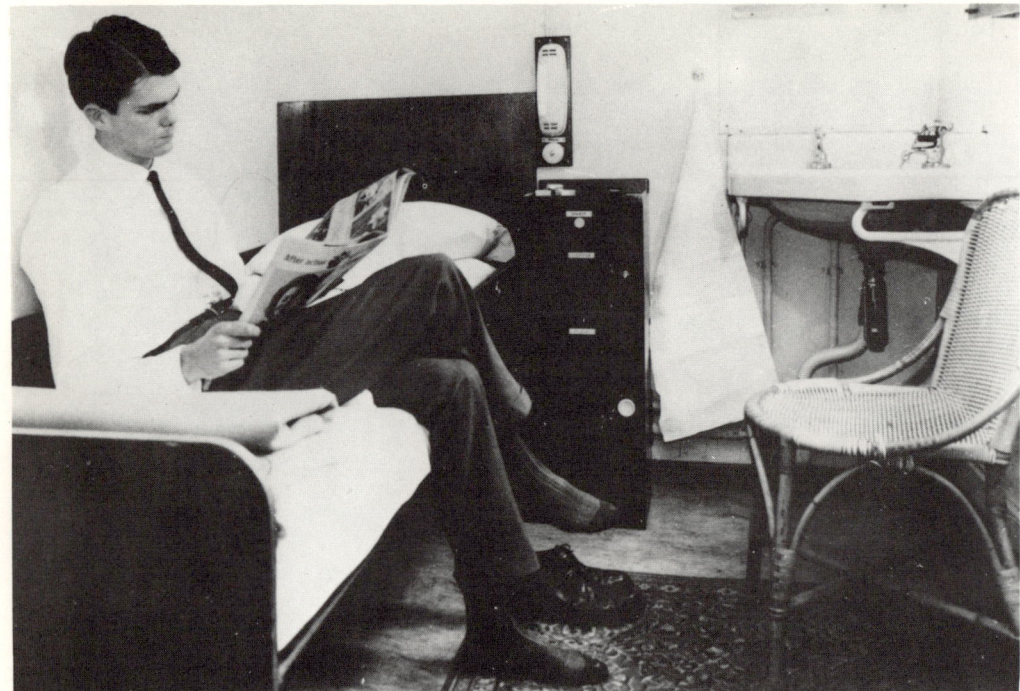

The standard of accommodation that could be expected in a single-birth cabin on B deck in the last *Maori. Union Steam Ship Company*

February 1947 that was to continue until the ill-fated *Wahine II* arrived in August 1966.

Hinemoa had a tough baptism to the run. A few days after starting service she was eight hours late getting to Lyttelton in a southerly, arriving with two bridge windows smashed. Her arrival meant goodbye to the long-serving *Maori*, which was sold to a Chinese concern and was eventually sunk in a hurricane in January 1951. The first *Wahine* now became relieving vessel. She was used as a barracks for air-force personnel during the 1951 waterfront strike and met her end in August 1951 when she struck a reef in the Arafura Sea north of Darwin, *en route* for the Korean War with 500 New Zealand servicemen on board. Her loss, and the fact that the Union Company wanted a new partner for *Hinemoa* anyway, paved the way for the introduction of the new *Maori*.

The 8,303-ton *Maori III* was launched by Princess Margaret at the Newcastle-upon-Tyne yard of Vickers Armstrong in November 1952. After clocking 21.7 knots (40.1 kilometres/hour) in speed trials, she entered service in November 1953 and was a success on the run despite initial criticism of her lines. She was involved in two incidents over the next decade. On Christmas Eve 1954 she struck a submerged object thought to be a whale. The impact put her bow rudder out of action. Then, in February 1962, she crashed into the auxiliary scow *Motu* while berthing at Lyttelton.

Maori's interior continued the reputation for passenger comfort on the Wellington-Lyttelton run. *The Dominion* on 25 October 1953 reported:

> The interior fittings of the *Maori* enhance the illusion of a luxury yacht. Her saloons, staterooms and officers' quarters are veneered in a variety of woods. For the passengers' interest they are all labelled — French walnut, sapelle, figured sycamore, maple, oak, Indian rosewood, mahogany . . .

But with the needs of wartime still fresh in people's minds *The Dominion* also reported:

> The *Maori* is fitted for conversion into an armed merchant cruiser in case of war. Sections of her deck can be lifted to provide gun emplacements. Her hull is lined with wires setting up a demagnetising field to protect her from mines.

By the 1960s, change was imminent on the Wellington-Lyttelton steamer express service — change that was ultimately to lead to the route's demise. Rail ferries were shortly to take over the Wellington-Picton run and the Strait's Air Freight Express was taking a chunk of the interisland goods trade. The Union Company was running its Wellington-Lyttelton service with *Hinemoa* and *Maori*, with the *Rangatira* as a relief ship, but the company was planning a new type of vessel for the run. In September 1961 the *Evening Post* reported the Union Company's chairman and managing director, Mr H.H. Dobie, as saying that *Rangatira* would be sold, *Hinemoa* would become the relief ship and a new ship would be built. Two months later, Mr Dobie announced that the new ship would be an 8,000-ton ferry, with ramps to allow vehicles to drive on and off.

Thus the age of the "do-do" (drive-on, drive-off) or "ro-ro" (roll-on, roll-off) ship arrived, when the company's new managing director, Mr F.K. Macfarlane, announced at the beginning of 1964 that the Fairfield shipyard in Glasgow was to build a twin-screw ferry of about 9,000 tons, with accommodation for 927 passengers in one, two-, three- and four-berth cabins and space for about 200 cars. Cars and cargo trailers would be loaded through the stern door. Until then cars had been loaded and unloaded by tray. They were driven on to the tray, left in gear with the hand brakes on and lashed to the tray. Watersiders claimed they could complete a lift in three minutes.

The name chosen for this new turbo-electric ship was *Wahine*, a revival of the name of one of the service's earlier favourites. The new vessel was to have stabilisers installed to counter rolling at sea. But before taking to the water she had to overcome a near-disaster when the Fairfield Company went into the hands of receivers. The pro-

Inside the engine room of the *Maori* III. *Union Steam Ship Company*

spects were for long delays in the completion of the ship, but the outlook improved with the formation of a new company called Fairfields (Glasgow) Ltd. This new concern took over the *Wahine* job and the 8,944-ton ship finally arrived in Wellington on 24 July 1966.

In the meantime, the Union Company had decided to convert *Maori* to a "ro-ro" ship to ensure compatability in the service. She was sent to a Hong Kong shipyard to have a door built in her stern and cabins ripped out for the installation of a vehicle deck, returning to service in December 1965. Her car-carrying capacity had risen from 70 to 100, but passenger capacity had dropped from 962 to 790. She was also now able to use the "ro-ro" link-spans specially built for the service at

The sharp lines of the ill-fated *Wahine* II. *Union Steam Ship Company*

Wellington and Lyttelton. The two ships began their partnership on 1 August 1966 with *Wahine's* first trip to Lyttelton. Within a month, the new arrival had hit the headlines when a freak wind dislodged a gangway at Lyttelton and threw some passengers into the sea. They were quickly rescued.

Even into the late '60s, the Wellington-Lyttelton run preserved its reputation for punctuality. Captain Alan McIntyre served with the Union Company for 40 years in a career that spanned 67 ships — including 41 as master. He told how during a week on board *Maori* in the late 1960s the ship made 10 trips a week — seven night runs plus daylight runs on Tuesdays, Thursdays and

Saturdays. On daylight runs the turn-around had to be accomplished in something under two hours, so there was bedlam as freight was off-loaded, new freight was taken on and the Union Company's laundry supplied hundreds of new pillowcases and sheets for the ship at each Wellington call:

I think punctuality was just a fad with these old skippers on the Lyttelton run. You had up-to-date ships with reserve power and you kept checking the ship's position through the night and would increase or reduce speed as necessary. You set your time to pass Pencarrow or Godley Head [Lyttelton] at 6.18 a.m., so you had

42 minutes to come in, swing and berth. Coming up the harbour you might meet shipping that would hold you up, or if it was blowing a bit it would take longer to berth. On the rare occasion when it was really bad weather, and you couldn't get in first go, you had to come out and try again. Once at Lyttelton I couldn't swing the ship outside the breakwater, so I had to steam out, come in head first and swing the ship round inside the breakwater with the help of a tug.

That trip happened to be the worst that Captain McIntyre experienced on the Lyttelton run. He recalls:

There was a rugby test in Wellington and I brought a full complement of passengers up on the old *Rangatira*, and when we arrived in Wellington a real southerly blew up. The passenger list going back to Lyttelton was something like 700 men and 40 women, it was all the men coming back from the test. New Zealand won, and these chaps came on full of the joys of spring, celebrating victory. By the time we cleared the heads it was a very different story. They were quiet. They had made a terrific noise coming up, and the bar had done a roaring trade, but coming back we had a terrible trip. We shipped a lot of water and the stewards' accommodation was flooded out. It was blowing so hard that I was five hours late getting alongside at Lyttelton. They were a sorry lot then.

Lyttelton ferry captains had a long day in those times. Captain McIntyre says he would be called at 5.15 a.m. and be on the bridge at 5.45.

We would be at the heads about 6.15, the gangway would go down at seven, I would have breakfast at 7.30 and shower. If we were staying in port I'd change and stroll down to the office about half past nine, saying "hello" to the harbourmaster on the way. We would have midday dinner at 12 — a revolting idea but we had to have it mainly to keep the Cooks' and Stewards' Union happy. Then we would have tea at five — whoever heard of eating at five? I would be on the bridge when the ship was within harbour limits, then when we cleared the heads I'd set the course and revolutions required to get us to the other heads at 6.15 a.m. I would go down below and usually have the odd passenger or VIP

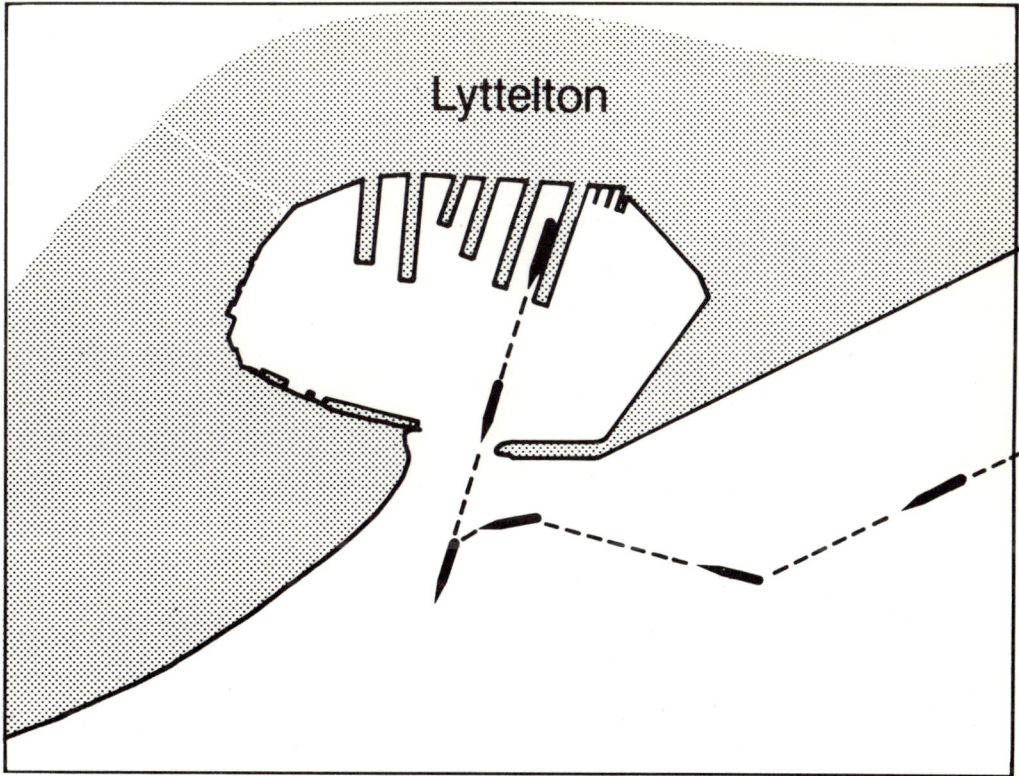

Approximate course followed by the steamer expresses when berthing at Lyttelton

to entertain. I usually made a point at 10 p.m. of giving a broad hint that it was time they went to bed. I would write out my night orders and hoped to be in my bed with lights out by 11, because I would be called at 5.15. The master of a ship is the only job I know where you can have a sleep in the afternoon, either in port or at sea. I would get my head down for an hour

or so. You needed to because you never knew when you might be up all night anyway. Nowadays, I couldn't sleep in the afternoon if I tried.

The growing challenge from the rail ferries was causing problems for the Union Company and those problems were compounded by the loss of *Wahine II* at Wellington Heads

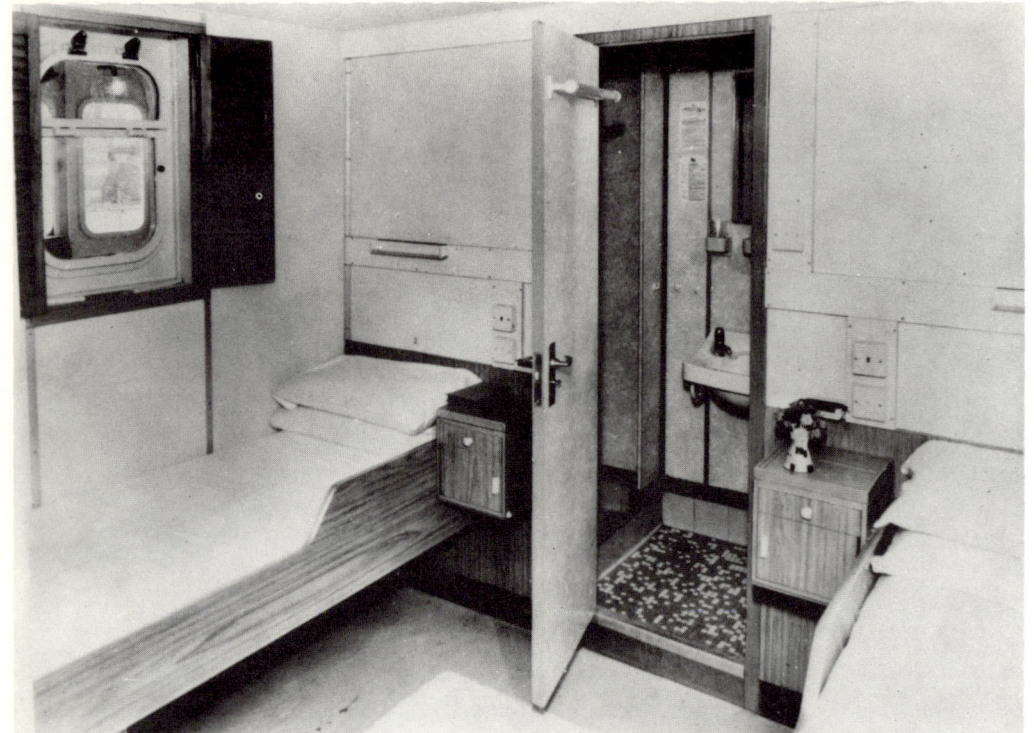

Interior of a two-bed cabin with shower and toilet on board the second *Rangatira*. Union Steam Ship Company

in April 1968. The *Wahine* disaster is the subject of a chapter in this book, but from an organisational point of view it meant the Union Company was scratching to find a partner for *Maori* (*Hinemoa* had been sold to the Tasmanian Government in October 1967 as a floating hostel for a power projeect). A stop-gap solution came in June 1970 when the small 1,053 ton *Holmlea* (formerly *Seaway Princess*) was chartered from the

Holm Shipping Company, but she was a cargo-only vessel and the Union Company decided to bring in a real replacement for *Wahine*. Thus the $12-million *Rangatira II* came into service in March 1972, with capacity for 768 passengers and 200 cars. Captain McIntyre flew to Britain with chief engineer Mr Bill Hall to take delivery of the new ship. The debut voyage from Wellington to Lyttelton, he recalled, was something of an

ordeal due to fog:

I had everyone on board — top management, VIPs and even television cameras. I wrote up my night orders and got to bed between 11 and midnight, but I was hardly asleep before we ran into fog. I was called to the bridge between one and two when we were off Kaikoura, and I stayed up all night. I felt like the wreck of the *Hesperus* when we got to Lyttelton, but of course we had functions there, entertaining the local populace and introducing the ship. We had the chairman of the harbour board, and the chairman of the Union Company there. I think I eventually got clear of that lot by 3 p.m. I just went up to my room, locked myself in and made sure no one could get at me.

Although *Rangatira* was the most modern ship on the Lyttelton run, she was not Captain McIntyre's favourite, nor did her handling characteristics escape criticism:

My favourite ship on that run would be the *Maori*. She was the best to handle of the lot. The *Wahine* was very good but I was only in her for six or seven weeks relieving, so it is difficult to say how she compared. The *Rangatira* was more difficult to handle than the *Maori*, because the older ships used to have a bow rudder to help you back into the berth. You could come in full speed astern, in fact the faster you came in the easier she was to handle, particularly if it was blowing.

With the *Rangatira* you couldn't do that. She was also turbo-electric powered, but if you came in full astern you would never stop her — and probably you'd end up in the post office at Lyttelton. You had to do the procedure slowly, and if it was blowing it would be a damned nuisance. The ship would be blown out of position. When you made your swing you had to allow for where you would be by the time you got up to the wharf, knowing full well the wind was going to take charge one way or the other. You had to be very alert with the *Rangatira*. I didn't do any damage to her but there was a time when I was backing in and the chief engineer said, "You are coming astern too fast". He couldn't pull her up. I rang half-ahead, and nothing happened. Then I rang full-ahead, and he just managed to pull her up.

One good feature of the *Rangatira* was her gyro stabilisers. These acted like fins and you could keep her steady in the swells. The *Wahine* had a stabiliser system as well, but these were flume tanks. She had these tanks which contained "slack" water, which was supposed to tip over when the ship rolled, and helped keep her steady. It was supposed to dampen the roll, but you had to have a good roll going to activate the flume tanks in the first place.

Captain McIntyre left *Rangatira* after her settling-in period, when Captain Ray Pugh-Williams of Christchurch and Captain John Cleaver of Lyttelton were ready to take command.

But even before *Rangatira II* made her debut the writing was on the wall for the Wellington-Lyttelton service. In May 1971 the *Evening Post* reported that *Maori* and *Holmlea* were sailing with half-empty cargo holds. The Union Company's assistant manager, Mr Peter Maxwell, talked of a "slowing down in the tempo of business". In addition, there was a ban by watersiders on sea freighters (pallets with collapsible sides) packed at consolidated stores and, most critical of all, there was to follow a Government-initiated freeze on rail ferry charges. This meant that the Union Company was caught in a "catch-22" situation. If it increased cargo rates, customers would flock to the rail ferries. If it did not charge more it would make a loss on the service. In fact, it made a loss, despite small rate rises.

As trade dropped the company decided to lay up *Maori* in March 1972, when *Rangatira* came into service. *Maori* was eventually sold to a Hong Kong shipping line in January 1974, after nearly two years full of ideas, such as using her as a floating hotel at the Christchurch Commonwealth Games, turning her into a trade-fair venue and even a power-generation plant. At one stage the evangelical group, Youth with a Mission, put a deposit on her, but they could not raise the buying price. The New Zealand director of the group said later, *Maori* (which they planned to rename *Agape*, the Greek word for love) was the only ship they felt led towards, adding, "We will continue to pray about the whole situation".

By September 1973 *Rangatira* was said to be losing $1 million a year and the Government was looking at the possibility of replacing her with two smaller ships. On 21 February 1974 Union Company chairman Sir Peter Abeles told a press conference that *Rangatira* had made losses of up to $3.5 million since she began service less than two years before. He said *Rangatira* would be withdrawn after June and that there would be no plans for a replacement. The Minister of Transport, Sir Basil Arthur, chipped in with the comment, "It's not the service that's at fault, it's the type of vessel".

Nevertheless, it was the Government which came to the temporary aid of the service. It announced in May that it would charter *Rangatira* for six months, possibly longer, and would bear the losses. In July the service was reduced to one ship, with the cargo-only *Holmlea* taken off the run. (It is interesting to note that *Holmlea* had no bow rudder or bow propulsion and therefore had to be assisted by tugs when berthing at Wellington. This occasionally led people to think she was in difficulties.)

The Government's financial backing of *Rangatira* stretched on for another year until finally, in January 1976, the ship's losses were estimated to be running at $3.25 million a year. Then the new Government announced that *Rangatira* would be replaced by a cargo-only vessel. The decision caused a storm of protest. More than 33,000 people signed a petition by the Canterbury Progress League to keep a *Rangatira*-type service between Wellington and Lyttelton. The Wellington Chamber of Commerce estimated that 150,000 paying passengers would still use a service each year. But the final death knell sounded on 15 June 1976 when the new minister, Mr Colin McLachlan, announced that the Government had bought the 2,300-ton *Hawea* from the Union Company for $2.75 million, to be operated as a cargo-only ship on the Wellington-Lyttelton run by the

The beautiful *Rangatira* II, the last ship on the Wellington-Lyttelton run. Was she really the right ship for the run in the 1970s? *Union Steam Ship Company*

fledgling Shipping Corporation of New Zealand.

So *Rangatira* made her final sailing on 14 September 1976 from Wellington to Lyttelton. She had started her service on 28 March 1972 to the strains of the Onslow Brass Band playing on the wharf and maroon-jacketed waiters taking passengers' orders for celebration champagne, imported wines and steaks. Now she bowed out, with Union Company spokesman Mr David Graham ruefully saying:

We have a fine ship sailing from Wellington to Lyttelton tonight for the last time and a lot of people are feeling sad about it, wondering why it is happening and saying it should not be. It should not be happening. There is a public demand for the service, the ship is the right one and there is a need for such a service between Wellington and Lyttelton. The ship can no longer make a profit and that is the reason the *Rangatira* is doing the last trip tonight.

Even a proposal to use the last voyage of *Rangatira* to raise funds for Operation Waterloo (the Wellington City Council's fund-raising effort towards a new town hall) had to be dropped because of the costs involved in the charter. (A similar fund-raising Lyttelton cruise that April had been a success.) So *Rangatira* disappeared back to the Union Steam Ship Company (U.K.) to reappear later as an accommodation ship at the North Sea oil installation in Sullom Voe, in the Shetland Isles.

Her going marked the arrival of *Hawea*, renamed *Coastal Ranger*, to run a cargo service which lasted until December 1977. That service, too, was run with a costly Government subsidy and the Government was eventually glad to see the Union Company take over from *Coastal Ranger* with its trans-Tasman vessels *Union Hobart* and *Union Lyttelton* — again on a strictly cargo-only basis.

The circle had been completed. The Wellington-Lyttelton service had begun a century before, with vessels making calls *en route* to Australia or other coastal destinations. Now, trans-Tasman vessels were again serving the route, albeit with several strictly Wellington-Lyttelton voyages in the time-table. But for the passenger, the service was dead. The causes? Perhaps a mixture of air and rail-ferry competition, high wage costs, perhaps the wrong type of ship, falling trade due to the economic conditions of the day, the fuel price boom, and — not least by any means — political interference in the freight rates of the railways. Whatever the reason, the passenger service was over. For the traveller to the South Island the option of an overnight sea voyage was gone. Now he or she may fly or take a ferry to Picton. The only alternative is not to go at all.

Chapter VII

The Nelson run dies; the Picton run lives

IF THE Wellington-Lyttelton route is the story of a business trade turning full circle, then the other major Cook Strait shipping routes, from Wellington to Nelson and Wellington to Picton, provide a story of contrasts. Whereas the Nelson run was a favourite which flowered then died, the Picton run was the opposite. It was perhaps the lesser of the two services that suddenly blossomed with the advent of the rail ferries and it grew to such an extent that it shut out much of the remainder of New Zealand's coastal trade. Today, it has taken a huge bite out of the once-prolific Safe Air services from Wellington to Blenheim and Nelson and, as a major shipping service on the Cook Strait crossing, it stands alone.

A direct and lasting passenger shipping link between Wellington and Nelson dates from August 1909, when the Anchor Company brought in *Nikau*, but before then there was a host of small and irregular operations. Some of these linked the two centres as part of a more complex coastal trading pattern. The Union Company, for example, provided a weekly service after 1875 between Dunedin, Lyttelton, Wellington, Picton, Nelson, New Plymouth and Onehunga with the steamers *Hawea* and *Taupo*.

Later, both Dunedin and Lyttelton were dropped as ports of call, although the Union Company kept a Wellington-Onehunga service going until 1909. Similarly, in the 1880s the company started a mainly coal-trade service between Greymouth, Westport and Wellington, calling at Nelson and occasionally Picton *en route*. These services were later supplemented by a Union Company service between Wellington, Picton and Nelson, with vessels such as *Mapourika* and *Pateena* making three return journeys a week.

Many of the earlier Cook Strait services had been important at the time, but they either died young or did not have the capacity to stay in business once steam ships began to challenge sail. An example of the former was that started in September 1852 with the schooner *Henrietta*, owned by Hervey, Johnston and Company of Wellington. She ran a fortnightly mail and cargo service arranged by the colonial government, but only five weeks later, on 27 October, she was totally wrecked while entering Port Nicholson.

She was followed in March 1854 by the 250-ton S.S. *Nelson,* which was owned by the British shipping company, H.H. Willis and Company. She began a trade linking various ports in the two islands, including Wellington and Nelson, but was withdrawn to England in August 1855 because of *Zingara's* entry to the coastal trade. *Zingara* did not last long either. She worked spasmodically between March 1855 and June 1857, when she was withdrawn to Melbourne. Afterwards the Wellington-Nelson link remained tenuous. The 84-ton paddle steamer *Tasmanian Maid* ran occasionally on the route from 1857, but shortly afterwards she was commandeered by the Government during the Maori-European land wars.

There were other small shipping lines which made brief appearances on the scene. The Wellington-based Black Diamond Line owned five steam ships capable of carrying passengers and cargo. It traded between

The *Mapourika* in Union Company colours. In 1922 she was bought by the Anchor Company for the Wellington-Nelson run and renamed *Ngaio*. *Union Steam Ship Company*

125-ton S.S. *Waverley*, mainly a cargo vessel but with room for 10 passengers.

Another Anchor vessel doing the Cook Strait crossing was the 178-ton steam ship *Tasman*, which had room for 36 passengers. She maintained a nightly service between Nelson, Motueka and Wellington from 1907 to the middle of the following year, delivering mainly fresh fruit to the Wellington market. This paved the way for the real milestone on the run, the introduction in 1909 of the 247-ton *Nikau*. Operated by the Anchor company *Nikau* could take 26 passengers and 130 tonnes of cargo. She made return journeys direct between Nelson and Wellington on three nights of the week. These night journeys earned her the title "The Cook Strait Ghost". Her funnel was illuminated and, as she ploughed through rough seas, the light shone through a fine mist of spray.

At this stage the Anchor fleet still had some stiff competition from the Union Company on the Wellington-Nelson run. The *Penguin* was a Union Company favourite on the route until she was tragically shipwrecked on 25 February 1909. Later the Union Company faded from the scene and let Anchor dominate the Wellington-Nelson business. More recently things have changed markedly. Anchor's seagoing interests were absorbed into the Union Company fleet in 1973. (The Holm Line was also taken over by the Union Company in 1972.) *Nikau's* record was so good that in 1911 the Anchor Company decided to give her a partner on the trade. The chosen ship was the 304-ton *Kaitoa*, then two years old and running at a loss on the West Coast coal trade. She was

Wellington, Nelson and the West Coast before being absorbed into the Union Company in July 1885. Among the owner-operator ships was the 60-ton *Wairoa*, built in Wairoa in 1882, which in the late 1880s plied between Wellington, Nelson and Motueka under the ownership of the Ricketts brothers of Nelson.

But this was the era of the growth of the Union and the Anchor fleets, and the Cook Strait runs came directly under their influence. The Union services have already been referred to, but Anchor ships also began to make an impact in the 1860s. When it was formed in 1862, the Anchor line had the name of Nathaniel Edwards and Company. It became the Anchor Line of Steam Packets in 1870. For the first 40 years of its life the Anchor line owned a small fleet of steam ships which conducted a passenger and cargo trade, mainly between the West Coast and the North Island ports — for example, the

converted into a passenger ship and joined
Nikau for the 1913-14 summer season.
Together they kept the service going until
1922, when Anchor bought the Union
Company's 1,203-ton *Mapourika*, which in
earlier days had been a competitor of
Nikau's. Now, renamed *Ngaio*, she took over
from the *Kaitoa* and ran in conjunction with
Nikau until December 1925, when *Nikau*
was replaced by the much bigger ex-Union
vessel, the 1,596-ton *Arahura*. There was
accommodation on *Arahura* for 155 saloon
and 66 second-class passengers. She was
captained by W.A. Wildman, whose son
Arthur took over the *Ngaio*.

Such constant replacement with bigger
and better ships continued in the 1929-30
season, when *Ngaio* was taken off in favour of
the two-funnelled twin-screw steamer *Matangi*. *Arahura* and *Matangi* began a partnership that was to symbolise the service
between Wellington and Nelson. They
remained together until after the war, doing
a crossing in about 10 or 11 hours. Their only
mishap occurred in February 1943, when
Arahura ran aground on Cape Stephen in the
early hours of the morning with 112 passengers on board. There was no loss of life
and *Arahura* refloated herself. Repairs took
only a couple of weeks. Before the outbreak
of war in 1939, Anchor had prepared sketch
plans for the next round of vessel re-
placements, but the international situation —
with shipyards committed to defence orders
— meant the company could not proceed.

After the war, both *Arahura* and *Matangi*
were overdue for replacement, but again the
Anchor company had difficulties with
orders. This time overseas yards were

The tiny coaster *Picton*, built in 1916, which operated on Cook Strait traded for years before being
laid up following the advent of the rail ferries. *"Evening Post"*

booked solid for years ahead as the world's
shipowners made up for lost time. *Arahura*
was put on Wellington's floating dock in May
1949 and the resulting survey showed that
most of her hull needed replacing. She was
laid up at Shelly Bay and scuttled in Cook
Strait in 1952.

Having decided that it could not afford to
repair *Arahura*, the Anchor Company

decided to buy a replacement, the 3,566-ton
Hualalai, an oil-burner then in Honolulu.
She was renamed *Ngaio* and made her first
trip on the Wellington-Nelson run in May
1950.

There was further trouble for the company
in the meantime, because *Matangi* went in
for her survey and got the same thumbs-
down that *Arahura* had received. She was

Aratika backs into her berth. Such shipping size and might has forced small coasters out of Cook Strait trade. *New Zealand Railways Publicity*

away as ever.

Cargo-only shipping between Wellington and Nelson survived the collapse of the passenger service (indeed today, the Union Company continues to call at Nelson). However, the passenger service was sorely missed. On 30 August 1956 the *Evening Post* reported that in her last year of operation *Ngaio* had carried 56,000 passengers and 3,000 motor vehicles. That was a lot of traffic needing alternative routes across the strait and it prompted efforts to revive a Wellington-Nelson passenger link.

A local committee was established in Nelson, which proposed the formation of a new company called the Cook Strait Ferry Company Ltd. Its idea was for a single-screw diesel-powered ferry of 2,000 tons, with cabin accommodation for 150 passengers and hold space for 60 cars and 300 tonnes of cargo. The committee went to great lengths to push its proposal. By 1956 it had worked out a weekly schedule of three return trips, which would yield £185,250 against a cost of £166,056. A basic point put forward by the group was that since the *Ngaio* had been taken off, the number of car registrations in Nelson had doubled, so there was more trade to be had than earlier. These ideas got as far as presentation to the Government before they were discarded.

In more recent times, the Transport Nelson Ltd (TNL) group came up with the bold jetfoil proposal which showed real signs of reaching the water until it, too, failed. The Boeing jetfoil that TNL had in mind was a waterjet-propelled craft, which raised itself on a foil above the water once it picked up speed. It could zip over the surface at 43 knots

also laid up at Shelly Bay, later dismantled in Pelorus Sound and her hull was towed to Hong Kong for breaking up. So the Anchor Company was left with *Ngaio* as its sole representative on the run — a run which by now was meeting increasing air competition and was losing money. The *Evening* Post of 23 October 1954 reported that *Ngaio* had been running at a loss of about £50,000 a year. Faced with such bleak returns, the Anchor Company had taken *Ngaio* off the

run on 17 April 1953. In his farewell speech, Captain Norman Collins said that passenger traffic by sea was giving way to passenger traffic by air. He envisaged a time when helicopters would whisk passengers from Trafalgar Park in Nelson to the Basin Reserve in Wellington in a matter of minutes — Captain Collins was speaking before oil price shocks were a matter of real concern. Little did he realise that 30 years later his vision of regular helicopter flights would be as far (about 80 kilometres/hour) and could accommodate up to 300 passengers, depending upon the operator's requirements. TNL's belief in the jetfoil was such that it commissioned computer analysis of the craft's ability to handle Cook Strait weather conditions. This was specifically to counter one of the first objections to be raised to the venture, namely that the jetfoil would not be able to cope with the strait's rough seas. Boeing's analysis, which covered 20,000 strait weather reports over a 20-year period, predicted that the jetfoil would run smoothly for 95 percent of scheduled crossings.

TNL raised the jetfoil proposal in 1978 and pushed it hard through 1979, actually receiving in July of that year Cabinet approval to import jetfoils at a cost of about $11 million each. The company even made one provisional order, based on plans for a definite Wellington-Picton service and a possible Wellington-Nelson run. TNL's real hope was that it could corner the passenger market, making an 80-minute trip across the strait compared with the three hours 20 minutes taken by the rail ferry. In order to see this dream reach fruition, the company needed an assurance from Government that when the Railways Department replaced *Aramoana* it would not be with a ferry that had great passenger-carrying capacity. Otherwise, Railways would continue to undercut the ticket cost of the jetfoil in order to maintain a share of the passenger market. In June TNL was said to be looking at a one-way fare to Picton of $12.50, compared with the Railways' ferry fare at the time of $8.35. TNL failed to get the assurance it sought. On 23 July the Minister of Transport, Mr Colin

JETFOIL
The new exciting way to cross COOK STRAIT

TNL GROUP LTD
BOEING
JETFOIL

TNL's hopeful advertising brochure which preceded the company's abortive plans for a jetfoil service. There were hopes of serving Nelson as well as Picton. *Boeing/TNL Advertising*

The *Tamahine*, one of the best-remembered coastal ships of all time and the forerunner of the rail ferries on the Wellington-Picton run. *Union Steam Ship Company*

McLachlan, commented: "Any decision to invest in a jetfoil or any other type of fast craft is purely that of TNL exercising its commercial judgement. The approval of an import licence does not in any way imply a judgement by the Government about the viability or desirability of the service or its exclusive nature."

On 31 August TNL announced that it had abandoned its plans. Managing director Mr Garth Butler said Mr McLachlan had written to him, saying that the Railways would reduce its ferry fares rather than lose passengers to the jetfoil.

"It is apparent that a highly-competitive situation could arise with the existing ferry service resulting in the jetfoil being unable to attract sufficient passenger volume to sustain a profitable operation."

He added: "While Governments for social or political reasons may from time to time see fit to invest capital at minimal or nil return, private enterprise is unable to pursue such a course and survive."

With his announcement, hopes of a renewed Wellington-Nelson passenger service died, along with the prospects of competition for the rail ferries between Wellington and Picton.

The history of the Wellington-Picton shipping service is dominated by two eras — the historic and long-lasting service provided by *Tamahine* and the sudden grip applied by the rail ferries in the last 20 years. Undoubtedly, it is the rail ferry operation which has transformed the Picton link into the country's most important coastal sea route and in so doing has stifled competition in other services.

The beginnings of the Picton run have already largely been covered, being mostly linked with the development of services between Lyttelton, Wellington and Nelson. The Union and Anchor Companies held the reins of these services, which until the 1920s included Picton in an overall coverage of South Island ports, linked to Wellington. The Union Company's three-times-a-week service from Wellington to Nelson via Picton was an example. The voyage to Picton took about four hours, followed by a break of between two and four hours, and then another six-hour trip on to Nelson. The Nelson-bound traveller therefore spent a whole business day on board ship. Many tourists also made the trip early this century to see the dolphin Pelorus Jack, whose antics alongside ships near French Pass we have described in detail in Chapter V.

The consolidation of the service into a direct Wellington-Picton run came in the 1920s; it was not too well received at first by the people of Picton. In December 1922 the Union Company withdrew from the Wellington-Nelson run, leaving that to the An-chor Company who had just bought *Mapourika* (later *Ngaio*) from the Union fleet. Picton travellers, who had lost the services of the bigger and more comfortable 1,203-ton *Mapourika*, had to make do with the 35-year-old and more cramped *Wainui*, of just 640 tons. They were pacified only when the Union Company placed an order with Swan Hunter Wigham Richardson, of Newcastle-upon-Tyne, for the 1,989-ton *Tamahine*. Specially built for the run, *Tamahine* registered 17.3 knots (32 kilometres/hour) on speed trials before her debut on 21 December 1925 for a service of three return trips a week.

The *Tamahine* did not always have the service to herself. An example of competition was the cargo-only run provided by the 681-ton *Holmdale*. She plied a trade between Dunedin, Oamaru, Timaru, Lyttelton, Wellington, Picton and Wanganui from 1922 to 1957. Picton and Lyttelton were dropped in the later years of the service. The *Holmdale* was actually in the employ of the Dunedin-Wanganui Shipping Company, but she bore the green funnel colours of the Holm line and was manned by Holm officers.

Tamahine's service was to last until the rail ferries took over in 1962, apart from wartime requirements which saw the ship seconded to the Wellington-Lyttelton run. Her introduction prompted the Union Company to make good use of the scenic attractions of the Marlborough Sounds for a while, offering a weekend excursion that left Wellington at 1.15 p.m. on Saturday. The ship arrived at Picton at 4.30 p.m., and, after a look around, the passengers went back on board for a meal

Old-style passenger comfort on board the *Tamahine*. The portholes even had curtains. *Union Steam Ship Company*

served at 6.15 p.m. An after-deck was lit up with coloured lights and a dance was held until midnight, when the passengers went off to their berths on board. Early next morning the ship steamed to Pelorus Sound, anchoring in Tennyson Inlet. Fishing or bush walks filled in time until the return to Picton at 1 p.m. Extra passengers were then picked up

for the return trip to Wellington.

Tamahine was nearly involved in a collision with the trans-Tasman steamer *Maunganui* on 3 February 1928. Both ships left Wellington at about the same time and followed parallel courses until the area of Tom's Rock, when *Maunganui* seemed to be edging over towards *Tamahine* and overtaking her.

The quayside scene on one side of the Tamahine's busiest sailing days. *Union Steam Ship Company*

When *Maunganui* was only about 20 metres away from the smaller ship she suddenly crossed *Tamahine's* bow. *Tamahine* was sent full speed astern and the wheel was thrown over. The officers on duty believed that another four seconds' delay would have spelled disaster. The Union Company issued a statement to say that both masters had breached company regulations. Each was accordingly relieved of his command and transferred to cargo ships.

Tamahine had the first woman radio operator to be carried by the Union Company — Miss Gladys York. According to one story Miss York objected to wearing a skirt on board because of the danger of it blowing up in the wind when she was attending to batteries. Although she had struck a blow for the equality of the sexes, she was unsuccessful in this further fight. Captain W.J. Hill refused to let her wear trousers and compromised by getting the bosun to attend to the batteries.

The two-funnelled *Tamahine* could berth 117 passengers when required, and the length of her service provides testimony to her popularity. She was generally economic for her owners, too, despite the constant challenge of the auxiliary scow *Echo*, which traded between Wellington and Blenheim.

The *"Tam"*, as she was called, had some unique and notable characteristics — particularly a heavy list. According to Captain Alan McIntyre, who served on *Tamahine* as a junior officer, the reason for this lopsided look was the weather.

"It was only a result of strong winds at Wellington," he said. "As she was going into Wellington Harbour the southerlies would make her heel right over to port. Coming out of Wellington she would heel right over the other way, and have a list to starboard until she got to Halswell Point."

Signs of *Tamahine's* impending obsolescence came in the early 1950s, by which time she could not cope with the increasing demand for vehicle traffic. For the summer of 1953 onwards she was replaced seasonally by *Rangatira* for this very reason. A decision to retire *Tamahine* was then inevitable and it duly came from the Union Company in April 1956. The announcement was that *Tamahine* would be withdrawn towards the end of 1957 because the costs of keeping her in service longer than that would be prohibitive.

It is from this point that the influence of politics began to shape the future of the Wellington-Picton service. Initially, in July 1956, that influence was behind the Union Company with the offer of a £1.5 million loan to enable the company to buy a car-and-passenger ferry as a replacement for *Tamahine*. During the next year the Postmaster-General, Mr Tom Shand, revealed that the terms of that loan were to have been 25 years, free of interest. However the loan never changed hands, because in February 1957 the Prime Minister, Mr Sidney Holland, announced that instead of granting a loan the Government would meet the Union Company's losses (possibly £50,000 a year) on the Cook Strait service for up to four years after 1958 if *Tamahine* remained in service. Holland explained that after discussions with the Union Company it had been decided to postpone the decision to build a ferry until a study had been made of likely transport developments in the Cook Strait trade.

In April 1957 a Cook Strait transport inquiry committee was duly set up by the Government to report on the best form of link between Wellington and Picton. The final report, tabled in December of the following year, really prepared the ground for the future service. It recommended a "drive-on drive-off" rail and road vehicle ferry steamer. The service should be daily both ways, it said, carrying up to 80 cars, or 40 cars and 20 rail wagons, and up to 1,200 passengers. The new Prime Minister, Mr Walter Nash, gave his blessing to the recommendations, but no decision was made on who should operate it. That question was answered in May 1959, when the Government announced that a 4,000-ton rail-road ferry would be brought into operation by the Railways Department in 1962. For some reason — which shall be covered later — the Union Company had failed to push hard enough to keep the service within its own ranks.

The decision to make the Railways Department into a shipowner was a momentous move, but not a new idea. As far back as July 1898 the general manager of Railways, Mr T. Ronayne, had told a parliamentary committee of inquiry that his department had from time to time brought down recommendations on the running of a fast steamer between the islands. This committee of inquiry recommended there should be a daily shipping service between Wellington and Lyttelton and also that the Government should invite tenders for such a service. These ideas had gathered dust on the shelf as the Union vessels began to increase their interisland trade.

In 1924 a Royal Commission of Inquiry into the New Zealand railway service, headed by English civil engineers Sir Sam Fay and Sir Vincent Raven, came up with the view that an interisland rail-ferry service would have to be established sooner or later in order to provide rail transit from one end of the country to the other. They favoured a southern terminal at Clifford Bay, near Cape Campbell, with the South Island main-trunk line being extended to that point. The Fay-Raven proposals were shelved the next year when a committee of railway officers presented the pessimistic view that a train-ferry passenger service would be less satisfactory than the existing interisland steamer expresses.

The idea had not died entirely, however. A Railways board of management reviewed the matter in 1931 before deciding again that a rail ferry could not compete against the steamers. This was more than just a case of the Railways keeping the pot boiling. The *Evening Post* of 5 November 1939, reported that a South Island Travel Association meeting in Christchurch had resolved that:

> We can see a train ferry across the strait would be of tremendous advantage. Such a service must come in time, and it will involve a great development in Picton . . . a train ferry is a bridge, and South Islanders should regard this development as one in which the future of tourist traffic is directly involved.

A similar call came in March 1944, when the Government M.P. for Marlborough, Mr E.P. Meachen, advocated a takeover of the interisland service by the Railways. The completion of the South Island main-trunk line made this proposition a possibility for the Railways, to the extent that the department made another review in 1947 before again deciding that it was too early to take any action.

The changing fortunes of the *Tamahine* kept the option constantly before the Railways, and on 17 May 1956 the *Evening Post* reported that National Roads Board engineer, Mr L.C. Malt, had recommended Wellington and Picton as the best terminals for a drive-on drive-off interisland ferry. The roads board had examined a possible route between Karehana Bay at Plimmerton and Deep Bay, a distance of 51 kilometres. This was dropped because a new 33-kilometre road would have been required to extend to Linkwater in the South Island. Karehana Bay was dropped as an entirely new terminal would be needed — the depth of the water

The first Cook Strait rail ferry, *Aramoana*, sails past Pencarrow Head with flags flying on her delivery voyage from Britain in July 1962. *"Evening Post"*

was insufficient and the harbour was exposed.

With the carrot dangling before it for so long, Railways was quick to take a bite when the political climate was right in 1959. The department worked quickly once the Government go-ahead was given, sending a team to England to study the design and operation of vehicle ferries. In March the next year the designs were put to tender and in July the contract was let to a company with strong New Zealand connections — Wm Denny Bros. of Dumbarton, Scotland.

The first ferry, *Aramoana*, duly arrived on 26 July 1962, to take over when *Tamahine* made her final departure from Picton on 11 August that year. *Tamahine* was bought by the Hong Kong Shipping Company and renamed *Kowloon Star*.

Even after she had been retired, the *Tamahine* — or at least some anonymous members of her former crew — made sure she was never forgotten. During the period she was awaiting sale, the *Evening Post* ran an editorial on the *Tam* which described her as ugly. Shortly after, the following letter appeared in the paper:

The massive stern door which provides entry for vehicles and rail wagons on the Cook Strait ferries.
"Evening Post"

Sir, I'm flattered and I'm humiliated. Its not many ships that get noticed in newspaper editorials. It was good of you to put me on such a pedestal but why make me an ugly duckling? Surely you don't mean that! Me ugly? What a thing to say. I'm old I know, but ugly? Sir, you must be thinking of someone else. And as for my stern — it's improper to mention a lady's stern. Anyway there isn't anything wrong with it. Abbreviated you say, but if it had

been any longer I might have lost it. Though I can't see it myself, I really don't think there is anything wrong with it and I'm quite pleased that my builders gave me a pretty little counter. I've never liked these modern chopped-off affairs.

Since I've been sitting here in Evans Bay these four months I've seen some sights go by — that brazen snub-nosed hussy they've put in my place [*Aramoana*]. Just wait till she gets a smack on her glassy face from one of those southerlies I've

bounced off.

Sir, I am not ugly though I have to say it myself. Look at my funnels. They're nicely spaced and they give me a neatly balanced profile. I'm glad I was born before they got the idea of turning funnels into inverted pudding bowls. My nose is sharp and slender, my lines are just what they ought to be for a lady of my size. The only defect I'll admit is that my bridge has just a bit too much on top.

I may not be quite as beautiful as my big

Brilliant lights illuminate the scene as the Aramoana spends her first night at the Wellington rail-road ferry terminal. *"Evening Post"*

sister *Rangatira*, but you must admit I'm much prettier than that *Hinemoa* woman. What an ugly mouth — just like somebody who has lost her teeth. And that *Maori* with her great fat nose and a funnel that's much too big. She hasn't even a decent mast. Call that tripod arrangement a mast! Look at mine, they're nice and neat and slender, just what they ought to be.

I'm sorry you don't like my list to port, but it's just my way of being coy and I mean to keep it. And, anyway, I dare say you'll have a list to port yourself this week and you won't look half as coy as I do — I am, etc., *TAMAHINE*.

Railways was precise in its requirements for *Aramoana*. She would have to be sturdy enough to withstand strong winds and rough seas, together with tides of up to 6 knots when making the 81-kilometre journey from Wellington to Picton. A nominal service speed of 17 knots (31.5 kilometres/hour) was decided upon, to give a crossing time of three hours 20 minutes, which is still the same today. In one hour it would have to be possible to discharge 55 cars, 30 wagons of average length and up to 800 passengers, and then reload with the same payload. Loading of freight had to be confined to the stern, and reliability was an essential element because *Aramoana* would at that stage be a one-ship "fleet". Her stern had to fit into and be closely held by the berth so that rail tracks on the ship and link span could be aligned. The Union Company would man and manage the ferry.

The *Aramoana* had hardly started her run when she proved an almost embarrassingly huge success. In its last year of operation, *Tamahine* had carried 60,000 passengers, 11,000 cars and 14,000 tonnes of freight. Railways had hoped for 85,000 passengers, 20,000 cars and 100,000 tonnes of freight from the *Aramoana*. The actual return on the first year was 207,000 passengers, 46,000 cars and 181,000 tonnes of freight. The profit return was even more startling. On 5 July 1961 the *Evening Post* reported that Marine Department figures presented to Parliament indicated that *Tamahine* had lost £81,044 in the year ended 31 March 1960 — money which the Government had to pay. Later figures compiled by the Railways (expressed in New Zealand dollars) showed that in the first three years of rail ferry operations the net cumulative return was in the order of over $2 million.

Strangely, interisland ferries have had a habit of getting into scrapes early in their careers and *Aramoana* was no exception. Two days before she began the service she was on a demonstration trip and was crowded with VIPs. As she berthed at Picton, watched by a 5,000-strong crowd, she was buffeted towards Waitohi Wharf by a strong wind. The captain had to take evasive action to avoid a small boat with four people on board that had turned out to greet the ship. She ended up swiping the wharf side-on, smashing about 9 metres of concrete and causing minor damage to the ship's side.

That piece of bad luck apart, she was an astounding success and, within a year, Railways was planning a sister ship. Dennys had gone out of business and were not able to quote for the contract. It landed instead with Vickers Armstrong, of Newcastle-upon-Tyne, and *Aranui* was duly delivered in early 1966. Trade growth rates on the run continued virtually unchecked and Railways' expansion plans soon moved on to a third ship.

By this time container shipping had begun to make its mark on the world and Railways toyed with the idea of making the third ferry a semi-container ship. This was eventually scrapped because the existing labour set-up made it impractical. But it was clear that more rail freight space was needed. The first two ships had often been down to their full load-marks in the water and, in some cases, wagons had to be taken off before sailing.

A review of the successful layout of the first two ships was made and Railways came up with the idea of lengthening the design and providing four rail tracks instead of three. Passenger traffic growth seemed to be adequately catered for by the first two ships, so a maximum passenger capacity of 40 was fixed for the next vessel. This capacity allowed dangerous goods to be carried on the open upper deck and allowed for accommodation of the drivers of road vehicles which would be carried on the ship. An order for the vessel, to be named *Arahanga*, was placed with Upper Clyde Shipbuilders Ltd,

of Glasgow, towards the end of 1969. Unfortunately the shipyard went into liquidation when the *Arahanga* was about one fifth completed. It was only by the perseverance of the department, its consultants and U.K.-based staff, that it was obtained at all (albeit at £500,000 more than the original contract price of £3.7 million).

Arahanga entered service in 1972, one year after the Union Company had ceased to manage and crew the ships. She equalled the success of the first ferries. She has more reserve engine power, which coupled with her extra length, enables her to handle heavy southerly storms better than the older vessels. She was the first ship on the New Zealand coast with controllable-pitch propellers. Her captains took a little while to master these before declaring their preference for such propulsion. Traffic forecasts indicated to Railways that a fourth ferry would be needed by 1974 and that this ferry should again be devoted mainly to rail wagons. The lowest tenderer, Dubigeon Normandie of Nantes, France, was given the contract in 1971 to deliver *Aratika* to start service in early 1974 as a sister freight ship to *Arahanga*. In 1975 two developments prompted Railways to convert its newest ship to a passenger-road vehicle configuration. First, both *Aranui* and *Aramoana* required major overhauls of their electric propulsion systems following breakdowns, and Railways considered two passenger ships were required for the service. *Aratika* was the obvious choice. Second, the Union Company announced that *Rangatira* was to be withdrawn from the Wellington-Lyttelton service, which meant the Picton ferries would

The *Aramoana* ploughs into rough seas as she passes the forbidding rocks of Wellington Heads. *"Evening Post"*

Aramoana, was actually laid up and the service reverted to a three-ship operation. This was a cost-cutting exercise, which the department said was necessary because an attempt to bring in a reduced sailing schedule for four ships had failed to win unanimous approval from maritime unions. A total of 135 seamen and cooks and stewards was paid off. However, *Aramoana* came back for the Christmas-holiday period that year and remained in service because freight volumes improved.

However, the unpredictable freight situation has not prevented Railways' planning for future needs. In December 1981 the Government approved a tender for a new ship — temporarily nicknamed *Ara Five* — to replace the *Aramoana* and enter service at the end of 1983. The $45-million ship is being built in Denmark by Aalborg Vaerft, and the significance of the order is that the *Ara Five* will be the biggest ship on the Cook Strait run. It has a length of 146 metres, a beam of 20 metres and a two-deck layout similar to the *Arahanga*. The upper vehicle deck has a headroom of 4.3 metres to enable larger vehicles such as trucks and caravans to be carried on that deck. There is room for 1,000 passengers and 60 rail wagons or 130 cars on the rail deck, plus 100 cars or equivalent on the vehicle deck. The wider beam means that vehicles have more room to turn on deck.

To complete this account of the Wellington-Picton service it is necessary to backtrack 20 years and ask why the Union Company did not push harder to keep the Picton service when *Tamahine* was retired. At the time, the Union Company maintained a discreet silence and it is difficult to get an official

have to carry more passengers and cars.

Normally, Railways has allowed three to four years for the planning and delivery of a new ship, but *Aratika* was a rush job. The total time from commencement of planning until the ship re-entered service, just before Christmas 1976, was 14 months. She was taken to Hong Kong with the intention of incorporating space for 800 passengers and 70 cars, to add to that existing for 50 rail wagons. In her first three weeks of operation *Aratika* carried 27,000 passengers. Railways considered the $7-million conversion cost to be money well spent, particularly as competition from the Wellington-Lyttelton trade had died off.

Since then, Railways has been hit by the fall-off in freight movements between the islands and, in late August 1980, after the round of annual surveys, the oldest ferry,

All four rail ferries group around the Wellington terminal. Such a sight is a rarity as the ships would normally be scattered at either the Wellington or Picton terminals or out in the strait. *New Zealand Railways Publicity*

The foreshortening effect of the telephoto camera lens makes it appear that the *Aramoana* has run aground at Point Halswell in Wellington Harbour. *"Evening Post"*

answer to this question. However, there is one theory which came from a Union Company source which seems to be plausible. The theory goes that when *Tamahine* was being withdrawn, the Union Company was naturally wary of entering another unprofitable service, so it required a commitment from Government concerning the Railways Department, which was competing for the new ferry service. The commitment was that the Railways would not develop their Cook Strait air service to the extent that sea freight trade would be scuttled. The Union Company was naturally wary of being drawn into competition with an air service that could possibly undercut its charges. Railways, of course, needed no such safeguard if it took over the ferry contract because it controlled both sea and air freight. The Government would not make any promises to the Union Company on the amount of sea freight that would be available and consequently, the Union Company disappeared from the scene. From now on it was to be a Railways undertaking . . . or nothing.

Chapter VIII

A modern ferry voyage across the strait

. . . off for a "drive" across the strait . . .

11.40 a.m. John Mansell, 10 years a captain on the Cook Strait rail ferries, gives the order to "Let go for'ard", and the latest — most say the best — ferry in the rail fleet, *Aratika*, edges slowly away from the link span at Picton. The link span is the umbilical cord that connects the ship to the railhead and the southern state highway at this South Island town, tucked deep inside one of the many coves of the Marlborough Sounds. Captain Mansell is on the bridge, situated high on the forward section of the ship, which gives a panoramic view across the bows and provides even a narrow back view down the sides of the ship. On the bridge with him, by Railways regulations, is one other deck officer plus the quartermaster (helmsman). At departure the third mate provides the company, but soon it will be the turn of the mate, Phil Norman, to take over the "drive".

"The whole day is broken into 'drives'," John Mansell explains. "Other ships might call them watches, but for some reason they have always been drives on the ferries.

Shortly the mate will come up for this morning's drive to Wellington. He will be on deck for the whole crossing. I'll be here in the Sounds, and from the Wellington harbour entrance onwards."

11.46 a.m. *Aratika* has slipped the berth and its surrounds. Captain Mansell has ordered the ship to pick up speed:

From the time we leave, the first thing we look at is the tides for the whole crossing. They make a big difference. If the tides were against us the whole way we could use 50 per cent more horsepower than if they were with us. Here, in Queen Charlotte Sound, we have slack water [the inert water formed when one tide has ebbed, and another not yet begun] at present, then the tide in Tory Channel will only just be starting to be with us. It should be slack water again in the strait, and in the harbour it will just be starting to ebb against us. We also have to take into account the weather. There is a 30-knot

[55.5 kph] southerly which will be against us to some extent. So we have to decide on our power setting, remembering that we want to leave a bit up our sleeve if we fall behind on time. We have also got to remember that for a three-mile stretch in Tory Channel, we have to reduce from the service speed of 17 knots [31.5 kph] to 14 knots [26 kph] to reduce the wash we form. We don't want to wash away the frontage on people's real estate. We'll be keeping a check on geographical landmarks as we go past, to check whether we are on time.

11.50 a.m. The mate, Phil Norman, comes up for his drive. He reports a forward draught (depth of hull under the water) of 4.9 metres and an aft draught of 5.1 metres. Big ships tend to perform better with a deeper draught at the stern. Across the strait and in the sounds *Aratika* will have plenty of water underneath her. At Wellington harbour entrance there will be a clearance of about 7 metres. Crossing the Falcon Shoals off the

The *Aratika* heads for the Wellington ferry terminal. In the background is the striking architecture of St Gerard's monastery on Mount Victoria. *New Zealand Railways Publicity*

Miramar peninsula, there will be less than 3 metres of water between the sea bottom and the ship. However, John Mansell is not concerned with the shoals because the water there is calm and the ship will not roll and pitch. But the harbour entrance, where tides converge with wind-driven swells to form big waves and troughs, can be a worry:

If you pitch heavily you can come within a few feet of the bottom, but it would be desperately bad weather to actually hit the bottom. In that kind of weather, I doubt if we would be going out anyway. More often than not it is the weather at the harbour entrance that causes cancellations, not the weather in the strait. In the strait, a big sea is a big sea. You just accept it. But the harbour entrance can be difficult. One of my worst trips was in the freight ferry, the *Arahanga*. There had been a very bad southerly for four or five days, and it was blowing about 70 knots [129.5 kilometres/hour] with very heavy swells. I hove to off Sinclair Head, but the forecast was for the weather to get worse, so I had to have a go at getting through the heads, and we got in okay.

Southerlies are always the worst weather. You can be in 80 knot [148 kilometres/hour] northerlies off Karori, but there won't be much of a swell because the sea is sheltered by the lie of the land. The strait has a bad reputation because the wind can change so quickly. A southerly gale can blow up a big swell very quickly, and then you will be heading straight into the seas when you leave the sounds. That's when you have a rough

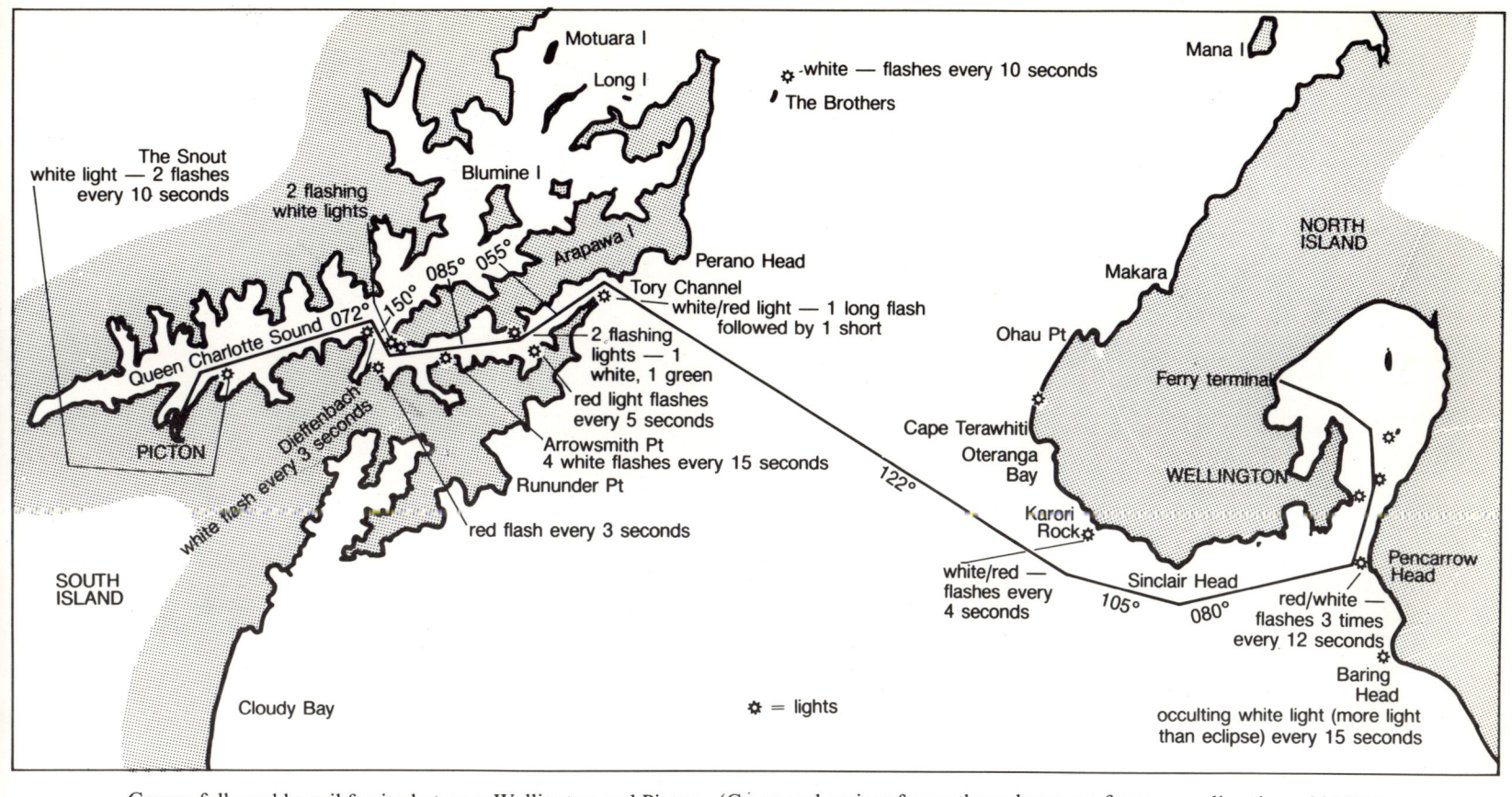

Course followed by rail ferries between Wellington and Picton   (Compass bearings for eastbound voyage: for reverse direction add 180°)

trip. You get this rough patch of unnatural water called the Karori Rip, where the wind and seas meet the tide head-on. We can even pick it up on radar. The passengers feel sick and so can the crew. But if you regularly cross the strait, you must expect a hiding now and again.

12.10 p.m. Captain Mansell orders a course change to take *Aratika* into Tory Channel. The ship is making 17 knots (31.5 kilometres/hour) the engine power being controlled directly from the bridge without the aid of telegraph. The older ferries, *Aramoana* and *Aranui*, have diesel-electric

engines. The new *Arahanga* and *Aratika* are straight diesels. They have twin rudders and twin variable-pitch propellers, with blades that can turn at different angles to change the power output. Placed sideways through the hull at the bows are two "bow thrusters", propellers which push the bow from side to

On the bridge of the *Aratika*. Captain John Mansell is at the right, quartermaster Dale Weeks, centre, and third mate John Oliver, left. *David MacIntyre*

At the controls of the ship. The big levers control engine settings. *David MacIntyre*

side when the ship backs into her berth. These are also controlled directly from the bridge. On her first trip of the day from Wellington, leaving at 7.20 a.m., *Aratika* crossed the harbour at only 12 knots (22 kilometres/hour) because the master did not want to strain the engines when they were cold.

12.13 p.m. Captain Mansell gives the order to slow down to 14 knots (26 kilometres/hour) in Tory Channel to avoid shore damage from the ship's wash. He is concerned because sister-ship *Aranui* is late leaving Wellington — there is a fear the ships will meet at the narrow entrance to Tory Channel. Captain Mansell wants to avoid the problems of reducing steerage way and also the inconvenience of losing time on the voyage. Just behind the bridge in the radio room, radio officer Ken Grace is in morse code contact with *Aranui* to check on her progress. Morse is used in most of ship-to-shore and intership communications because there are fewer problems with it in terms of interference.

12.14 p.m. *Aranui* is sighted, off in the distance at the channel entrance. There will obviously be no conflict between the courses of the respective vessels, and they can pass in the channel with room to spare.

12.21 p.m. Passengers on board *Aratika* and *Aranui* wave as the ships pass. Down below, chief steward Mike Young is overseeing the preparation of meals and snacks for the passengers' cafeteria. There is a light load of passengers on this mid-winter, mid-week trip, with about 80 on board. The cafeteria does not provide freshly cooked meals, but it does offer a curry, a casserole and an assortment of savouries, sandwiches and ice cream.

12.29 p.m. Captain Mansell gives the order to go up to 17 knots (31.5 kilometres/hour).

He is proud of the rail ferries' ability to turn around (discharge passengers and cargo, reload and sail again) in an hour:

In the summer holidays we can get a full load of 800 passengers. At that time of the year you don't get much rail freight coming across, because the factories have closed down, but instead of rail wagons we can get 200 cars on board. If we were using all four rakes [lengths of rail track on the rail deck] of rail, we would discharge 50 four-wheeled rail wagons, 65 cars from the two garages on B and C decks, maybe 10 more cars or half a dozen trucks plus a luggage truck from the rail deck, and all the passengers, then get an identical load back on and sail in an hour.

Compared with overseas, most European ferries would take two hours to turn around. We might have an advantage in that the berths we use are tailormade for us, whereas in Dover you would have ships of all shapes and sizes using the same wharves. Even so, it is still a remarkable achievement and we are proud of it.

12.33 p.m. Second mate Robin Bramley broadcasts a warning to all shipping that in

Wagons on the ship's massive rail deck are firmly lashed down. *New Zealand Railways Publicity*

10 minutes' time *Aratika* will be leaving Tory Channel entrance. The warning is for small craft, so they will avoid meeting the ferry in the narrow entrance.

Aratika has four decks of garages and passenger rooms, then a rail deck, then an engine room and below that fuel and ballast tanks. The engine room spaces are divided by bulkheads. If anything should go wrong, the flick of a switch on the bridge will close the watertight doors after a brief period when warning bells have sounded. The ship is

designed to stay afloat even if two adjacent engine-room areas are flooded. Built into the sides of the ships are four "heeling" tanks. These contain 300 tonnes of water on each side. When the ship is being loaded with heavy trains, the first mate on the rail deck will transfer water from one side to counterbalance the weight of the trains. If this was not done, a very heavy train coming onto the outside rake would make the ship heel violently to one side, causing the link span to be twisted.

Vehicle access is via a drive-on link span attached to the stern of the ship. *New Zealand Railways Publicity*

12.36 p.m. John Mansell gives the engine-room staff five minutes notice of "stand-by". The engineers are not allowed to do anything that will affect the running of the ship, such as changing fuel lines, during the navigation of the channel entrance.

12.41 p.m. Standby is ordered. Orders to quartermaster Dale Weeks come more quickly as *Aratika* emerges into Cook Strait. The water is choppy as the tides meet. A 25-knot (46 kilometres/hour) southerly is blowing. John Mansell decides to steer a straight course across to Wellington because the tides and wind are not going to cause problems on this trip:

> We will set a course to take us a mile-and-a-half off Karori Rock, and the third mate, John Oliver, will take over from me. We will allow 3 or 5 degrees on the course for leeway [being blown off course by wind] but nothing for set [being taken off course by tides]. Half-way across the strait the third mate will check with radar to make sure we are in position, and we will decide then whether to make any alterations. We can't afford to drop behind on time, not just because it inconveniences the passengers but because it puts a pressure on the whole schedule.

12.45 p.m. John Oliver takes over on the bridge and John Mansell goes off to his cabin, situated just aft of the bridge. While the ship is in the strait both the steering motors, which control the twin rudders, will be tested to make sure everything is in order for manouevring in Wellington Harbour.

Aratika is carrying a crew of 67. She has a master, three mates, a radio officer, four pursers (who look after the clerical work, do the crew's time sheets, pay the wages and collect the tickets), a chief steward, two second stewards, three cooks who prepare the crew's meals, 21 stewards, two stewardesses, a chief engineer, four engineers, two electricians, four motormen (general workers in the engine room), 14 able seamen and two ordinary seamen. The seamen do the general maintenance, steering, keep lookouts, lash the cargo and tie up the ship. The cooks, stewards, mates, electricians and engineers work four days on and eight off. The seamen work four on and six off.

The cooks work a long day, beginning at 5.30 a.m. The seamen and stewards are on duty or on call roughly between 6 a.m. and midnight. The master's day begins with a call at 6.45 a.m. Rail freight and cars start coming aboard at 6.30 a.m. and passengers at 6.45

In the captain's cabin, situated aft of the bridge. The cabin has a shower and a bunk. *David MacIntyre*

Radio officer Ken Grace prepares to tap out a morse message in the radio room, located immediately behind the bridge. *David MacIntyre*

a.m. The captain must be on the bridge by 7.20 a.m. at the latest.

Relaxing on the comfortable sofa in his cabin, John Mansell explains why the ship needs such a large crew:

One big worry on a ship of this size, where we could be carrying 867 people at the height of the summer season, is organising everyone and getting them off in an emergency. That could be a collision, a fire, a stranding, anything. I was involved in reorganising the emergency routine for the ship, and we now have a set plan where everyone on the crew has a duty to perform. Unless we had our present crew strength, we would be stretched when it came to passenger control. We have reckoned on having 24 crew to organise up to 800 passengers who could be spread through different areas of the ship. Those crew members would seal off areas such as the cafeteria and use them as mustering areas to distribute lifejackets and usher passengers to the nearest life raft. We have drills every week to practice this. We get passengers to try on lifejackets. The stewardesses will show the inflatible cots we have for babies. But in an emergency, we would only have those 24 crew members available to organise the passengers. The others would have different duties to perform. The seamen, for example, would be dealing directly with the emergency, fighting the fire or whatever. We could not make do with a smaller crew strength.

The *Aratika's* fourth engineer, Graham Spall, at the engine-room control console. Television screens monitor the engines.
David MacIntyre

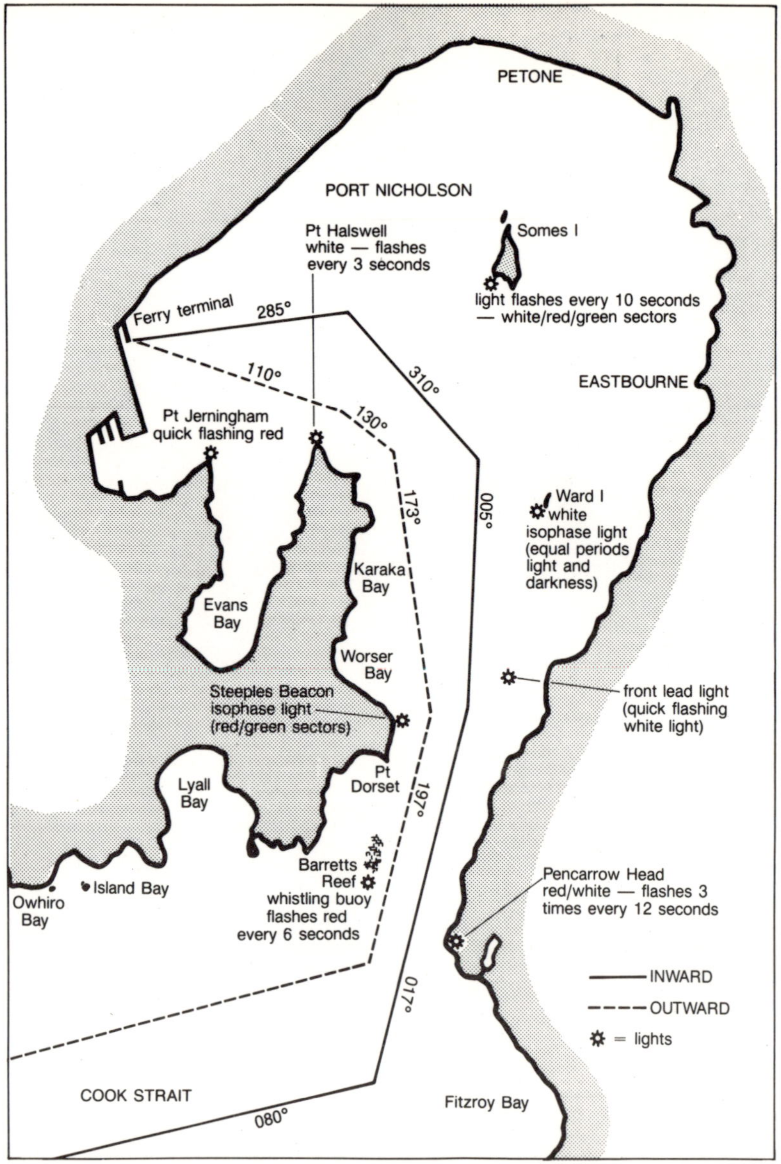

PETONE

PORT NICHOLSON

Pt Halswell
white — flashes
every 3 seconds

Somes I

light flashes every 10 seconds
— white/red/green sectors

Ferry terminal   285°

EASTBOURNE

110°

310°

Pt Jerningham
quick flashing red

130°

173°

005°

Ward I
white
isophase light
(equal periods
light and
darkness)

Evans
Bay

Karaka
Bay

Worser
Bay

Steeples Beacon
isophase light
(red/green sectors)

front lead light
(quick flashing
white light)

Lyall
Bay

Pt
Dorset

197°

Island Bay

Owhiro
Bay

Barretts
Reef
whistling buoy
flashes red
every 6 seconds

Pencarrow Head
red/white — flashes 3
times every 12 seconds

017°

INWARD

OUTWARD

= lights

COOK STRAIT

080°

Fitzroy Bay

Approximate courses followed by rail ferries in Wellington Harbour

1.16 p.m. John Oliver reports to the captain's cabin. *Aratika* is exactly half-way across the strait. She is running three minutes late, mainly because of the earlier speed reduction in Tory Channel.

John Mansell is proud of the rail ferries' safety record. In 20 years there has not been a collision, a grounding or a life lost:

Fire is our biggest worry — fire and the fear of getting water on the rail deck. That deck is a massive open area, and a film of water across it will cause "slopping". You know how difficult it is to carry a baby's bathtub full of water, when the water slops from side to side and the weight shifts? That's how it could be if we got water on the rail deck. We shouldn't get any water there, but in severe weather you might get water coming down the ventilators or squirting through the stern door. We have got very large scuppers [drains] on that deck, with non-return valves, to clear the water quickly. They are tested every week. If there was a fire on the rail deck, we have a powerful drencher system installed, and the scuppers would get rid of that water, too. Elsewhere on the ship we have sprinklers installed as a precaution against fire.

2.04 p.m. *Aratika* is six minutes late passing Sinclair Head. Unexpectedly, the tide was against the ship on the second half of the strait crossing. John Mansell is not too concerned, however, because time can be made up in the harbour. The radio operator checks on traffic with the harbour radio and learns that *Union Rotoiti* is waiting to berth. *Aratika* is meant to head for a position about 3

kilometres south of the Barretts Reef buoy to avoid any conflict with outgoing traffic. Then, the leading light in the channel entrance must be lined up with the rear light and the ship follows the course. Once in the harbour there are prescribed courses to follow.

2.15 p.m. John Mansell returns on the bridge to take command of the ship when she navigates the entrance.

2.42 p.m. *Aratika* passes Halswell Point on the northern tip of the Miramar peninsula. The ship is beginning to make up her six-minute deficit.

The Cook Strait service as a whole has a bad reputation with the travelling public, so far as its strike record is concerned. Partly that is due to some well-publicised and silly disputes over things such as the supply of chocolate biscuits for the crew, but those disputes happened some years ago and the industrial record is good now. Unfortunately, the ferries can be cancelled for reasons outside their control. For example, harbour-board workers at either Picton or Wellington can be in dispute and consequently the ferries can't tie up. Weather conditions may cancel some sailings and even the Railways department itself may decide to cancel a trip because freight loadings are low. In such situations, the public reaction is generally one of complaint that "the ferries are off again". This is usually associated with the belief that there are too many strikes.

The facts, however, do not fit that picture. In June 1981 Railways minister Colin McLachlan presented figures to Parliament

John Mansell works the bow-thruster controls at the extreme wing of the bridge as he backs the *Aratika* into the Wellington terminal.
Peter Avery

to show that in the year ended 31 March 1981 only 195 of the 4,360 scheduled one-way crossings were cancelled because of industrial action. Of these, only 52 related to ferry disputes. The remainder arose from outside issues, such as the Mangere picket dispute or harbour-board strikes. During the same period, Railways cancelled 61 crossings because of a shortage of freight bookings. That gives the ferries a reliability rating of about 95 per cent.

The view down the side of the ship as the final few metres are negotiated. *David MacIntyre*

2.47 p.m. *Aratika's* engine room is put on stand-by again as the Captain prepares to swing the ship around, parallel to Aotea Quay, and back the ship into its berth. Speed drops to 12 knots (22 kilometres/hour) as *Aratika* noses towards Aotea Quay, then down to 10 knots (18.5 kilometres/hour) as she passes the floating dock.

2.52 p.m. John Mansell sends out his orders more quickly as the ship swings round to a command of "hard aport". The captain peers out the side windows to obtain a view down the sides of the ship to the distant rubber fenders on the wharf. At either side of the bridge are small consoles, which allow him to control engine speeds and the bow thrusters.

2.54 p.m. *Aratika* backs in at half-astern, giving her a speed of about 6 knots. The second mate is in radio contact with the bridge calling off the distance to be run in feet, first to the ends of the wharf and then to the fenders.

2.59 p.m. *Aratika* ties up on schedule, and the stern door drops on to the link span. In an hour she will be ready to sail again.

Chapter IX

The story of *Echo*

Feed 'em well, pay 'em well and work 'em bloody hard.

IN EARLIER days the auxiliary scow *Echo* ("auxiliary" in the sense that she had the use of an engine as well as her sails) became as much a part of the Wellington waterfront scene as any of the bigger and more vaunted ships that called regularly in the harbour. Her trade was to Blenheim, an unlikely thing in itself because the trip to Blenheim required a ship that could scrape over the Wairau Bar and then navigate the twisting, turning Opawa River up to the township.

Echo was owned and operated by the Eckford family of Blenheim, whose shipping company was founded by Captain Thomas Eckford in 1880 with the steamer *Mohaka*. In 1898 the family built the passenger ship *Opawa* for the Cook Strait trade, then in 1912 took on something of a handful in buying the scow *Wairau*, which under her former name of *Ronga* had a history of being a killer ship. Twice she capsized in Pelorus Sound and once, in 1906, she capsized on a voyage between Lyttelton and Wellington with the loss of all six crew (see chapter XI).

As it turned out, *Wairau* was an excellent buy. She had been converted to a steamer by the time the Eckford family bought her and was used in a variety of roles including the Wellington-Blenheim run. She was less suited to this run than *Echo*, however, because she had a slightly deeper draught (depth of hull under the water). In a situation where a matter of centimetres could determine whether the ship could cross the bar, *Echo* always had the advantage over *Wairau*. Even so, the Eckfords got more than 40 years of service out of *Wairau*. She spent about seven years swinging idly at her moorings at the Wairau Bar before being sold in 1961 to Captain Morrie Sawyer of the Sullivan Shipping Company. Captain Sawyer had her towed to Wellington and spent some time working on her in Shelly Bay. Plans for her re-use did not eventuate and she was taken to Motueka, to be hauled up on the mud-flats.

After the addition of *Wairau* to the company, the Eckford family continued over the years to make contributions to the so-called "Mosquito Fleet", which traded in and out of the Cook Strait ports. This was the fleet of small coasters, such as the 144-ton *Picton* owned by the Southern Cross Shipping Company, the Holm Company's tiny *Wakanui* and the 68-ton converted scow *Portland*, which earned the nickname "The Green Pea" because of her green hull and nondescript size. The Eckford company boasted that the family had driven the Union Company off the Blenheim trade. Although the little steamer *Tasmanian Maid* called at Blenheim as early as 1857, the Union Company opened the Blenheim route in 1883 with the 92-ton *Waihi*, followed by the *Kanieri* between 1886 and 1892. Incidentally, *Waihi* was the first command of Captain Walter Manning, who became something of a legend in the Union Company and whose role in the development of Cook Strait crossings is covered in the earlier chapter on the Wellington-Lyttelton steamer expresses.

Eventually, Eckford competition proved too much for the Union Company and the symbol of Eckford prosperity became the fine-looking scow, *Echo*, built in 1905 initially as a topsail schooner by William Brown and Sons at Te Kopuru, on the northern Wairoa River. Even then, she had an auxiliary engine, a 20-horsepower (15-kilowatt) Hercules. Her hull was of the square-bilge scow type, which had been developed in the

The *Echo's* beginnings, at the Brown and Sons boatyard on the northern Wairoa River. She was then registered in Auckland and did not begin her Wellington-Blenheim trade for several years.
Ron Palmer

to carry sail mainly to stop her rolling in the swells of Cook Strait, but her topmasts were later removed. She could carry 150 tonnes of cargo and was also one of the first coasters to have a radio.

Echo's history was one of minor scrapes. She had collisions with the Wellington tug *Toia* and the Eastbourne ferry steamers *Cobar* and *Muritai*, but the worst episode occurred in the 1930s when she was driven onto Pencarrow Head and holed. The crew abandoned her and some came ashore at Scorching Bay about midnight. The hull filled with water and drifted off on its side. Next day she was found upside down near Somes Island. She was later salvaged by the Wellington Harbour Board's floating crane and repairs were made to the hull. But behind the bare bones of this account lies an interesting human story.

At the time, the crew of *Echo* had bottles of cream given them as a kind of perk. During the grounding at Pencarrow, one crewman became so frightened at what was going on that he "froze" on board and had to be carried forcibly into the ship's boat. The story goes that he was landed at Pencarrow and eventually picked up from the farmhouse by a police car — still with a bottle of cream in his hand. He had been so scared that he clutched the bottle continuously in a death-like grip.

At the subsequent marine inquiry, Captain W.Q. Jarman, *Echo's* master, said that a heavy rain squall came on just as he was entering the harbour and obscured all the inside harbour lights. This left him without any sure idea of his position. The court exonerated the master and crew, saying that the accident was caused by a combination of

days when trade to rivermouths or up-river ports was a commercial necessity. Centreboards were lowered when the ship was at sea to prevent sideways drift. She is believed to have traded around the Auckland peninsula before being bought by Richardsons of Napier for the Hawke's Bay meat trade. She was fitted with two Skandia semi-diesels of

about 40 horsepower (30-kilowatts) each, making her one of the first diesel ships on the New Zealand coast. It was then that the Eckfords stepped in. Some accounts put the date of purchase in the early 1920s, but her late owner, Captain Tom Eckford (grandson of the line's founder) believes *Echo* was bought in 1918. A 131-tonner, she continued circumstances beyond their control.

During the war years *Echo* went through the most unlikely transformation, being requisitioned by the United States Navy in 1942 to serve as a supply ship in the New Hebrides (Vanuatu)-Solomon Islands-New Guinea area. She clocked up about 65,000 kilometres as the only United States sailing vessel actively employed in the war service.

She actually did see active service, too, being attacked by Japanese aircraft and joining in the chase for a submarine. She was also equipped with a couple of anti-aircraft guns and was rumoured to have two "kills" to her credit, although that story appears to be a case of mariners' exaggeration.

Echo's wartime experience led to another unlikely happening. In 1959 the Columbia Pictures Corporation asked if the ship could be taken to Honolulu to appear in a film based on her war role, but Eckfords could not release the vessel because she was needed on the Wellington-Blenheim run. The best Captain Eckford could suggest was to make her available for film sequences around the New Zealand coast. It eventuated that Columbia used a look-alike ship and produced the film, *The Wackiest Ship in the Army*, which appeared in Wellington in 1961. It was shunned by *Echo's* crew and owners. The Hollywood version of a land-lubber crew trying to handle a pure sailing ship was met with derision by those who knew that the film bore no relation to the truth.

When she returned from war service in 1944, *Echo* was in a poor state. her hull was riddled with teredo worm holes, and an almost entirely new hull was required before

In her early days the white-painted scow had high topmasts and a long bowsprit. *Ron Palmer*

she returned to the Cook Strait run. Shortly after, there was an unhappy milestone in the scow's career when she was caught in a real blow in Cook Strait and was driven miles off course. A north-west gale blew *Echo* down towards the Chatham Islands in 1948 and the Wellington tug *Toia* had to be sent out to bring her back.

By 1950 Mr Tom Eckford was holding the reins of the company, having taken over from his uncle Alex. He was running the business in conjunction with his engineer brother, Mr Bert Eckford. Most New Zealanders who recall *Echo's* service will identify with Tom Eckford's methods of operating the run, but an interesting "inside" account is given by Captain Ron Palmer. He is now well known in Wellington shipping circles, being assistant general secretary of the New Zealand Port Employers' Association and a member (and past deputy chairman) of the Wellington Harbour Board. He was also National

The *Echo* as she looked with sails up in her latter years. *"Evening Post"*

Party candidate for Heretaunga at the 1981 general election.

In March 1959 he left the trans-Tasman passenger liner *Monowai* to join *Echo*, later becoming her relieving master. He described his first day like this:

I joined the *Echo* in the morning and started work at 1 p.m. I was told we were sailing later that night. We finished loading at 8 p.m. and got the ship ready for sea. We weren't sailing until 11 p.m. and one of the crew said to me, "You'd better get some sleep; you're on the two to four watch." I wasn't used to the cramped conditions in the fo'c'sle and I found it hard to get to sleep. At 11 p.m. we cast off and I again returned to my bunk. This time I fell asleep but only for 10 minutes, when I got a shake at about midnight. It was one of the crew asking me to get up on deck and help put the sails up. I got up on deck and helped, and the *Echo* shipped a big sea and I got soaked. All of that for an hour's overtime.

Anyway, it was wet and cold and pitch black, darker than normal because the master had a thing about using torches on deck. He didn't like them and wouldn't let anyone use them, so first-trippers had to fumble their way around on deck. It was hard at first, but you soon got used to it. The master used to look out for landmarks a lot and claimed that a flashing torch would flash in his eyes and upset his night navigation. Anyway, I finally got back to my bunk, wet through, and knowing full well that I was going to be called at 1.45 a.m., so there was no chance of sleep. At two it was my turn to be on watch for two hours. I finished at four and went down to my bunk, very tired. I'd been asleep about 15 minutes when I was shaken awake and told it was time to get the sails in. By this time I was wondering if the crew was having me on, but I soon learned they weren't — that was a typical trip.

I only had two hours' sleep that night. I was woken up once more going through the bar, so by the time we arrived in Blenheim I was exhausted. We worked hard that day, unloading and reloading and I ended up having only another two hours' sleep on the way back to Wellington. As near as possible we would leave Wellington on a Monday night after loading during the day, arriving at Blenheim sometimes at four in the morning. We'd start working cargo straight away. Tom Eckford had his own store and his own wharf and the crew used to discharge the ship with the help of Tom's storemen. We'd tear into the cargo and discharge at an average 25 tons an hour, which is terrific for general cargo when you compare it with more modern equipment. In those days general cargo was being handled at between 10 and 12 tons an hour in other ports. The best we did was when we put up some sort of record by discharging 90 tons in two hours, with an old diesel winch and the swinging derrick type of system. It was all go. We used to work like hell. Anyway, we'd discharge and load and try and get out on the tide 12 hours later if possible on Tuesday night. We'd arrive back in Wellington in the early hours of Wednesday morning, discharging all day. In those days the wharfies used to work from 8 a.m. to 9 p.m., with a meal hour at midday through to 1 p.m. and a tea hour from 5 to 6 p.m. The overtime hours were 6 to 9 p.m. On Thursday we'd load all day and usually sail at 9 p.m. or 10 p.m. We'd get back over the strait and up the river to discharge her and reload on Friday. We'd leave Friday night or early Saturday and if the tides were right we'd be back in Wellington for an 8 a.m. start to discharging on Saturday. We'd discharge during the morning, knock off and then finish the job Monday morning. Saturday afternoon and Sunday was our only time off. The *Echo* existed on hard work. Tom Eckford had a saying which summed it up — "Feed 'em well, pay 'em well, and work 'em bloody hard."

The *Echo*, aground again at the beach near the Wairau Bar. A bulldozer and trolley unloads the cargo. *D.M. Furness*

The reference to the master of *Echo* disliking torchlight at night leads to a humorous revelation of the true story behind an incident in Cook Strait in the early 1960s. This was the time when New Zealand fishermen were up in arms about Japanese fishing boats allegedly poaching within the 3-mile limit in force at the time. On one occasion, there was a near-collision between a local fishing boat and an unlit craft, which was thought to be a foreign fishing boat. The local fishermen vented their feelings in the press next day. Ron Palmer recalls the incident like this:

The master in question was a great old Shetland Islander and very fine seaman. However, he hated torches being used and even disliked the slight shine inboard from navigation lights. On taking over the navigation watch I relieved the master and failed to notice that he had turned the lights off. Some two hours later I was watching this trawler bearing down on us when I realised we weren't showing any

This is how the *Echo* usually looked when she went aground on the bar. Notice how high she is out of the water. *Ron Palmer*

engineer shared a cabin just off the crew's messroom, which was aft as well; the other five slept in the fo'c'sle. The forward accommodation was fairly cramped and primitive according to Ron Palmer:

It wasn't uncommon to sleep with an oilskin on top of your blankets, to keep dry. When you were at sea she'd be shipping over a spray, and quite regularly good, hefty seas would wash aboard and the decking would leak a little. You were living and working in the conditions that existed when the ship was built in 1905, but the pay and food made up for it. I maintain the reason she was a happy ship is that the crew were so damned busy they were too tired to think of union problems or argue. Whenever you stopped working you'd stagger off to your bunk and sleep.

One of the things which made *Echo* a ship of real character was her ability to cross the Wairau Bar (the sharp rise in the seabed which acts as a natural barrier to shipping entering the Wairau River) and from there her navigation of the Opawa River to Blenheim. The bar would usually allow *Echo* to draw about 5 feet 10 inches (1.8 metres) of water, or in good conditions 6 feet 6 inches (nearly 2 metres). A clearance of 7 feet (2.1 metres) was a luxury. The ideal loading for *Echo* was a draft of 5 feet 6 inches (1.7 metres) forward and 6 feet (1.8 metres) aft, so if she did hit the bar it would only be with the stern hull and the ship's momentum would work with the prevailing seas to "bump" her across the bar. On occasions conditions would prevent a crossing; then she discharged at

lights and, as it was pitch black, he wouldn't be able to see a thing. I reached up and flicked the switch back on, and the trawler veered away. Next day this fisherman complained in the paper about these so-and-so Japanese who were wandering about Cook Strait without lights. It was really us, but we didn't let on about it.

At this time, the topmasts (extensions to the masts) had been removed from *Echo* and she sailed basically with a gaff foresail, a gaff mainsail and a jib. She worked with a crew of 10 — an ordinary seaman, four able seamen of whom one was made bosun, two engineers, a cook-steward, the chief officer and the master. The master, chief officer and chief engineer slept aft; the cook and assistant

Picton with the aid of watersiders. Tom Eckford cut down the percentage risk with his own soundings of the depth of the bar, which Ron Palmer describes:

> Tom would come out in his launch during the day, if we were going to cross it at night. As we arrived at the bar maybe at 2 a.m. he'd talk to us by radio telephone. He'd tell us he had sounded the bar at 4 p.m. and that the shallowest part was 5 feet 10 inches. He'd ask what draft have you got and we'd perhaps say 6 feet aft. "Oh well," he'd say, "that's not too bad. There's a wee bit of a lift. You should be able to bounce over." We'd come to accept this style of navigation.

On several occasions *Echo* did not quite make it across the bar. Her propellers — she finished up with 95-horsepower (70-kilowatt) Gardiner diesels fitted in 1963 — suffered occasionally from the groundings.

The ship would either get stuck on the bar itself or hit the bar and lose way (steerage momentum). If that happened the wind and sea would take control and blow her sideways onto the beach. Whenever *Echo* was stuck Eckfords used strong salvage tackle to winch her off. During Ron Palmer's five-and-a-half years on the ship, to late 1964, he recalls her being grounded six times, including one two-week grounding on the beach at the mouth of the Wairau River. This period of frustration gave rise to an incident which he tells like this:

> We were being pulled off the beach, and the strain and tension on these thick steel wires was tremendous. You could hear

The crew of the *Echo* about 1960. Ron Palmer is in the back row with arms folded third from right, and Captain Jock Dalziel is at the extreme right in the back row. *Ron Palmer*

them groaning. If one had snapped and hit you, it would have cut you in two. Anyway we were working amongst all these straining wires while we were being pulled off, and suddenly the strain started to pull the bulkhead [wall] off the side of the galley. The cook saw what was happening to his galley and he suddenly snapped. A fight developed between him and a German seaman on board. We tried to separate them and we held the cook down for a while. A radio message was sent out to Tom Eckford, who brought the police out and they led the cook away in a straitjacket. The funny thing was that the German seaman was a keen photographer and, while I was holding the cook down, I heard him say to me in cracked English, "Can you just hold him there for a moment, Ron, while I go and get the camera".

In order to withstand the knocks she took when getting across the bar *Echo* had to be a resilient little ship. On one occasion she managed to put into Wellington while the passenger liner *Canberra* could not get in because of bad sea conditions. This was in

The Anderson brothers, who were connected with the scow *Echo* for many years. "Jock" Anderson (right) was the ship's engineer before becoming Eckford's wharf representative in Wellington in the early 1950s, and brother Bob was a seaman before becoming a waterman on the Wellington wharf. *"Evening Post"*

The *Echo* as she is now, tied up at Picton and preserved as a clubhouse. *David MacIntyre*

1961 when the All Blacks met the French in a howling gale at Athletic Park.

Although resilient, *Echo* and her crew certainly were made to pay for putting to sea in rough weather, and Ron Palmer tells a story about another cook to illustrate what life was sometimes like:

On this occasion the weather was so bad the waves were coming right over the ship. The cook was working in the galley and there was a skylight ventilator above where he was standing. He was cooking a meal at the stove and suddenly with the force of the waves the skylight opened and water poured down onto the cook and the stove. The galley was turned into a steam bath and the cook could hardly see. His cabin was just opposite the galley, and suddenly someone noticed that water was pouring from under the cabin door. The cook was concerned to see what was happening to his quarters, and although someone shouted to him not to open the door, he went ahead and opened it. Water came pouring out, sending him flying back across the galley. What had happened was the force of the waves had knocked in his porthole, complete with frame. The cook shared his cabin with the engineer who had the top bunk, and when the door was opened you could see the engineer lying there in his bunk, watching the water rush past and unable to do a thing about it. The engineer's bunk was quite dry, but unfortunately for the cook, not only was his galley soaked, but so was he and his bunk.

At one time *Echo* was nicknamed "The Breakfast Ship", because her loads out of Blenheim would include bacon (live pigs) and eggs. She developed a mixed trade on her southbound journeys, taking aeroplane wings and aircraft parts for the Woodbourne aerodrome near Blenheim, steel, galvanised iron, washing basins and anything else on offer. Northbound from Blenheim she would carry a lot of salt from Lake Grassmere, chaff for the horses in the Wellington Milk Station and sometimes hay for the Somes Island animal quarantine station.

The introduction of the rail ferry *Aramoana* in 1962, followed by *Aranui* soon after, was the death knell for the old *Echo*. There was a poignant note to her passing. When Columbia Pictures made its bid for *Echo* in 1959, the studio actually made an offer to buy *Echo* outright. The sum at stake was thought to be tempting, but Tom Eckford turned it down because he believed his traditional customers would not desert him when the rail ferries began running between Wellington and Picton. Unfortunately his faith was misplaced and cargo dwindled to nothing.

Under the command of Captain Jock Dalziel, *Echo* made her last trip out of Wellington for Blenheim on 17 August 1965. For several months she was tied up in the Opawa River and was then sold to a Bluff owner for use in a crayfishing venture in the Chatham Islands. This did not last long and she was resold to Mr R.A. Mason, who returned her to Blenheim. After removing the engines, Mr Mason handed the ship over to a group of enthusiasts who wanted to preserve her. She was eventually towed to Picton, where she was restored and now serves as a clubhouse for the Marlborough Cruising Club.

Echo's demise did not mean we had seen the last of the scows crossing the strait. The auxiliary scow *Portland*, renowned for her timber and wool trade to Petone from Marlborough Sounds and Nelson, continued service until she went ashore at Island Bay on 12 December 1972. The last to go was *Te Aroha*. She finished her Nelson-Wellington trade on 20 July 1976.

Chapter X

Air travel between the islands

AS LONG ago as 1870 there was an interest in flying across Cook Strait. A man named Corrie is supposed to have been the first to attempt the crossing, with the aid of a pair of wings strapped to his body. He covered a distance of about 6 metres before he fell and broke his leg.

Nowadays, the relatively narrow crossing is no obstacle to air travel, but in the period of mushrooming interest in aviation, between 1910 and 1920, the strait was a formidable barrier which prompted showmen fliers to tout for sponsors for an attempt. New Zealanders were doubtful about their chances and it took a tragedy to sow the seeds for the first successful aerial crossing.

On the afternoon of 1 February 1919 the Canterbury Aviation Company's chief pilot, Cecil Hill, was doing aircraft stunts over the crowded Riccarton racecourse. At a height of about 300 metres one of the aircraft's wings collapsed and the biplane plunged to the earth, killing the pilot. He had been a valuable asset for the company, and the chairman, Henry Wigram, was hard pressed to find anyone able to take over the position.

Wigram turned to the Government for help and Government contacts in Britain put forward the name of Captain Euan Dickson, DSC and bar, DFC, Croix de Guerre. Dickson was duly appointed and asked to arrange the purchase of two Avro 504K biplanes for the company. He arrived in New Zealand in November 1919, just as the CAC began to feel uneasy about likely competition in the South Island from a service being proposed by the Mount Cook Motor Company.

This fear of potential competition was underlined by a concern that the Auckland-based New Zealand Flying School might cross the strait and begin operations in the northern part of the South Island.

Wigram considered an aircraft should be sent to Marlborough to put the CAC's name firmly at the head of the queue.

At 7 a.m. on 25 August 1920 Dickson set off for Marlborough with two passengers on board, including the company's chief mechanic, Mr J.E. Moore. After several stops, when the party took refreshments and refuelled, the Avro touched down just out-side Blenheim at 11.35 a.m. Fifty minutes later, Dickson took off for an undisclosed destination.

He climbed steadily to 1,800 metres, following the South Island coastline northward. When parallel with Perano Head (then named Wellington Heads), he made his crossing to the North Island.

The biggest fear in those days was engine failure, but the rotary engine never missed a beat. When half-way across, cloud forced Dickson to descend and he overflew Cape Terawhiti light (Karori Rock) at 1,000 metres. He then flew over the Makara hills and on to Wellington.

Some people knew he was coming, including Andrew Burns, chief reporter for the *Lyttelton Times* a paper owned by Wigram. Even in those days newspapers were keen to secure their own "scoops".

Burns reported: "Wellington was unaware of the intended visit, but when a machine came into view from the southward a few minutes before two o'clock, the crowds turned out in the streets and word soon got about the stranger hailed from Christ-church."

Over the city, Dickson put the Avro into some turns and stalls before heading for Trentham racecourse. There, an advance agent had lit a fire so the smoke would give Dickson an idea of wind direction. Burns reported:

> At Trentham the word had got round that the machine was expected, and as it hove in sight over the hills there was a rush of trainers and jockeys, men from the camp adjoining and nursing sisters to see the landing. Captain Dickson descended over the rifle range, took a preliminary circuit over the smoke fire and just glided down into the wind as if he had been up on a "guinea flip".

The Avro landed at 2.10 p.m., one hour and 50 minutes after leaving Blenheim. Parliament had been in session as Dickson came over the city, and M.P.s rushed out to see what was happening. The Prime Minister, Mr Bill Massey, learned that the pilot had come from Christchurch and hailed it as an important event in New Zealand's history. In actual fact, the CAC had stolen the glory of the first crossing from under the nose of the flying school. The school had a flight planned for the next day and were working on an aircraft at Petone when Dickson came over. Dickson flew back south on 28 August, doing the trip to Blenheim in an hour and five minutes.

In Blenheim, he made pleasure flights for 186 people, who paid a total of £505. He eventually got back to a rousing welcome at Christchurch on 4 September.

The men and the aircraft connected with the first crossing of Cook Strait in 1920. From left, pilot Captain Euan Dickson, aviation administrator Mr C.H. Hewlett and engineer Mr J.E. Moore. Behind them is the Avro 504K. *"Evening Post"*

Envelope and date-stamp markings used on airmail carried on the 1970 flights which commemorated the 50th anniversary of the first Cook Strait crossing by air. *New Zealand Post Office Publicity*

The *New Zealand Times* wrote of the occasion:

The feat takes its place among the records of aviation. It is to New Zealand what Bleriot's flight over the English Channel was to the aviation of the whole world.

The 50th anniversary of the first Cook Strait aerial crossing was commemorated in 1970. A committee comprising representatives of the aviation and oil industries, the RNZAF, the Air Mail Society, the Aviation Historical Society, press, radio and the Post Office organised re-enactment flights between Christchurch and Wellington, and Wellington and Blenheim. Special commemorative mails were carried, with the letters having special covers, and pictorial date stamps were used at Christchurch and Wellington. The commemorative flight was made in a Piper Cherokee, piloted by the Canterbury Aero Club's chief pilot, Mr C.J. Collins. Beside him was 78-year-old Euan Dickson, who took the controls from Rongotai to near the touch down at Trentham racecourse. When he stepped from the aircraft to a welcoming committee led by transport Minister Peter Gordon, he remarked that the crowd was well-disciplined.

"We couldn't keep them back when we landed 50 years ago," he said.

The commemoration of Dickson's first flight gave rise to another more unorthodox "first" for crossing the strait. On 25 August 1970 the president of the Golden Age Flying Society, Mr R.T. Alexander of Blenheim, made the first recorded crossing strapped upright on the wing of an aircraft. Mr Alexander performed the 1930s-styled stunt standing on the top wing of an old biplane, which flew from Omaka near Blenheim to Trentham. He was kitted up in woollens and a leather flying suit, but he still complained of the icy winds.

The Dickson crossing was not followed up to any great extent because aviation in New Zealand went into a lull in the mid-'20s. One or two ideas were hatched and became stillborn, such as plans for an international airship service. Studies showed that mooring the ship would be difficult in some cities, particularly in Wellington with its high winds.

It took Charles Kingsford Smith's crossing of the Tasman to create a new lift to the industry. In September 1928 he flew from Sydney to Christchurch and a month later made the return journey, this time setting out from Blenheim.

The flights made by Kingsford Smith had a direct effect on the development of a Cook Strait service because they prompted the City of Wellington to develop an aerodrome at Rongotai. Rongotai already had a flying field of sorts, but it was not considered good enough for *Southern Cross* to land on, so Wellington missed the glory of being a terminal for the two crossings.

The mayor at the time, George Troup

(later Sir George) and Air Board director Major T.M. Wilkes took Kingsford Smith's advice about developing Rongotai, which by then had seen only basic levelling. Subsequently, Rongotai became the site for major airport development.

By this time, efforts to send scheduled services across the strait were gaining momentum. One company, Dominion Airlines Ltd, was formed in 1929 to operate between Wellington and Blenheim, using a Saunders-Roe Windhover three-engined flying boat. The company did manage to begin flying operations between Gisborne and Hastings, using another aircraft, but its Cook Strait enterprise never got under way and the flying boat was never unpacked after it arrived in New Zealand.

Successful operations eventually started in the mid-'30s, when Cook Strait Airways and Union Airways made their appearance.

Cook Strait Airways got in first, starting a regular service in late 1935, linking Wellington with Nelson and Blenheim. CSA used de Havilland (DH)89 Rapides, and later provided connections to Westport, Hokitika and Greymouth. Union Airways began a daily service between Palmerston North, Blenheim, Christchurch and Dunedin in January 1936, using DH86 Expresses with A.G. Gerrard as senior pilot. Later, Union turned to Lockheed aircraft, Electras and Lodestars.

It did not take long for group travel to make its mark. The Marlborough rugby team was the first rugby XV to travel by air in August 1936, when it arrived for a game in Wellington. The team had worked out it would cost £89 to send the party by air and

The *Evening Post* being taken to Nelson by aircraft delivery in May 1933. *"Evening Post"*

arrange board. If a backload of passengers could be organised for the aircraft's return journey the cost would be cut by a further £30. In comparison, the cost of travelling by steamer, plus the cost of hotel accommodation, ran to £95. But in addition, the players would be away from work for only half a day if they went by air, compared to four-and-a-half days by sea.

The creation of reliable Cook Strait air services had a spin-off effect — an interisland airmail service. Air Travel (N.Z.) Ltd had inaugurated in 1935 the first regular airmail service from Hokitika south to Bruce Bay, Haast and Okuru, one of the most isolated districts in the South Island. The first airmail actually carried in New Zealand was by seaplane from Auckland to Dargaville on 18

December 1919, with the avowed purpose of trying out this type of "ship".

In 1936 the Union Airways link provided a daily service from Palmerston North to Dunedin with intermediate stops, and CSA came in with a twice-daily connection between Wellington and Nelson and a three-times-a-day service linking Wellington with the railhead at Blenheim. When the Union Airways service began on 16 March 1936 the DH86 headed south from Palmerston North with 10 bags of mail from the city itself, weighing 34 kilograms plus another 9 kilograms which arrived overnight from Auckland. A large proportion of the mail was sent by philatelists who wanted first-day covers. At that time the airmail came in for some criticism from cost-conscious and De-

The first scheduled inland airmail service leaves Nelson on Monday, 16 March 1936 at 7.45 a.m. From left: chief pilot Flight Lieutenant G.B. Bolt, ground attendant Mr V. Nobbs, booking clerk Mr K.H. Jones and managing director Mr E.H. Thompson. *"Evening Post"*

pression-hardened New Zealanders, who reacted sharply to the twopence surcharge that such mail attracted on its introduction. Nevertheless, in the year ending 31 March 1936 domestic aircraft carried over 2,000,000 letters, so the service had obviously caught on.

Wartime requirements, and the requisitioning of aircraft, completely changed the face of aviation development. CSA's Rapides were commandeered by the RNZAF to form the basis of No. 42 Transport Squadron. Aero club operations were also absorbed for military requirements. The requisitioning of CSA's aircraft meant the end of its services, but CSA gave its blessing for Union Airways and Air Travel to provide an air link across the strait and on to the west coast. The effect of the requisitioning was the virtual amalgamation of Air Travel for the Hokitika-Nelson service, and of Union Airways and CSA for the Cook Strait link. After the war, Union Airways was supplied with surplus Lockheed Lodestars from the RNZAF, but already moves were underway to bring the re-emerging network of private airlines under a state umbrella.

The National Airways Act was passed by Parliament on 7 December 1945 and was aimed at exploiting the expertise of the 7,000 trained members of the air force who were being repatriated. The National Airways Corporation, or NAC as it became universally known, began with a capital of £1,200,000 and was under the chairmanship of Sir Leonard Isitt. Isitt was also chairman of Tasman Empire Airways Ltd, the forerunner of Air New Zealand, which had been formed in April 1940 (the two chairmanships were separated in 1965). There followed a period of transition, in which Union Airways and other smaller operators ran services which were supplemented by flights mounted by RNZAF Squadrons 40 and 41. But NAC gradually absorbed the smaller airlines such as Union Airways, CSA and Air Travel and by 1948 it had a near-monopoly of domestic air services. NAC actually began its own services in April 1947, to 18 centres with aircraft ranging from biplane Gypsy Moths to Lodestars, Electras and DC3s. Those 3 aircraft gave a seating capacity of 387, compared with the 1,500 seats it had available in the late 1970s with fewer aircraft.

NAC was still in its infancy when major decisions were made on the future of the principal airports of Wellington and Auckland, requiring each to find a temporary "home" while the first-choice sites were developed. A special commission from Britain, headed by Sir Frederick Tymms, was invited to report on all New Zealand's airport needs. The report, which came out in 1948, recommended the Rongotai isthmus as Wellington's best bet. After negotiations between the city council and the Government, Cabinet approved the development of the site, and reclamations began in Evans Bay in the early 1950s. This meant shifting the base of Wellington's major air traffic to Paraparaumu, an hour's car drive to the north. Hangars were built or moved onto the site and the old de Havilland Tiger Moth factory was converted to the domestic terminal and remains in use to this day. This factory had been set up in 1940 and at one time, produced three aircraft a week.

The new Wellington airport at Rongotai reopened to NAC's updated fleet of turbo-prop Vickers Viscounts on 23 July 1959, although the official opening was not until October of that year. In the meantime, services into Rongotai had not ceased entirely. In the early 1950s the Wellington and Marlborough Aero Clubs operated passenger flights across the strait with three-passenger Gemini and Proctor aircraft. This service died away in 1953 when NAC introduced the small DH Heron, which was capable of using the restricted runway at Rongotai for short trips across the strait. Wellington Aero Club came briefly on the scene again in the 18 months before the new airport opened. At that time, building work began to encroach on the runway surrounds and the Herons had to be taken off. The aero club began an operation called Wellington Air Taxis, which made passenger flights to Nelson and Blenheim until NAC took over once again when the runway works were complete.

While all this was going on the Straits Air Freight Express Service (SAFE for short and, since October 1967, officially known as Safe

A Douglas DC3 roars into Rongotai airport in 1959, the year Wellington Airport reopened fully for business. Workmen pour the concrete outline for the name of the airport. *Evening Post*

Air) had blossomed into the country's specialist freight airline. Safe Air had its beginnings in the air freight service operated jointly by the Railways and the RNZAF late in World War II, performed by DC3s which linked the railheads of the two islands. When NAC was formed it took over the service and continued with the DC3, but there was a growing realisation that a specialist freight

aircraft was needed.

The general manager of Railways, Mr James Sawers, was impressed by the claims of the new Bristol Freighter. He obtained Government approval to investigate a mechanised loading system, based on the Bristol's configuration. A Bristol Mark 21 was flown to New Zealand for operating trials. At the same time Mr Tom O'Connell,

Tom O'Connell, the first general manager of Straits Air Freight Express, seen here in his previous role as an RNZAF transport officer. Mr O'Connell died in the Bristol freighter crash of 1957. *Geoff Bentley Associates/RNZAF*

who had wide experience as an air movements officer for the RNZAF, was convinced that the Bristol was the right aircraft and he, too, had some original ideas for a streamlined cargo-loading system. With the help of Railways engineers, he produced the "cargon", a wheeled metal pallet which reduced handling costs and was a world first in the loading of palletised cargo. One man could load an aircraft with the use of a cargon, while DC3s required a team of muscular loaders.

Tenders were invited for the provision of an air cargo service across the strait after Railways found it could not legally operate an airline itself. Mr O'Connell's SAFE company won the contract as a subsidiary of Airwork Ltd, a British company which subsequently became British and United Airways. O'Connell was the first general manager, with James Sawers as chairman and Captain Robin Hamilton as operations manager. The sole contractor was the Railways department, which provided the freight for fast delivery across the strait. When SAFE began flying in 1951 it had to hire C-46s from Formosa (now Taiwan) due to a delay in the delivery of its Bristols, but the new freighters arrived a month later to create a high-frequency service between Rongotai and Woodbourne, outside Blenheim. A wide range of freight was carried, including cars and livestock.

Both Mr O'Connell and Captain Hamilton died when a Bristol crashed at Harewood, near Christchurch, in November 1957. The accident — the only flying fatality in the company's history — was caused by fatigue in part of the aircraft's structure. It led to a new system of determining the permissible life of the Bristol. Previously, the operating life had been determined by the number of engine hours flown, but this changed to the number of take-offs and landings completed. The new man brought in to succeed Mr O'Connell was Mr Des Lynskey, who had executive experience with a tobacco company and aviation experience in both active flying and instruction.

Mr Lynskey changed the image of SAFE. He decided that it should be recognised as a bona-fide airline and that his flight crews should wear uniforms instead of white overalls. In 1966, he moved SAFE away from a pure rail-air operation, dependent only on the rail contract, and took over some of NAC's freight operations. This enabled NAC to phase out its DC3s and prompted Mr Lynskey to go hunting overseas for low-life Bristol Freighters. He came back having signed up four from Pakistan and three from

Spain, which enabled him to retire some of the older aircraft and keep the operational fleet at 11. The next year SAFE expanded its operations by winning a Government contract to run passenger services from Wellington and Christchurch to the Chatham Islands.

In 1971 Safe Air (the change for SAFE had been made) began operating a night express-freight service linking Auckland, Wellington and Christchurch. Bristols were used, but these were later replaced by two larger Hawker Siddeley Argosys bought from Canada. Until late 1972 Safe Air was totally independent of the NAC network, but this changed when NAC bought the major shareholding from the British parent company, Air Holdings Ltd, which controlled British United Airways. This integration took another step forward in April 1978 when NAC and the international carrier Air New Zealand merged, leaving Safe Air as a wholly owned subsidiary of the new Air New Zealand. The final step towards total integration was announced in March 1981, when Safe Air's chairman, Mr "Skip" Watson, revealed that the Air New Zealand Board intended to have the freight airline totally integrated by the end of 1983.

Safe Air's importance as a cargo carrier across the strait has diminished with the success of the rail ferries, but at one time the positions were almost reversed. In May 1956, when the debate was raging over the need for a roll-on roll-off ferry service between Wellington and Picton, the director of Civil Aviation, Mr E.A. Gibson, presented figures which suggested that it was cheaper to send goods by air than by sea. He said a ship

The Bristol Freighter, long-time workhorse of the Safe Air fleet, seen here in the airline's original colours. *Geoff Bentley Associates/Safe Air.*

Des Lynskey, who has guided Safe Air through all except its formative years as an airline. *Geoff Bentley Associates/Safe Air*

The striking twin tails of the Safe Air Argosy are unmistakable as the aircraft is loaded through its stern door.
Geoff Bentley Associates / Safe Air

costing £1.5 million would be able to take 80 cars and make one return crossing per day. An air freighter costing £120,000 could take three cars and make 13½ return trips. The ship would therefore have capacity for 160 cars against the aircraft's 81. But the real costs of transporting were far less for the aircraft, he said.

While Safe Air was consolidating its Rongotai-Woodbourne run in the late '50s and '60s, NAC was also making strides with its fleet. It moved away from the piston-engined DC3 and opted for the Dutch-built Fokker Friendship, the aircraft that still services the Wellington-Nelson and Wellington-Blenheim routes. This was a courageous decision for NAC to make as it was under strong political pressure to buy the British Handley Page Herald; but the Friendships started arriving in 1960. Later, NAC again resisted the buy-British lobby by opting for the Boeing 737 as its main-trunk jet, instead of the BAC1-11.

Cook Strait has always been a difficult sector for profitable operation by airlines. This is because it has static costs at the terminals for things such as airport and airways dues, baggage handling and ticketing. Between the two islands there is only a short expanse of water to cross, but the relative seat-kilometre costs of the journey are higher than is the case with, say, an Auckland-Wellington trip. Smaller airlines, in particular, have found this to be so, although even Air New Zealand runs at a loss on its Cook Strait services. The Wellington Aero Club, after some years out of scheduled operations across the strait, was drawn back into the service in the mid-'60s when it bought a Piper Aztec to ferry hospital cases to a specialist in Dunedin. No sooner had it bought the aircraft than the specialist moved to Wellington, so the club decided it should get some use out of the Aztec by ferrying newspapers, some passengers and small amounts of freight across the strait.

This heralded the formation of the club's Capital Air Services Ltd offshoot in 1965, which gradually built up a fleet of other aircraft, including Cessna 402s. Capital worked on a shoestring basis, initially achieving modest profits before things got harder and the club decided to offload the operation. A major factor in this decision was believed to be a lack of working capital, but the company was also finding the going tough and, when James Air took a controlling interest in November 1975, it had trading commitments of $65,000. Capital lapsed into receivership in 1978. A report made at the time listed its debts as $820,000 as at 5 October 1977. Since, James Air has operated its own services across the strait, but schedules were cut back because it could not make a profit in competition with Air New Zealand's Friendships.

Only now is the future looking rosier for small "commuter" airlines. The facts of economic life have started to tell on Air New Zealand, which is looking to jettison some of its loss-making provincial routes — or cut down the frequency of operations. The way appears to be opening up for smaller airlines to operate aircraft in the 10-20 seat range on these routes. Without Air New Zealand stealing their traffic, these smaller airlines will be hoping to trade at a profit. If and when the door does open, the Cook Strait crossing should be a prize target for the smaller carriers.

Chapter XI

Graveyard for mariners — shipwrecks in Cook Strait

COOK STRAIT, with its unpredictable and powerful tides, its high winds and sometimes appalling weather, has been responsible for scores of mariners' deaths. Some of the worst shipping accidents New Zealand has known, particularly the *Penguin* and *Wahine* disasters, have occurred in the strait. At times, the scene of the disaster has been ridiculously close to shore, at a distance which on a calm day would seem to be easily in reach of the shipwrecked crew and passengers; but experience has shown that proximity to the shore does not mean survival. The *Wahine* tragedy, because of its recent and still-enormous impact upon the nation, has a chapter of its own in this book.

However, it is worth remembering that some of the biggest and best-remembered shipwrecks or strandings did not involve any loss of life — for example, the *Devon's* demise in 1913 and *Wanganella's* stranding in 1947, and the grounding of *Pacific Charger* in 1981.

Most New Zealanders have little idea of the huge number of shipwrecks that have occurred around the nation's shores and particularly in Cook Strait because of its peculiar weather and tides. Marine records go into the thousands. This in part is due to the classification of relatively minor wrecks, such as fishing boat accidents in which there is no loss of life, as "shipwrecks". But it is equally a result of the huge number of casualties which occurred in sailing-ship days, when vessels were more at the mercy of weather and sea conditions.

Records of Cook Strait shipwrecks range from the ridiculous to the tragic. Perhaps some humour can be seen in the plight of Mr Athol Perano of Picton, who in September 1953 put a kettle on the primus of his fishing boat in Tory Channel, then shortly afterwards noticed smoke coming from the cabin which contained the primus. He tried to put out the fire with sea water, but lost his bucket over the side. He managed to beach his boat, *Mahau*, before the fuel tank exploded. Mr Perano suffered minor burns. At least he had a good idea of what had caused his vessel to founder and he lived to tell the tale. This was not the case in a good proportion of Cook Strait's shipping tragedies.

One of the worst unexplained shipwrecks in the strait occurred just before the turn of the century. The steamer *Ohau*, owned by the Union Company and carrying a crew of 22, left Greymouth on 12 May 1899, carrying a cargo of coal and timber to Dunedin via Cook Strait. The next day she was sighted by the lighthouse keeper at Cape Campbell, but a terrific gale blew up which caused several vessels in the area to run for shelter. As a result, several ships were late completing their voyages and no immediate worries were held for the fate of *Ohau*. Eventually, a steamer was sent off to search the coastline, but nothing was found. Confirmation of *Ohau's* fate came when wreckage and lifebuoys bearing her name were washed ashore.

Six years earlier, in September 1893, an unexplained tragedy of similar proportions struck the iron barque *Evelyn*, which was bound from Newcastle, New South Wales, for Lyttelton with a cargo of coal. The Wellington Pilot Station received a report that a large barque had been seen southbound through Cook Strait at a time when a

One of Cook Strait's biggest tragedies was the disappearance of the steamer *Ohau* and her crew of 22. *De Maus Collection, Alexander Turnbull Library*

northerly gale switched into a real southerly. A steamer found the sea strewn with wreckage, including ship's rails, cushions and a sextant case, which was identified as coming from *Evelyn*. Later, Captain C. Neilson of the ketch *Huon Belle* reported that he had been in the company of two vessels to the south of the strait when the weather worsened. One of these ships was reckoned to be *Evelyn*. Captain Neilson ran to Port Underwood for shelter and the *Evelyn* was seen heading east, apparently making for Cape Palliser or Palliser Bay. Three years later a lifebuoy marked *"Evelyn, Liverpool"* was picked up by a steamer *en route* from Wellington to the Chatham Islands.

A similar fate met the schooner *Phoenix*, which sailed from Nelson to Wellington in thick fog in November 1846. The ship was wrecked somewhere between Stephens and D'Urville islands, with the loss of all seven people on board. The first confirmation of the shipwreck was the finding of a paper parcel belonging to a Mr Perry, a merchant on board, along with other items and wreckage near D'Urville Island. The following year, the keel of a ship, thought to be from *Phoenix*, was seen floating off Port Gore.

Another schooner, *Colleen Bawn*, sailed off and was never heard from again. Under the command of Captain Louis Pike and carrying a crew of six, she sailed from Wellington in May 1880 bound for Havelock. About the time she was at sea, residents in Wellington's Vogeltown saw two distress rockets fired well out in the strait. Whether that was the last act of the crew of *Colleen Bawn* is unknown.

The story of the loss of the barque *Timaru* in August 1902 comes to a similar abrupt end. She sailed under the command of Captain Alfred Johansen with a crew of 10, bound from Lyttelton for Kaipara. She was last seen off Kaikoura.

Although there was nothing found to indicate the fate of *Timaru*, there was at least wreckage left as evidence of the third-worst shipping loss in the Cook Strait, that of the steamer *City of Dunedin* in May 1865. She left Wellington for Nelson with a complement of about 40 on board and was never seen nor heard from again. The *City of Dunedin* was a schooner-rigged paddle steamer, and it was rumoured that she must have hit a rock and gone down quickly. Wreckage that came from the ship was washed through Cook Strait and found in Palliser Bay.

A more recent loss was the *Ripple*; she went missing in August 1924, leaving few clues about the reasons for her foundering. She sailed from Wellington to Napier under Captain J.A. Norling with a crew of 15. A heavy south-east gale sprang up and the ship managed to get a signal to the Cape Palliser lighthouse keeper asking for assistance from Wellington. About half an hour after the first signal was sent a second was given asking if assistance had been sent for. The lighthouse keeper could see *Ripple's* deck and cabin lights, but when he went to signal a reply, the lights had disappeared. At least six ships searched for *Ripple* and search parties combed the coast for survivors. A few days later a boat from *Ripple* was found on shore with a seaman's body inside it. The body was clad in a lifebelt, indicating that the crew had taken to the boats when *Ripple* went down. On the same day, Captain Norling's body was found near Castlepoint lighthouse. The subsequent court inquiry could not point a finger at specific causes for the shipwrecking. It was believed that the steamer had some mechanical problem and was overwhelmed by rough seas.

The unexplained loss of the schooner *Ronga* in April 1906 is a mystery with a difference, for while the crew of six were lost, the ship itself survived. *Ronga* had a reputation as a killer ship, having already capsized twice in Pelorus Sound. She sailed under Captain E.O. Petersen from Lyttelton to Havelock, and next day the steamer *Pateena* reported passing an upturned scow or schooner off Cape Campbell. Eight days later the derelict had passed through Cook Strait and was found near Kapiti where it was taken in tow. Some fishermen from Paraparaumu righted the vessel and confirmed it was *Ronga*. There was no sign of the crew. The remarkable thing is that the ship was recovered, converted to a steamer a few years later and renamed *Wairau*. Even more remarkable, she survived a second sinking in 1911 when she collided with the steamer *Himatangi* in the Manawatu River. *Wairau* was recovered yet again and repaired for another half century of active service. Subsequently she became a partner to the scow *Echo* in the fleet owned by the Eckford

All hands were lost when the *Ripple* foundered in Cook Strait in August 1924. *Alexander Turnbull Library*

family of Blenheim.

At the bottom of all these mysteries, of course, is the tendency for Cook Strait to turn on some of the world's most hazardous sailing conditions. There are other stories which amply testify to horrendous combinations of wild seas and gale-force winds. In January 1861 the brig *Shamrock* was voyaging from Auckland to Otago, and had reached Lyttelton. She set off on the last leg of her journey and ran into hurricane conditions. Every piece of sail was blown out and the ship driven way off course. Two days after setting out, *Shamrock* was approaching Turakirae Head at 11.5 knots (21.2 kilometres/hour). The master, Captain Thomas Dixon, tried to check her progress, but could not prevent her being driven into

Palliser Bay. Captain Dixon decided to beach the ship in order to save the lives of the crew and passengers, who included three women. *Shamrock* beached in sand, with the crew leaving their holds on the rigging to plunge into the surf. The women were lowered by rope and all on board survived the ordeal.

The tendency for wind and sea conditions to drive vessels to a graveyard in Palliser Bay was shown again with the wreck of *Zuleika* in April 1897. The ship was bound from Lyttelton for Wellington when a strong gale blew up. Captain J.R. Bremner tried to wear the ship (put the ship about, or change course) when she neared Palliser Bay, but she hit rocks. Waves came over the side and swept everything movable overboard. Efforts to

Not every shipwreck is a disaster — some can provide a decent day out for the family. Such was the case when the Fijian freighter *Tuvalu* went ashore near Honeycomb Rock on the Wairarapa coast in January 1967. Her load of high explosives was salvaged, but the ship was given up as lost. *"Evening Post"*

after the ship had passed Palliser Bay. *Maria* was bound from Lyttelton for Wellington with six passengers and a crew of 22. She was being steered for the Wellington harbour entrance when she passed over a reef and ran aground. She maintained some steerage way, but then hit a rock which smashed through her hull. The masts broke away and the ship broke her back, separating into two halves. Everyone gathered in the aft section and those not on board tried to cut away a lifeboat containing 24 people. But the davits (the uprights which suspend the ship's boat and lower it over the side) gave way and the boat was smashed to pieces. All aboard the boat scrambled back onto the aft section, but that finally went to pieces and the crew and passengers were left to try and make the shore by swimming or clinging to pieces of wreckage. Only two survived. Of the 26 dead, 12 bodies were recovered. Among the dead was William Deans, who in 1843 with his brother John had been one of the first settlers in Riccarton, near Christchurch.

It is fair to say that while wind and sea conditions are blamed for the majority of shipwrecks in Cook Strait, several have resulted almost entirely from human error. Tough decisions handed down by marine courts of inquiry bear testimony to that. Usually, the responsibility remains with the master, but an example of a wrecking that was not the master's fault was that of the barque *Subraon*, in October 1848. The ship was leaving Wellington for Sydney and was making headway into the fresh wind from the south when the pilot tried to take her through Chaffers Passage (between Barretts Reef and the mainland at the entrance to

launch the lifeboats failed when the boats became badly damaged, so the crew clung to the rigging until the masts started to be swept away and the ship lurched to one side, sending them into the sea. Some managed to swim to shore; others clung to wreckage. Some were unfortunate enough to be hit by

heavy pieces of wreckage and were drowned. Twelve of the crew of 21 died.

It would be wrong however, to suppose, that Palliser Bay was the worst black spot for marine accidents. One of Cook Strait's worst tragedies, the wrecking of the barque *Maria* in July 1851, occurred near Cape Terawhiti

Wellington Harbour), despite a warning from the captain that *Subraon* would not stay. Sure enough, the ship missed stays in tacking and the pilot's attempts to rectify the error failed. (To miss stays is to fail in an attempt to alter course by tacking — that is, sailing on a zig-zag course into the wind.) *Subraon* struck the rocks about 100 metres from shore. The passengers and crew were landed safely, but there was no chance of saving the ship. Her rudder had been washed away and she was taking a lot of water in the hold. However, the accident did have its ironic side. The passengers on the ship were actually fleeing Wellington. They had been frightened by an earthquake and were trying to quit the town for good. Eight days before the shipwrecking, an earthquake estimated at 7.1 on the Richter Scale struck north-east Marlborough. The shock waves caused serious damage to buildings in Wellington destroying more than half of the small settlement.

Subraon's demise was unusual, in that the fault appeared to lie with the pilot, but the site of her shipwrecking was not unusual. Some of the biggest, most tragic, and best-remembered of Cook Strait's wrecks occurred close to the Wellington Heads . . .

St Vincent, February 1869   Twenty-two people died when the fully rigged ship *St Vincent* was wrecked in Palliser Bay, after sailing from Wellington to take on wool at Lyttelton. The day after sailing, the ship was blown back into Palliser Bay by a strong south-easterly and went on the rocks north of Cape Turakirae. The chief officer, Mr J. Stringer, survived the wrecking and later recounted how the master had tried first to run into Wellington and, when that was unsuccessful, to stop the ship drifting by dropping both anchors. This failed too, and she struck at 10.30 p.m. A big sea washed over *St Vincent*, throwing her almost onto her side, smashing the lifeboats and carrying away the bosun. The anchor cables parted and the ship went fully onto her side and onto the rocks. Another huge sea hit the ship and gutted her, carrying away masts and decking and leaving just a wooden shell. The crew huddled together for warmth, but about 3 a.m. Mr Stringer was washed away. He was washed up on the shore unconscious, and when he came round he saw part of the hull about 100 metres offshore. He made for the nearby lighthouse and found the other survivor at a shepherd's hut. A total of nine bodies was later recovered, but some had received such a battering against the rocks that only four were identifiable. A court of inquiry was held at Wellington the following week, at which Mr Stringer testified that he had offered to take the ship into Cloudy Bay for shelter, but the master, Captain James Barron, had refused the offer. The court found the cause of the tragedy was the master's error of judgement in not seeking shelter at Cloudy Bay or Wellington.

City of Newcastle, November 1872   The wrecking of the barque *City of Newcastle* near Tory Channel was the result of total confusion about the position of the ship. She was towed out of Wellington by a steamer to start a run to Newcastle, but the wind changed and the barque sheltered in Cloudy Bay where she stayed for four days. Eventually the weather improved and the voyage started, but in the early hours of the morning it was found the ship had stranded. There was no sudden shock, and it appeared she had slid between two rocks. No-one knew where she was, but the order was given to abandon ship. The largest boat was lowered, but it dropped bow-first into the water and was swamped. Next was the captain's gig, which held four women passengers, three children and three seamen. The one remaining boat was then lowered, holding eight people including the master, Captain John Bain. There followed an argument about whether the boat could hold so many, and one man climbed back onto the wreck. Those in the boat were not particularly safe, anyway, because it was leaking and had to be bailed constantly to prevent it being totally swamped. They managed to rig a sail, negotiate a narrow passage and attract the attention of the schooner *Canterbury*, which picked them up four hours after they left the wreck. Meanwhile, the gig containing 10 people had been lost from sight and a week passed before information came to hand that they had been saved. The survivors had been picked up by the barque *John Knox*, en route from Lyttelton to Sydney. But the six unfortunate people left on the wreck were unable to get away because their boat had been swamped. Two drowned trying to reach the shore, including the man who had given up his place in the overcrowded boat. The surviving four were picked up by the steamer *Rangatira*. The wreck of the *City of Newcastle* quickly went to pieces on the rocks. The court of inquiry at Wellington found Captain Bain guilty of extreme negligence and cancelled his certificate. It appeared that the Pencarrow light had been mistaken for the Mana Island light and this confusion was seen as the major cause of the shipwreck.

***Lastingham*, September 1884**   Eighteen people died when the iron ship *Lastingham* was wrecked at Cape Jackson, at the very end of a voyage from London to Wellington. She struck bow on and swung around so her side was exposed to the big seas whipped up by the north-west gale. The waves washed over the ship, which was thrown off the rocks and sank. Captain Alexander Morrison, his wife, five passengers and 11 crewmen were drowned. Confusion on board the ship at the time she ran aground and the sheer noise of the gale contributed to the loss of life. The captain and his party had gathered in the aft part of *Lastingham*, whereas another party had assembled in the forward section and soon found they could climb along the bowsprit and drop onto the mainland. Once safe, they yelled to the others on board, but the noise of the gale drowned their voices and the captain's party stayed put, until the ship came off the rocks and sank. The surviving party numbered about a dozen. They spent about 40 hours without food. Many were cut and bruised and the few clothes they had were soaked. The survivors huddled together at night for warmth. On the third day after the wrecking they managed to attract the attention of the ketch *Agnes* by waving a piece of blanket fixed to a pole. Several steamers had passed close to the shipwrecked party on the previous two days, but they had not seen the signal. The survivors were landed at Wellington.

***Taiaroa*, April 1886**   Two years after *Lastingham's* wrecking came an even bigger tragedy, the loss of the steamer *Taiaroa* with the death of 34 passengers and crew. The ship, owned by the Union Company, was on her normal run between Wellington, Lyttelton, Akaroa and Dunedin under the command of Captain George Urquhart Thomson. Her departure from Wellington was delayed three times because of passengers being late and because on one occasion a warp snapped, injuring a seaman.

When she sailed, a north-westerly wind was blowing, which changed to a south-easterly when *Taiaroa* was off Cape Campbell. There was heavy rain, the sea rose and wind increased. Before Captain Thomson went below he instructed the first mate to tell him if the ship got closer to the land or if the land was obscured by thick weather. Half an hour later the mate reported seeing land, at which point the master came onto the bridge, turned the vessel away and put the engines into full astern. It was too late; the ship struck the rocks and began taking water. She had struck at the mouth of the Clarence River, whereas the master apparently thought he was in Halfmoon Bay near Kaikoura. Efforts to run a line ashore failed, so all four lifeboats were launched, including the captain's which had been holed and was stopped-up with bits of blanket. A line had been dropped over the stern and three of the lifeboats were secured to it. However, the captain's boat failed to follow suit and was cast adrift. The 11 people in the boat, including the captain, were involved in an 18-hour struggle involving constant bailing caused by the leakage through the blankets. After making its way

up the coast, this small craft eventually landed safely at the Wairau River the day after the wreck. The other three boats were not so lucky. Each capsized sending 37 people into the sea. Only three reached the shore alive. Nine bodies were recovered.

The court of inquiry criticised the captain for not taking cross-bearings at Cape Campbell. It was also critical of his failure to check the compass and his certificate was suspended for two years.

***Devon*, August 1913**   *Devon's* shipwrecking at Pencarrow Head was the scene of night-long rescue efforts which eventually successfully rescued the 40 or so people on board. The liner was entering Wellington harbour in a strong southerly and heavy rain when she went on to the rocks about 100 metres from shore. Distress rockets were fired, but water came into the stokehold and all the ship's lights were estinguished. It was about 8.15 p.m. when *Devon* grounded, so the ship was in darkness until the Fort Dorset searchlight was played on her to assist rescue attempts. Those on board went to the fore part of the vessel. They could hear the shouts of would-be rescuers and tried to fire lines across, but these fell short. Similarly, lines attached to lifebuoys floated off and became tangled. A "special reporter" from the *Evening Post* wrote on 26 August:

It was readily seen that the task of bringing off a line would be a perilous one, but volunteers were not wanting for the work. Captain Johnson and Captain Hayward, with Messrs Edmondson, Peters and

Kinvig, struggled waist deep in the water amidst the treacherous wash of the waves attempting to reach the line. For some hours they proceeded, but the work was extremely difficult. Then one of the bulk heads was pressed into service and, making their way from rock to rock, some of the party at last got close to where the wires were entangled amongst the pinnacles. To get within reach, however, it was necessary to place a plank between two jagged outstanding rocks over which the sea was breaking perilously. This dangerous task was safely accomplished, however, the feat being breathlessly watched by those on ship and shore alike.

Eventually a line was made fast, and the first man ashore brought the ship's two kittens with him. The mother cat came with the next survivor. A basket was used to haul the crewmen ashore, with spectators, newsmen and photographers being pressed into action. Everyone was safely landed, although the last two off weighed over 96 kilograms (15 stone) each, and the *Evening Post* reported euphemistically, "the pulling was hard". The ship was battered by the surf and became a total wreck.

At the magisterial inquiry it was found that sufficient way (steerage momentum) had not been taken off the vessel for navigation in shallow waters, that the captain mistook the harbour lights and that *Devon* was taken too near the shore. The certificate of Captain A.H. Caunce (he had actually been chief officer, but had taken over command when the master contracted typhoid *en route* to New Zealand) was suspended for three

The *Devon* hard aground. *"Evening Post"*

months and he was ordered to pay the costs of the inquiry. A Supreme Court hearing overturned these findings. It was found that the master had mistaken the lights, but in the circumstances he was not to blame.

Omaka, January 1921   One of the saddest shipwrecks of Cook Strait — sad because the deaths of some of the crew were witnessed from the shore by the keeper of the Pencarrow lighthouse, who was powerless to assist — was that of *Omaka*. She was an auxiliary schooner owned by the Eckford line of Blenheim and was coming into Wellington with a cargo of chaff and peas from Blenheim. She arrived at the heads about 5 a.m., when she was hit by the combined strength of

a strong south-easterly gale and heavy seas. The schooner capsized, only about half a kilometre from where *Devon* went down. The lighthouse keeper witnessed four of the six crew struggling to reach safety. One man made it into the ship's dinghy, which was swamped and sank. Another clung to a floating drum, but was eventually washed off. Two more hung on to the ends of a floating plank. These two were passed by two steamers, *Wairau* and *Baden Powell*, at distances of about 300 metres and 100 metres, despite their frantic efforts to be seen. People on shore also tried to attract the ships' attention. The seamen tried raising themselves on the plank and pulled clothes off to enable them to swim more freely, but their efforts

The *Progress* begins to break up under the battering of the Cook Strait waves. *Alexander Turnbull Library*

were in vain. Eventually, they lost their grip on the plank and were swept away. All six men on board died. Five were from Wellington and the ship's boy was from New Plymouth. Three of the men were married with young families. In a press interview later crewmen from *Baden Powell* described the seas in Cook Strait that morning as the biggest they had ever seen.

Progress, May 1931   Sheer bad luck, rather than bad seamanship, was the root cause of the shipwrecking of the cargo steamer *Progress* at Owhiro Bay, Wellington. Under Captain A. Copeland and a crew of 11, the converted dredge had been bound from Lyttelton for Wellington when her tailshaft broke and she lost her propeller near the Pencarrow light. Sails were set, but *Progress* was not able to steer properly with just sail power and she drifted towards Lyall Bay. Morse signals were sent to the Beacon Hill signal station and the ship was also in contact with passing vessels, but the captain declined offers of help because he understood the tug *Toia* was coming out to give a tow. The first signal had been sent at about 7 p.m., but *Toia* did not arrive until half an hour after midnight. By that time the weather had worsened, the wind had strengthened and a heavy swell was running. *Progress* was being held by her anchors, but in the conditions *Toia* could only get a light line attached and this soon parted. At about 5.30 a.m. *Toia* gave up and steamed off, passing the other tug *Terawhiti* on the way. *Terawhiti* decided not to proceed to *Progress* and turned back. The later court of inquiry found that the stranding of *Progress* could have been avoided if the tug masters had carried out the duties expected of them.

Progress rode out the storm until 11 a.m., by which time three of her four holding anchors had been carried away. Captain Copeland decided to try sailing the ship into a more sheltered bay, so the sails were set, the remaining anchor was cut adrift and *Progress* headed towards Owhiro Bay. Unfortunately, she struck a submerged rock and the next sea lifted her up and dumped her down on the rocks with a mighty bang.

Within a few minutes she had broken in two. There followed a desperate rescue attempt, in which the rescuers on shore were often in as much danger as the crewmen clinging to the rocks and the wreckage. Constable F. Baker of Island Bay tried to reach the crew in a boat, but the boat capsized and he was injured. Constable Wally Hammond of the Taranaki Street police station was beaten back when he tried to take a lifeline out. A boat manned by Italian fishermen managed to pick him up, along with a crewman. On 1 May 1981, the 50th anniversary of the wreck, the *Evening Post* ran a story of a reunion between Mr Hammond and that survivor, Mr Fred Dergerholm. Mr Dergerholm was the last to come ashore, and he recalled being smashed against the rocks, breaking his ribs and injuring his left arm, making it useless for swimming.

Mr Hammond remembered taking a swig of whisky, putting the bottle in his pocket, then setting out with a line to try to reach Mr Dergerholm.

"I tried to swim out to the rock, but after climbing on to one rock I was washed off and the bottle in my pocket smashed. I was knocked about and cut and bruised but nothing serious," he said.

All the crewmen received a battering on the rocks — seven of the eight survivors were taken to hospital. Four men died in the accident. The court of inquiry found the wrecking was directly attributable to the fracture of the tailshaft.

Wanganella, January, 1947 *Wanganella's* stranding at Barretts Reef was a major accident, which fortunately did not result in any loss of life, but was a good example of how one simple slip can result in a major maritime casualty. The Huddart Parker passenger liner was resuming her civilian trade after the war, taking 400 passengers from Sydney to Wellington when she struck Barretts Reef at the entrance to Wellington harbour at 11.30 p.m. on a dark, clear night with a calm sea. The rocks held her fast and she had been badly holed in the forward section of her hull. Three tugs tried to pull her off, but they failed and it was left to the forces of nature to free the ship.

Passengers and crew were taken off by the harbour ferry *Cobar*. Among those passengers was 69-year-old former jockey L.H. "Tod" Hewitt, who complained that he had been allowed to sleep in. When *Wanganella*

Wanganella on Barretts Reef, Wellington. *Smith Collection, Alexander Turnbull Library*

went aground, Tod realised that women and children would be first off, so to fill in the time he went back to his cabin and to bed. Next thing he knew, he was shaken awake by a steward. All the other passengers were off the ship and he had been overlooked. He had breakfast with the crew and then clambered down a rope ladder to *Cobar*. As the passengers left the ship, half-metre-long pink streamers were still fluttering from her as a reminder that she had left Sydney to a joyous send-off after her reconversion from a wartime hospital ship.

Eighteen days after the stranding, on 6 February, a strong southerly swell lifted the ship clear of the rocks. Amazingly, the summer weather had held up all that time, otherwise the ship would probably have been

lost for good. However, she was salvaged and taken to the Wellington floating dock, then to Clyde Quay. Labour disputes held up her repair, and it was nearly two years before she was back in service. By then, the court of inquiry had sat at Wellington and had put the blame for the stranding squarely on the shoulders of the master, Captain R. Darroch. It found that he had mistaken the Barretts Reef flashing buoy light for the southernmost leading light into the harbour, about 4 kilometres north. Examination of the charts should have shown that the leading light would have been hidden by land and that the flashing light that was visible to the ship could only have been the reef buoy light. Captain Darroch's certificate was suspended for three months.

The crippled bulk steel carrier *Pacific Charger* is battered by the southerly winds and high seas which drove her on to rocks at Baring Head in May 1981. *"Evening Post"*

Pacific Charger, May 1981   Baring Head claimed another victim when the Japanese bulk-steel carrier *Pacific Charger* ran aground in the early hours of 21 May in atrocious weather. The ship was on her maiden voyage, carrying about 4,000 tonnes of cargo plus 800 tonnes of heavy marine oil, when she crashed into rocks side-on, about 100 metres offshore. Mr Steve O'Neill, the Baring Head lighthouse keeper, was radioed at 3.10 a.m. by the Wellington harbour radio to say there was a ship aground. A rescue headquarters was set up beside the light-house. *Pacific Charger* was lying parallel to the beach, wedged against a rock. But despite being buffeted by high seas she seemed in little danger of breaking up. Fifteen hours after the accident 23 of the 26 Taiwanese and Burmese crewmen were safely ashore. The master, Captain R.Y. Chiou, elected to stay aboard with the first mate and chief engineer.

Singapore-based salvage company, Selco, led by salvage master Captain Hugh Murray, was called in to attempt to release the ship from the rocks. This was finally accomplished in a hazardous five-hour operation. *Pacific Charger* had been stuck for 15 days and 18 hours before she came off, to be towed first to Kings Wharf and then to Glasgow Wharf for discharge. Even this was not the end of her troubles. She was holed again when steel girders plunged from a cargo sling to the bottom of her No. 2 hold. About 2,000 tonnes of harbour water gushed in, settling at a level of about 3.5 metres in the hold. The fire service pumped it out and the hole was patched by a diver next day. The ship finally began the tow back to Japan on 31 July 1981. A subsequent court of inquiry found that the master and deck officers of the ship were grossly incompetent, with the master never having had any proper training in the use of radar.

Penguin, February 1909   Overshadowing all other tragedies in Cook Strait, including that of *Wahine*, is the loss of the steamer *Penguin*. Of the 105 people on board (64 passengers and 41 crew), 75 died. *Penguin* was on the Union Company's run from Picton to Wellington under the command of Captain F.E. Naylor.

When they entered Cook Strait the weather became very thick, and Captain Naylor believed he had set a course that would take *Penguin* well out into the strait and that they would sight the Pencarrow light at 10 p.m. Instead, at about 9.45 p.m. the ship struck in the vicinity of Tom's Rock, off the mouth of the Karori Stream. The starboard hull was torn open. Pumping was started, but it was obviously a hopeless task. Captain Naylor had decided against beaching the ship because the coast was strewn with rocks, and from the bridge he organised the launching of the five boats and two rafts. The first boat was smashed to pieces when it was

After being salvaged, the *Pacific Charger* was towed to the Wellington wharves for temporary repairs and the discharge of cargo. Note the boom spread around the ship to contain spills. *David MacIntyre*

dropped into the sea, but the second got away despite being partially stoved in. One of the crewmen, Able Seaman Charles Jackson, likened the sound of the vessel's grounding to the tearing of a giant piece of calico. In an interview in the *Evening Post* on 13 February 1909, the day after the shipwrecking, he recalled no panic as the captain gave orders. Mr Jackson said he helped get one of the rafts ready and he described the scene like this:

Being a strong swimmer, I was the first to jump. I had no lifebelt, but I was quite prepared to depend on my ability as a swimmer. I stuck to the painter (the rope attached to the bow of the boat) and I looked up to the vessel. She was down by the nose with her stern high out of the water. Some of the men on the deck were afraid to jump, but they soon recognised that the ship was fast settling down.

One by one they commenced to leap over the side and, happily, all managed to reach the little craft which was being buffeted about in the waves. Altogether 12 people clambered aboard the raft, of which I took charge. We had a full complement aboard and were just drifting away from the ship when the boiler burst with a tremendous explosion and the ship slipped out of sight. Fortunately, we were a sufficient distance from the vessel to prevent us from being sucked in. The other raft had also managed to get clear. By a stroke of luck we managed to secure two oars and with these we guided the direction of our frail craft during the long hours of the night. We drifted for three hours, and about three o'clock saw the land looming up through the haze and mist.

I shall never forget that night as long as I live. We were overturned on three occasions. Once I got away from the raft about 20 yards, and again my ability as a swimmer was responsible for saving my life. It was really pitiable when the raft overturned to see the men struggling in the water, but it was magnificent to see them helping each other once more to a place of safety.

Mr Jackson said that they occasionally caught glimpses of Captain Naylor, who was clinging to a smashed lifeboat with a young male passenger. The young man's hand had been torn off and Captain Naylor was seen to bandage the wrist with his handkerchief. All the people on the two rafts were saved, but those on the boats were not so lucky. The only woman to survive was Mrs J.H. Hannam of Blenheim, who lost her husband and four children.

She said later that when she got in a lifeboat, "There were four men, six women and several children in our lifeboat. As we got into the boat it capsized right alongside the *Penguin*. It was dreadful. I clung to my two-year-old baby and saw three other

Seventy-five people died when the *Penguin* went down in 1909 in the strait's worst shipping tragedy. The question of why she foundered has never been fully answered. *Union Steam Ship Company*

children drowned before my eyes".

Mrs Hannam drifted ashore by holding on to an overturned lifeboat, with a 17-year-old boy, Ellis Matthews, hanging on to her dress. She had tied her baby, Ruby, to a thwart of the lifeboat, but when the boat reached the shore and was righted she found the baby was dead. Mrs Hannam was taken in shock to

the homestead of Mr John McMenamin.

The ship sank an hour after grounding. A search of the coastline revealed 52 bodies, 25 of which were identified. A further nine bodies were recovered later. Those not claimed by relatives were buried in separate graves at Wellington's Karori Cemetery. In the grief-stricken city a public funeral was

held. Crowds lined the route and the City Mission band, with muffled drums, played the *Dead March*.

The subsequent court of inquiry resulted in the suspension of Captain Naylor's certificate for a year. The court found there had been an exceptionally strong flood tide and the master should have headed out into the strait sooner than he did. However, the story did not really end there. It was generally assumed that *Penguin* had wrecked herself on Tom's Rock. But rumours abounded that the ship might have actually struck the drifting hulk of the *Rio Loge*, an auxiliary brigantine which had foundered between Kaikoura and Banks Peninsula four weeks before. The fact that her wreckage could have been in the vicinity was proven by the finding of a lifebuoy bearing the name *Rio Loge* at Island Bay, not far from *Penguin's* last resting place. Also, the previous experiences of *Ronga* and *Hydrabad* had proven that wreckage off the east coast of the South Island could work its way through the strait and up to Kapiti.

There is another reason to suggest that *Rio Loge* was the true cause of the tragedy. When searchers combed the coastline for bodies they were surprised to find large quantities of timber scattered along the shore. *Penguin* was not carrying any timber cargo, but *Rio Loge* had been carrying timber when she was lost. It is likely that if *Rio Loge* had capsized her hull would have been kept afloat by the timber in her holds. A strange hulk that looked like a derelict was spotted in Cook Strait in early February that year, but was never seen again after the *Penguin* disaster. If *Penguin* had rammed *Rio Loge*, the collision

would have split the hulk open and emptied the timber contents into the sea — hence the large amounts of timber found on shore.

So two questions arise: was Captain Naylor right in his claim that he had steered *Penguin* away from the coast and into the centre of the strait, and was it therefore the drifting hull of *Rio Loge* that was struck, not Tom's Rock? The mystery remains unanswered.

A memorium card printed after three members of the Toomer family had died in the *Penguin* tragedy. *Alexander Turnbull Library*

One of the rafts that brought *Penguin* survivors ashore. *Dickie Collection, Alexander Turnbull Library*

Chapter XII

The *Wahine* disaster

We are abandoning ship . . . .

IN THE hot and humid Solomon Islands the gentle breeze would have been noticed only for the mild relief it gave. Yet five days later it turned into a terrible hurricane and, at the height of its power, crashed head-on into one of the finest ships to serve New Zealand.

At 8,994 tons, *Wahine* was the largest ferry ever to sail across Cook Strait and along the South Island between Wellington and Lyttelton nightly for the Union Steam Ship Company. Built in Glasgow and under the command of Captain E.G.K. Meatyard, she arrived in Wellington in July 1966 after the British Government bailed out the shipbuilders when they ran into financial problems.

She was the second vessel to bear the name *Wahine* — because it means "woman" in Maori some seamen thought the name was unlucky. The first *Wahine* had an incident-free life until 1951 when she ran aground on a reef in the Arafura Sea north of Darwin while carrying units of New Zealand's K-Force to Korea. She was abandoned without any loss of life.

The new *Wahine*, described in an *Evening*

Captain Gordon Robertson, master of *Wahine.*
"Evening Post"

Post headline as "almost too good to travel in", was a contrast to the old faithful *Maori*, which also plied the route. After Captain Meatyard initiated *Wahine's* new run, the ship had only one master, the experienced Captain Gordon Robertson. Aged 57 at the time of *Wahine's* last voyage, he had sailed for 41 years and had served as a master of the ferries *Hinemoa* and *Maori* as well as taking a spell on the Railways Department ferry *Aramoana*. While serving on a Pacific liner he met a Canadian girl, Anne, who later became his wife.

"His first love of course was for his passengers," Mrs Robertson told us while we were preparing this book.

"I had to admit that, but I knew it instinctively."

Her husband, she said, demanded perfection, but while he was a hard taskmaster he was also a fair one.

Wahine was to make the voyage between the two cities 156 times without once being late. She now and again cast off late, especially in Lyttelton where departure was timed with the arrival of the express train from Invercargill, but thanks to ample reserves of power the ship was never late in port the following morning. In many respects the *Wahine* exceeded its Lloyd's "Plus 100 A1 Ferry" classification and was truly an ocean-going vessel because of the conditions it was designed to encounter in the Cook Strait.

Tuesday evening 9 April 1968, it was overcast in Lyttelton when *Wahine*, 43 minutes late because of the train, cast off and headed out to sea. On board that night were 123 officers and crew, 610 passengers and one stowaway — a sailor who was to be dead within 24 hours. On *Wahine's* vast vehicle deck were 74 motorcars, 17 sea-freighters and eight trailers. Two of the open-topped containers held 19 tonnes of coke, while another was loaded with 25,110 dozen eggs. A cargo of tombstones was also carried that night.

After taking *Wahine* out to sea and heading north, Captain Robertson had coffee with an old friend, Father James McGlynn, and Alfred Rutland, an Australian traveller with a love for ships. The Australian was to be dead at the end of the next day.

On bidding them good night Captain Robertson went to bed and slept as soundly as possible for a man whose whole body was tuned to the whims of the sea and the safety of his ship. However, this was not the case with Mrs Robertson in the Maungaraki house they had moved into on 1 April from their flat in Lower Hutt. The new house was in a suburb on steep hills overlooking Wellington harbour, the city and, in the distance, the harbour entrance where a great drama was to take place. They had moved

Drama as *Wahine* makes final entrance into Wellington Harbour

(A) Off Baring Head all appeared normal until (B) the ship's radar suddenly failed and the ship was thrown off course in high seas and a wild wind. For some 30 minutes (C) the ship followed an uncertain course before hitting Outer Rock (D) and being blown across Barretts Reef (E). Coming clear (F) *Wahine* was able to drop anchors, but this was to no effect and the ship drifted, coming close to Point Dorset (G). At 11 a.m. a tug passed a line to *Wahine* (H), but it soon parted and *Wahine's* fate was sealed.

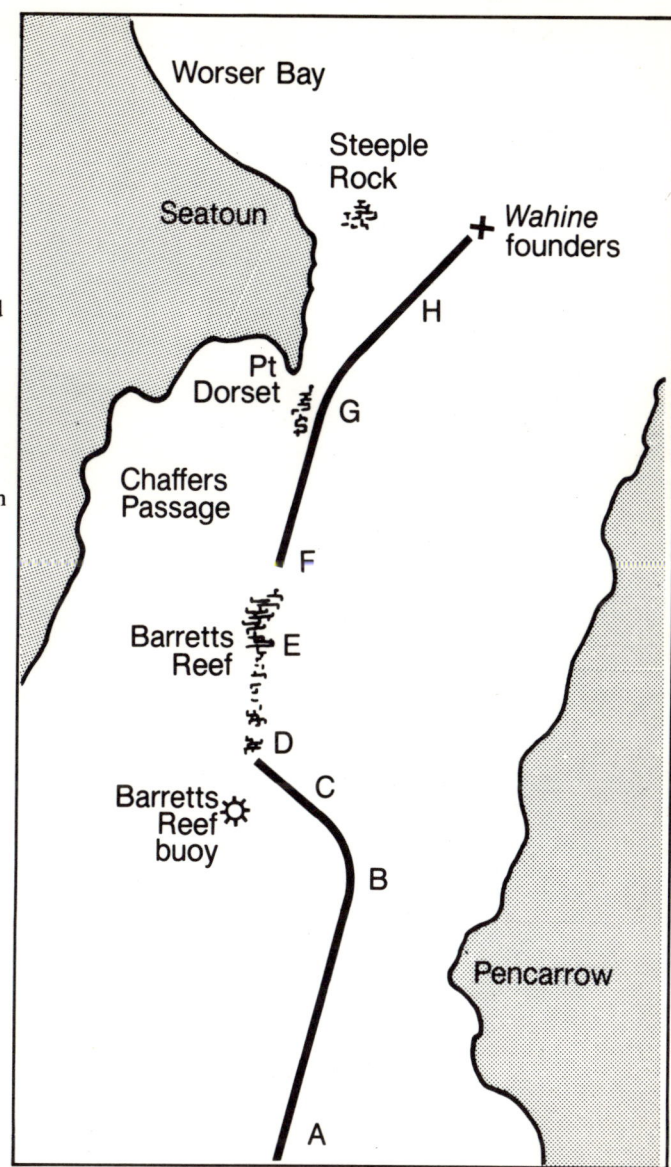

Wahine's radio officer, Robert Lyver.
"Evening Post"

Wild Cook Strait conditions were not unknown to Captain Robertson, as this photograph of *Aramoana* pitching deeply shows. It was taken in 1963, south of Wellington. Captain Robertson was commanding the rail ferry at the time. *"Evening Post"*

onto the hill so that Captain Robertson could signal his wife each time he sailed out of the harbour.

As Captain Robertson slept, his wife paced around her new home, worried.

On *Wahine*, Radio Officer Robert Lyver monitored Radio-ZLW, a Post Office station on the Tinakori Hills overlooking central Wellington, for the weather forecast. It stated, in part:

Storm warning: Severe tropical depres-

sion . . . about 60 miles east of North Cape is moving south south-east 20 knots . . .

Forecast for Central Area (Cook Strait): Strong northerlies changing to southerly after midnight tonight, the southerlies gradually increasing to gale or storm force from tomorrow morning . . .

Captain Robertson, who saw the forecast, noted that winds of 55 knots were predicted — nothing especially unusual in the lives of ferry captains, or Wellington commuters for

that matter.

Three days earlier, the depression had been confirmed as a tropical cyclone, centred around 240 kilometres south-east of Guadalcanal. Earlier in the day, when *Wahine* sailed, it was placed off Norfolk Island where the experts believed it was beginning to weaken. But when nightfall came on 9 April the cyclone made a totally unexpected move: it turned southward, accelerated and intensified and, by 10 a.m. on

10 April, it would be off the eastern entrance of Cook Strait. But as *Wahine* sailed north nobody had any way of knowing that this was to be the case.

At 1.30 a.m. on 10 April *Wahine* passed the Lyttelton-bound *Maori*. Chief Officer Rodney Luly arrived on the bridge at 4 a.m. to commence his watch, noting, as he did so that there was heavy rain, rough seas, a moderate to heavy swell and a wind from the south of around 35 to 40 knots. "Vessel rolling easily," he wrote in the log at the start of his watch, but an hour later he noted "rolling heavily" and reported that the ship was scending, which meant that the swell, running from behind, was lifting the ship out of the water, exposing the rudders and propellers.

At 5 a.m. Radio Officer Lyver tallked with Beacon Hill, the Wellington Pilot Station overlooking the harbour entrance. They told him that winds in the harbour were up to 60 knots and as a tug was to be out to move a ship in the harbour it would also be available for *Wahine* if necessary. Half an hour later Lyver took the first weather forecast since the previous night and heard that the cyclone was apparently off to the east of Hawke Bay.

Captain Robertson came onto the bridge at 5.45 a.m., ready to take the ship into port. *Wahine* was abeam Baring Head at 6 a.m. In the following 10 minutes, between Baring Head and Pencarrow, Captain Robertson could have safely turned his vessel out to sea. But while conditions appeared unpleasant, as far as Captain Robertson could see there was nothing that *Wahine* had not been designed to handle. But one aspect of *Wahine's* design led him to gain a false impression of conditions. The ship's bridge was totally

Passengers sitting on B-deck during the morning as *Wahine* struggled through the storm. The photograph was obtained from film recovered from the wreck. *"Evening Post"*

enclosed, leaving an experienced seaman more reliant on technology than his own proven instinct.

Up ahead at Beacon Head they knew something dramatic was occurring to the weather. In the 10 minutes before 5 a.m. the average wind speed had been 55 knots, but at 6 a.m., as *Wahine* approached a point of no return, that average soared to 75 knots. The signalman at Beacon Head did not think to tell *Wahine* of the sudden change.

Abeam of Pencarrow, *Wahine*, at a speed of 10 knots, suddenly went blind when the radar failed. Then, within seconds she was thrown 23 degrees to port. The rudder was hard to starboard, but it had no effect. *Wahine* was at the mercy of a wild storm, heading uncontrollably towards the rocky Barretts Reef.

Captain Robertson, now unable to see anything from the bridge, ordered full speed ahead in an attempt to gain control, but this tactic did not work. Just as he was about to give another order the ship sheered mightily,

This photograph, obtained from film recovered from the wreck of *Wahine*, indicates the amount of sea water leaking on to the vehicle deck in the morning. *"Evening Post"*

An unknown *Wahine* seaman took this photograph of the tug *Tapuhi* on the morning of 10 April 1968. The tug was attempting to get near the ship to pass over a tow line. This photograph, more than any other, illustrates the wild nature of the weather that day. *"Evening Post"*

tossing the captain and Chief Officer Luly across the bridge. Captain Robertson hit the useless radar console. Picking himself up, he ordered the port engine to be put astern in an effort to get the ship to swing full circle — but nothing happened.

At 6.41 a.m., 28 minutes after the violent sheer, the starboard quarter of *Wahine* hit Outer Rock, the southernmost exposed rock of Barretts Reef. The starboard propeller and part of the shaft was smashed off and moments later the vessel's port engine died. As *Wahine* was driven across the reef by the wind and sea, badly damaging her hull, the watertight doors closed and Captain Robertson gave orders to drop anchors.

Fourteen minutes after *Wahine* hit the reef, police received an emergency call from Seatoun residents Stuart and Jennifer Young, whose home looked out over the reef. Catching glimpses of *Wahine* through the storm, they realised she was being blown sideways and was in great danger. Around the same time an SOS was being sent from *Wahine*. On board, it had taken Chief Officer Luly and a seaman 20 minutes to execute the order to drop anchors. The machinery for doing so was out on the exposed forecastle head, battered by high winds and a wild sea. The anchors were finally dropped when *Wahine* was at the northern end of Chaffers Passage, between the reef and Worser Bay. The passengers, shocked by the harsh ringing of alarm bells, were told by Captain Robertson to go to their cabins, don lifejackets and reassemble on B-deck. Passengers greeted the news first with incredulity, but for the next six hours their time was spent in uncomfortable boredom, sitting around in

Wahine, in her dying moments, begins to capsize. *"Evening Post"*

the cold and dark conditions wondering what would happen next.

Wahine had already sustained mortal damage, but abandonment was simply out of the question because of the violence of the elements all round the ship. Few would have survived if the lifeboats had been launched in the morning. Powerless and taking in water, *Wahine* was dragging her anchors and

threatening at times to be washed ashore at Point Dorset. The wind was damaging the ship. At nearby Wellington Airport the average wind-speed for the 10-minute period 6.50 a.m. to 7 a.m. was 66 knots, with the highest gust reaching 82 knots. Later in the morning the highest wind gust reported at the airport was 101 knots, while down the coast at Oteranga Bay a gust was recorded at

145 knots, a record wind-speed for the country. A huge swell also created problems, which were to have a fatal impact in the afternoon. The seas were building up the tide in the harbour, where gauges recorded sea levels 30 centimetres higher than normal. Later the court of inquiry into the disaster described the weather in terms of "awesome violence, beyond anything hitherto recorded anywhere in New Zealand".

Mrs Anne Robertson heard on the radio that *Wahine* was in trouble and, later in the morning, a Union Company official telephoned to tell her not to worry.

"During the day I didn't think once about Gordon's safety," she told the press later. "I thought about the battle he was facing out there in that terrific storm. He always felt a great responsibility for his passengers. He loved the ship and I knew what he must be facing."

With anchors down and *Wahine* seemingly out of immediate danger, Chief Officer Luly went on damage inspection. On the vehicle deck, coke and broken eggs were spread across the floor while more significantly, water was seeping in. According to engineer Stanley Spiers, by 10 a.m. the water was "blowing out" of the ventilators and an hour later the water was knee-deep at the after-end of the vehicle deck. The ship's double bottom and other compartments were also flooded and an estimated 3,000 tonnes of water lay in the ship. The inquiry later found that *Wahine* officers, believing the water could be pumped out, underestimated the danger it posed. Ultimately it was the steady flooding of the ship that produced the fatal capsize.

Captain Galloway, the assistant harbourmaster who leapt aboard *Wahine*. *"Evening Post"*

During the morning, harbour board vessels, including a tug, attempted to reach *Wahine*, but the force of the storm sent them racing for shelter. Later in the morning the tug *Tapuhi* made it and with great bravery passed across a tow line, which snapped within minutes when seas tossed the tiny tug away from *Wahine*.

At around 12.30 p.m. a harbour board pilot boat made it to *Wahine*. On board was the deputy harbourmaster, Captain Bill Galloway, who, with remarkable courage, leapt from the pilot boat to a lifeboat ladder hanging down the starboard side of *Wahine*'s bridge. After climbing up in a howling gale with waves crashing around him, he joined Captain Robertson on the bridge. On coming aboard he noticed, as the passengers had realised at noon, that *Wahine* had begun to list. The ship was in grave danger and her only hope rested with *Tapuhi*, which was sheltering in a nearby bay as a second tow rope was prepared.

At 1 p.m., as Captain Galloway stood on the starboard side of *Wahine*'s bridge and Captain Robertson on the port side, the ship began to swing, creating a lee or sheltered area on the starboard side. It offered the first chance to abandon ship and Captain Robertson was quick to give the order. It was 1.20 p.m. when Captain Galloway told Beacon Hill, "We are abandoning ship. We are abandoning ship." *Tapuhi* was told to forget the tow and return quickly to *Wahine*'s side in order to save lives.

As the order was given to abandon ship, miraculously the violent gale dropped off in a moment, although the raging sea was another matter. Despite the grim seriousness of what was about to take place, a purser with a remarkable sense of humour called out calmly, "Tickets please".

As the ship swung, the list steepened, leaving the port lifeboats useless. Passengers were told to go to lifeboat stations on the starboard side, but some passengers did not wait and instead jumped immediately over the side, hampering *Tapuhi* in its efforts to get close in to *Wahine*'s side.

On the deck Mrs Shirley Hick of Shannon stood confused with her three children, six-year-old David, three-year-old Alma and Gordon, who was marking his first birthday on that very day.

"One of the passengers came round and took Alma," she said later. "I do not know what happened to her. He went round and down the low side. Gordon and David were with me. David was there screaming and would not move."

Alma died that day. Gordon suffered extensive brain damage while in the water. Two children under four died. A steward, Bryan McMaster, told the inquiry of one of them:

I floated on my back with the baby on my chest. It had on very little clothing — a singlet, a tee-shirt and some napkins or shorts, not very much at all. The clothing wasn't adequate. I would estimate that I was in the water for from between 30 and 40 minutes. The tide was going out and we floated well to the port of the vessel. I would say the child died while I had hold of it. It coughed and foamed at the mouth, then it was washed out of my hands by a wave.

Ian Bull and his wife from Waikato were caught in a crush as the order came to leave the ship. Hanging on to baby Judy, Ian found himself protected by a big Fijian, who took time out to calm a man who was making a noise by threatening to thump him. Ian was also helped by a group of passengers, who formed a human chain across the steep and slippery deck.

"I think it was just a lot of 'hang-of-a-nice' Maori people who were not concerned about their own safety and stayed where they could help." The Bull family made it safely.

A photograph obtained from film recovered from the wreck of the *Wahine* shows Mrs Shirley Hicks of Shannon. Beside her is her son David who survived, and in Mrs Hicks' arms is Gordon, who also survived but sustained permanent brain damage. *"Evening Post"*

Alma Hicks (centre) of Shannon, who died in the sea on the afternoon of the wrecking of *Wahine. "Evening Post"*

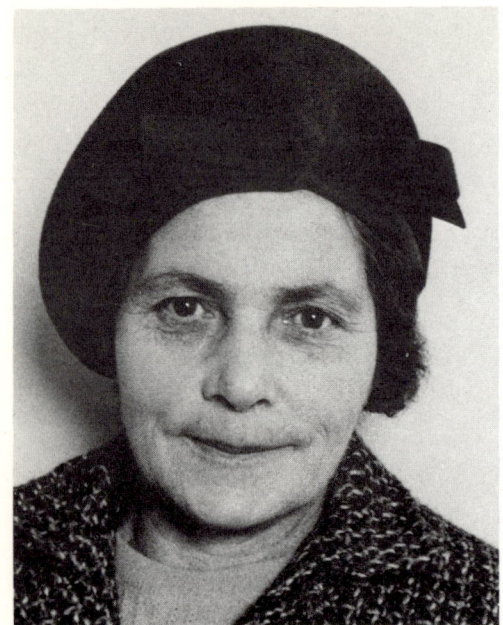

Mrs May Hickman, whose husband died when the *Wahine's* motor lifeboat was swamped. *"Evening Post"*

Wahine, her useless port lifeboats swinging high, heels over as the rail ferry *Aramoana* attempts to recover people from the water. *"Evening Post"*

Some passengers found that their initial good luck in getting into *Wahine's* motor lifeboat did not last for long, as the boat was swamped. Samuel Folkard sat in the lifeboat as it moved away from *Wahine*, noticing crying women still on the deck of the ship:

It was something I couldn't comprehend. I wondered whether I had missed an announcement over the public address system stating that women and children should have entered the boat first.

Mrs May Hickman of Ashburton was also in the lifeboat with her husband:

When this wave came somebody said she was going over, and over we went. I was still with my husband then. I was quite convinced he was knocked out because he went absolutely limp. I came up and the boat was upside down. A crew member caught hold of me and pulled me over to the boat. I looked around. I never saw my husband, I never saw him again. My husband just slid away.

Mr and Mrs Folkard hung onto the upturned lifeboat with eight others until around 3 p.m. when a pilot boat came within 10 metres of them. Mr Folkard said:

I had trouble hearing, for I had water in my ears, but I understood the chappie in the boat to say, "when we get close, grab the ropes".

When I looked again I saw there were what appeared to be small strands of rope surrounding the pilot boat, so I said to my wife, "When it comes near, you jump and

grab the rope. We will do this together."
We held hands, we jumped and grabbed.
I grabbed a rope, then all I remember then
is that I felt myself slipping.

He was plucked from the water, but his
wife did not survive.

Among those picked up was Wellington
lawyer Bernard Knowles, who later went on
to become general manager of the New
Zealand Dairy Board. It was his second experience of disaster. Six years before he had
been one of 13 to survive an aircraft crash on
a Honolulu runway in which 27 people died.

Although *Wahine* went over quickly,
Captain Robertson ensured that everybody
had left the ship. He and Captain Galloway
were the last to leave. Captain Robertson,
jumping into the sea in full uniform, felt
"sadness and frustration".

They were picked up 10 minutes later by
the launch *Cuba*. A steward, also picked up,
gently wiped a thin stream of blood from
Captain Robertson's face.

With a howling southerly blowing it was
reasonable to expect that all in the water
would have been blown into the harbour,
coming ashore on Petone beach. Some did
get ashore at Seatoun beach and at Eastbourne, but in the afternoon the much higher
tide than usual began to run out along the
rugged eastern side of the harbour. It carried
many of the survivors onto the wild rocks of
the coastal area south of Eastbourne, a place
difficult to reach, even in the best of weather.
Of the 51 people who died that day, all but
four of the bodies came up on the rocky coast,
many with significant bruising and abra-
sions.

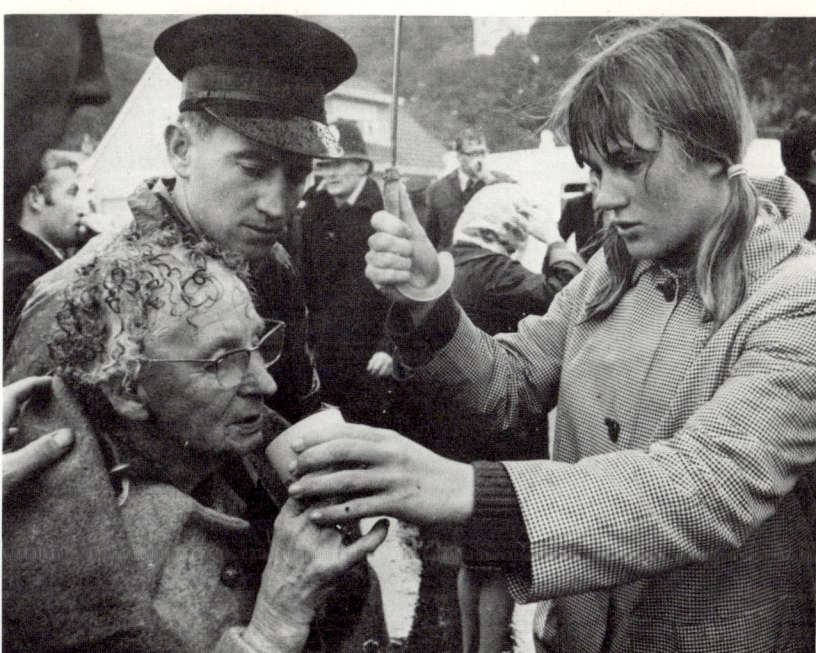

A young helper
holds an
umbrella over
one of the
survivors while
a Salvation
Army officer
watches on.
"Evening Post"

One Eastbourne resident who went along
the coast saw people being smashed on the
rocks, but was unable to do anything.
One survivor came ashore in a liferaft:

The raft capsized in the first line of
breakers. I went overboard then, and so
did a lot of others. This was about 500
yards offshore. There were breakers from
then on until we got to the beach . . .
There were bodies rolling round in the
waves. I went back until I was absolutely
finished. I dragged out three people. They
were all right, and then there were three or
four deeply unconscious people. They
may have been all right. And then there

were bodies. I gave up in the end. I could
not go on.

Engineer Spiers was in the same raft when
it overturned. He told the inquiry:

When I managed to get back to the raft I
could hear people talking underneath. A
man swam out with a baby in his arms. I
asked him if he had a knife and he gave me
a pocket knife. I cut through the raft and
the first person I got out was a small boy.
I assumed he was dead. I pulled out a
woman. She was also dead.

The police were initially caught off-guard
when people came ashore on the eastern

Wahine's starboard number two lifeboat, loaded with survivors, came ashore at the Seatoun wharf. *"Evening Post"*

Young survivor Clarence O'Neill stands frightened, wet and cold in his adult-sized lifejacket after safely making it ashore. *"Evening Post"*

coast, and then, when they moved, wild conditions hampered their efforts. But the police officer in charge of operations on that coast, Senior Sergeant Brian Courtney, made it clear that when the police acted, their efforts were superhuman:

Many survivors were being smashed against the offshore rocks by the huge waves when in sight of shore. Members of the police were wading into the surf, often up to chest height and dragging out as many bodies as possible, and every assistance that was humanly possible was being given to those in the water.

One constable who was assisting survivors from a liferaft found that an elderly woman had been trampled by the abandoning survivors and lay face down, floating in the bottom of the raft. He dragged the woman from the raft and attempted to revive her, but such was her condition that it was unlikely that she lived.

Another constable assisted an elderly

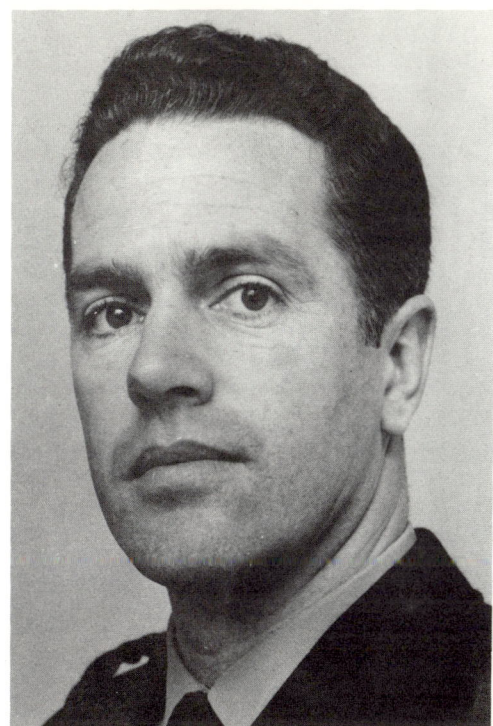

Senior Sergeant Brian Courtney told of survivors being washed ashore and then swept out to sea again before anyone could reach them. *"Evening Post"*

A young child is gently lifted ashore at Seatoun. *"Evening Post"*

man from a raft to a position near the roadway. He had no sooner left the man than a huge wave swept him out to sea again and the constable did not see him again . . .

Another woman who was found floating face down was dragged from the sea by another constable. She was an elderly woman who was frothing at the mouth and who appeared to be dead. She was dragged to a place of what was thought to be safety near the road, only to be swept out to sea again.

On another occasion, a constable dived into the sea to assist a woman, but before he could grasp her she was swept back out to sea and forced in on the next wave. She was thrown onto one of the jagged offshore rocks and her head was seen to split open like a broken egg. She was dragged from the shore, and it was presumed she was dead.

Another young male person was found completely submerged in the sea and had

The working end of the *Wahine* salvage vessel *Holmpark*. *Michael Field*

slipped through his lifejacket. He had been battered against the rocks, and was found to have a gaping hole in his forehead. He was presumed dead . . .

A constable, who was wearing gumboots, dived into the sea to bring out an elderly woman who was greatly distressèd and nearly stripped of her clothing. As they emerged from the water, the woman was seen to be wearing the constable's gumboots to protect her already cut feet from the rocks . . .

I wish to state that I have never in my service in the police seen men display such courage, and, if the Court will excuse me, sheer guts and unity of purpose, as I witnessed on April 10 last. I am proud to be associated with them.

Captain Robertson came ashore at Seatoun and was taken home.

"He was in a state of great shock," Mrs Robertson said later, "but when he came home he didn't know anyone had been lost. When he heard over the air that an officer had been lost he wouldn't go to bed despite appeals to him to take a hot bath and lie down. He made many phone calls asking if the crew were safe. He never anticipated the loss of life."

At the end of that terrible day *Wahine* lay like a beached whale, with 12 big holes in her hull.

For a time, there were hopes that she could be raised, repaired and put back in service, but the salvage experts reported substantial damage. Their proposal was to pump the ship full of foam to refloat it and tow it out to sea where it would be sunk. The Wellington Chamber of Commerce showed a jarring mercantile insensitivity when it came up with the suggestion that the ship be towed to the southern end of Wellington airport and sunk to form the basis of runway extensions. But in the end nature had the final say — during a storm just over a year later the wreck was torn into three pieces.

"It was all over in a couple of hours," said salvage leader Captain Jock Anderson on the tender *Holmpark*. He was wrong and the wreck removal job was not finally completed until September 1973 at a cost of $3.5 million, paid by Lloyd's of London.

After an intensive inquiry Captain Robertson was cleared of any blame, a decision which, if public reaction is anything to go by, was widely supported.

Six months later he was back at sea, master of the 3,500-ton freighter *Kowhai*. He was to sail into Wellington harbour many times on that and other ships, despite a popular waterfront rumour which said he had been banned from the port. Another rumour, based on superstition and a belief that something similar happened to the master of the first *Wahine*, had it that Captain Robertson eventually died broken-hearted at the loss of his ship. His widow, Mrs Anne Robertson, who gave us a moving interview for this book, felt the disaster may have contributed to his early death, although he actually died from cancer.

Thirteen years later she was still living in the home they had moved into two weeks before the *Wahine* disaster. Those events have given her what she calls a deep appreciation of "the immense beauty of nature and the goodness of man".

The Robertsons received thousands of letters from around the world after the disaster and only one was critical. They felt there was something wrong with the writer:

Only one wrote an awful letter and my husband always opened the mail; he never let me open it because he was afraid I would be hurt.

Whenever you criticise or condemn others without knowing the facts or the truth you must be very dissatisfied with yourself. Now a greater understanding of human frailties has come to me. Many, undoubtedly, erred on that fatal voyage and I feel no resentment towards anyone.

Salvage experts prepare the *Wahine* for a refloating attempt using foam. Working from the *Holmpark*, divers cut away the ship's superstructure. However, the attempt to refloat the ship was never made because a storm a year after the disaster broke up the wreck. *"Evening Post"*

Pity and sadness, yes, for any who endure mental or physical wounds from that day.

And the lessons we learned. It was a wonderful experience to see the world behaving with such kindness, civility and love, easing one another's passage through this changeable and considerably brutal world.

I now understand what the avalanche of love means, and one has to accept pain as a condition of existence. That means everyone. Gordon's total acceptance of the whole thing amazed me. He suffered from shock for eight days as the specialist

Salvagers — and probably most of the seamen on board — did not know *Wahine* carried a cargo of tombstones until 1971 when divers brought them to the surface. Leading diver Stewart Doig felt they had been partly responsible for the bad luck that plagued the salvage. *"Evening Post"*

told me he would, but his personally seeing that all were off the ship, that was very important. He came home to me dripping wet and he knew that everyone had got off the ship safely . . . .

The head of the Seamens' Union telephoned me and said, "Don't forget Mrs Robertson — every single person got off that ship safely. So don't have too many worries. It's just one of nature's catastrophies."

Tragedy and pain is in everyone's life. It's not what happens to you that matters, it's how you cope. Fearful of hurts caused to others, and to each other, Gordon spared me from the knowledge of his cancer. He tried to spare me from this for months. I had to get the information from his specialist.

All stories have their "if onlys", and Mrs Robertson said the *Wahine* story was no different, especially in relation to the move into their new home two weeks before the ship was wrecked:

This was a great triumph, moving to Maungaraki where he could signal me. We only had one day to move and, strangely, . . . he had asked for two weeks' leave so we could settle comfortably into our new home. But the company couldn't spare him.

All the other captains said, there but for the grace of God go I. They all knew they

could have been chosen if he had been given those days' leave.

After the disaster Mrs Robertson joined many other people opposed to the idea of erecting a big memorial to the wrecking:

I was so much against it. It was bringing back the tragedy to the people and I felt tremendously that they should not be subjected to any further sorrow or distress. This business of something coming up every year to remind people of *Wahine* is very tragic and it was tragic for Gordon and for me.

She also felt strongly that if a memorial was to be erected one should be put at every street corner in the land where fatal road accidents had occurred.

Mrs Robertson did not return to her native Canada to live after the death of her husband and, to the puzzlement of a number of people, she remained in the same house. People used to quiz her on why she wanted to stay at a place where, they assumed, she saw the disaster.

"View it!" she replies. "I couldn't even see our fence."

Mrs Robertson clearly loves the rugged splendour of Wellington's magnificent scenery. Her love for the sea remains, safe in the knowledge that what happened to *Wahine* was, as she put it, "A oncer, thank God".

Chapter XIII

Incidents and achievements

We're making the crossing for the hell of it.

COOK STRAIT has a more colourful history than probably most people realise. The fact that it presents a physical challenge has led to crossing attempts by boat, by swims and by hot-air balloon. But the strait has earned itself a niche in history for more than this: it has hosted enemy submarines in wartime; it has been the scene of a tragic yachting disaster; it played a part in one of the most spectacular UFO sightings ever documented; and it had its own pirate — of sorts.

UFO sightings in the strait and surrounding areas put the public spotlight on Cook Strait — both nationally and internationally — during the summer of 1978-79.

Controversy has raged ever since television film was taken of supposed UFOs off the Kaikoura coast on New Year's Eve 1978. Official reports from the Ministry of Defence and the Department of Scientific and Industrial Research (DSIR) have pointed to "natural causes" as the explanation for the sightings, but these reports were emphatically and eloquently rejected by witnesses.

The series of sightings began in the Cook Strait/Marlborough Sounds area early on 17

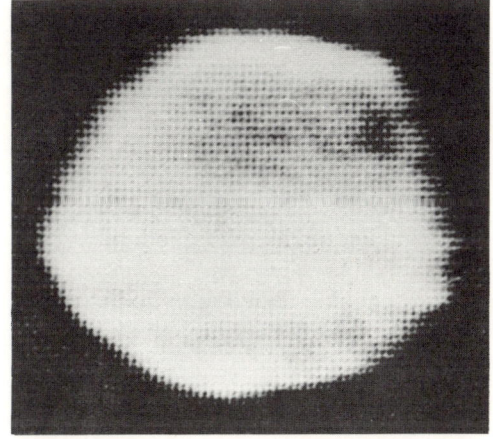

One of the strange glowing objects captured on film during the eventful Argosy flights of 1978. *"Evening Post"*

December 1978, when Waikawa freezing worker Frank MacDonald and his wife Peggy saw an immense light in the sky in the vicinity of the sounds. Mr MacDonald described the object as like a gigantic machine which appeared to be in trouble. Other

people living near Picton also saw it. Four days later, on the night of 20-21 December, Warrant Officer Ian Uffindell of the RNZAF and Flight Service Officer Bill Frame witnessed strange lights over the Woodbourne Aerodrome, outside Blenheim. They thought the lights were off Cape Campbell at the southern entrance to Cook Strait, although returns were picked up further down the coast by Wellington airport radar. Independent sightings were also made.

Early on 21 December a Safe Air Argosy flight from Blenheim to Christchurch picked up radar returns in the same area. Captain John Randle and First Officer Keith Heine continued their return-leg flight from Christchurch to Auckland and, after seeing strange lights, which were also picked up by Wellington radar, they made an orbit and saw one light which had apparently been tracking the aircraft. Captain Vern Powell, pilot of another Argosy, and First Officer Ian Pirie also saw strange lights.

The wave of sightings in the Cook Strait area prompted a Melbourne television channel to send reporter Quentin Fogarty on an Argosy piloted by Captain Bill Startup who was later to become president of the New Zealand Airline Pilots' Association, and First Officer Bob Guard. They were accompanied by cameraman David Crockett and his sound-recordist wife Ngaire. In the early hours of 31 December, just out of Wellington *en route* for Christchurch, the pilots began to see strange lights in the vicinity of the straits which were also being picked up by Wellington radar. All the way to Christchurch the flight deck crew saw what they considered to be UFOs and the television crew managed to take some film. Back at Wellington, air traffic controller Geoff Causer wrote in the official records that those on board the Argosy had indicated they had seen some unusual lights, but "did not elaborate that the sightings were UFOs". The experience so unnerved Ngaire that she refused to join the aircraft for the return leg from Christchurch to Woodbourne.

Her place was taken by Television One reporter Dennis Grant. The return leg was to provide the news "scoop" — the appearance of an immense lighted orb just out of Christchurch which was filmed by the television crew. On the aircraft radar, it showed up at a distance of 30 kilometres but later closed to 13 kilometres. When the aircraft was heading towards Kaikoura, Captain Startup decided to get a closer look and turned towards the UFO. The orb dipped below the aircraft and appeared on the other side. Eventually it moved off behind the aircraft. During the rest of the flight more unexplained lights were seen off the Clarence River and Cape Campbell, over Tasman Bay and in Cook Strait. The television film was developed to show frame after frame of un-explained images. On one frame the orb looked like a shuttle craft and on another like a spinning top. There was also a strange loop, like a squashed figure-of-8.

The RNZAF put an Orion surveillance aircraft into the air to investigate the area, but it found nothing in Cook Strait or over the South Island. Following that, a variety of semi-official statements were made suggesting the sightings were due to Venus or Jupiter rising, squid boat lights being distorted in the atmosphere, flocks of mutton birds coming in to land, windscreen distortions and radar anomalies. On 25 January 1979 the Ministry of Defence put out a news release blaming "natural and unusual atmospheric phenomena" which had refracted or reflected light. After that release was found unconvincing a second report was brought out by the DSIR in December 1979. Again, the finding was that there were no UFOs and that the main sighting outside Christchurch had been of a brightly lit fishing boat.

Other sightings were put down to lighthouses, navigation lights, city lights or planets. Captain Startup rejected these findings also. He pointed out that planets did not normally follow aircraft and that the radar returns were unexplained. He suggested the UFO report should be retitled "Unable to Fool the Observers".

If UFO sightings have provided some of the more sensational moments in Cook Strait history, other more conventional aerial crossings have added human interest. Ballooning, if it can be called conventional, took the limelight in January 1975 when the crew of a hot-air balloon managed to conquer the strait's high winds for the first time. Flight Lieutenant Roly Parsons and his Blenheim passenger, Mr Rex Brereton, lifted off from Cape Jackson in Queen Charlotte Sound and took their bright-orange balloon to an altitude of about 2,150 metres. The balloon measured 30 metres high by 18 metres across and cruised across the strait at about 7 kilometres/hour. The only problem faced by 33-year-old Flight Lieutenant Parsons was the high temperature, which made the balloon struggle to maintain altitude.

Less than three hours after lift-off, hundreds of sightseers watched the 2,200-cubic-metre balloon drift north towards Pukerua Bay, then turn back towards Paremata as the wind changed. Flight Lieutenant Parsons brought it in to land at the Whitby Golf Course at 6.40 p.m. A big crowd gathered to take pictures and congratulate the crew — but the balloon's recovery team was not among the crowd. The team had lost track of the meandering balloon and had to be informed of the landing by telephone. Flight Lieutenant Parsons said he had kept in touch with the Wellington Airport control tower throughout the journey. His main problem on landing, he said, was to find a safe place to put down in the built-up areas around Paremata.

The problems of tackling wind and weather across the strait are shared by balloonists and glider pilots, but gliders managed to conquer the conditions 18 years before the successful balloon attempt.

Christchurch topdressing pilot Keith Wakeman made the first crossing by glider at the end of October 1957. He took off in his 270-kilogram Slingsby Skylark II glider from

Lees Valley, near Oxford, North Canterbury, and landed in the grounds of Freyberg High School, Palmerston North, two hours and 50 minutes later. The 15-metre-wingspan glider reached a maximum height of 5,500 metres (18,000 feet) approaching Blenheim. An average speed of about 150 kilometres/hour was achieved on the 435-kilometre flight and it was hailed the fastest flight ever made by a glider at that time. It prompted Mr Philip Wills, the chairman of the British Gliding Association, to describe it as "the most startling glider flight in history".

The second crossing in January 1964 was also made by Keith Wakeman. He set off from Culverden in the South Island in search of a diamond distance badge (500 kilometres in one journey) awarded by the New Zealand Gliding Association. He caught on to a north-travelling cold front near Kaikoura, but landed 20 kilometres north of Masterton, short of his target. A later attempt to cross back to the South Island by glider failed with a landing being made at Titahi Bay.

Dick Georgeson made the third crossing in February 1977, with an attempt on the record for the longest distance to a specified goal. He glided from Five Rivers, near Invercargill, to Napier, but he did not achieve his target. Georgeson finally had luck on his side for his 27th attempt in January 1978 when he was one of three pilots to set a world goal record (furthest distance to a specified goal). With Dave Speight and Bruce Drake, all in open-class long wing-span gliders, he flew from Invercargill to near Hicks Bay on the east coast of the North Island, a 12-hour flight of 1,254 kilometres. They all crossed the strait at 5,500 metres (18,000 feet) above

sea level and lost 1,200-1,500 metres (4,000 feet) by the time they were over the Hutt Valley.

Crossing the strait by glider is no longer a big event in gliding, although a North Island-South Island crossing is much harder than the reverse because of prevailing winds. A major problem is the cost of towing the glider back to its home base — to retrieve the glider from a paddock and tow it back could cost several hundred dollars. Hence in 1981 when Wellington pilot John Vincent flew from Paraparaumu to Tory Channel at 1,500 metres (5,000 feet) he preferred to fly back to Paraparaumu and enjoy a 75-minute round trip rather than land in the South Island.

Although balloon and glider crossings have their difficulties, these are minor compared to the task of getting a parachute across the strait. There has never been a successful parachute crossing of Cook Strait, but four Nelson parachutists came close in April 1979. Paul Lewis, John Frew, Paul Kroupa and Morrie Campbell used airfoil canopies, which acted as substitute sails or wings to sweep them towards the North Island. They flew from Nelson to Perano Head on Arapawa Island and timed their jump at 10.08 a.m. from 4,900 metres (16,000 feet). Prospects looked good as their airfoil canopies picked up strength from the 30-knot northerly wind, and they began to glide over the calm sea. All four parachutists were clad in wet suits in case the attempt failed and their jump was monitored by boats and by two light aircraft.

Initial progress was good as they glided at about 70 kilometres/hour towards Ohau Point on the Wellington coast, about 22

kilometres away. But as their goal loomed ahead the four parachutists slowed and began drifting northwards. Their momentum dropped and they all landed in the water only 6 kilometres from Ohau Point. A helicopter picked up the four, but they had to leave their $5,500-worth of parachute gear in the strait. "Operation Island Hop" had failed, but the four parachutists remained philosophical about failure and its cost. Their comment before they set off was, "We're making the crossing for the hell of it."

Their comment after ... "There's no business like show business"

Although aerial crossings of Cook Strait have attracted attention and perhaps stolen some of the glamour attached to unusual feats, public interest has also been captured by surface crossings — swims in particular.

The swimming of Cook Strait has perhaps lost some of its magical qualities in recent years. More than 100 attempts have been made on the strait since 1963, of which slightly more than one in ten have succeeded. Maoris claim some early successes in swimming the strait, notably in the case of the frustrated wife Hine Poupou, who is reputed to have swum from Kapiti to D'Urville (see Chapter II). Another story has it that Te Rauparaha once had a man thrown overboard from his canoe in mid-strait and that he swam to shore, but like many stories regarding the great chief it may have suffered in the telling by Europeans who saw Te Rauparaha in negative terms.

The first European to swim the strait was Barrie Devenport who did so on 20 November 1963. He crossed to the South

An exhausted Barrie Devenport clings to the rocks of the South Island in November 1962 and gives a tired wave to signal the fact that he has just made world swimming history. Final pacers, Ian Greenwood and Jim Cornish, share his moment of exultation. *"Evening Post"*

Island in 11 hours 13 minutes. Two-and-a-half months later the feat was repeated by Keith Hancox in nine hours 34 minutes — a record which stood until Napier's John Coutts lowered it by 10 minutes in 1977. For 27-year-old Devenport it was a particularly satisfying swim. Nine months earlier his attempted crossing had failed an agonising 1,100 metres from the finish.

Even on his second attempt it seemed a touch-and-go effort. With less than 50 metres to shore, Devenport suddenly turned onto his back with his legs kicking feebly. Yells and screams from his supporters in the boats surrounding him made him look around.

"Get cracking, Barrie," someone shouted and, sluggishly, without apearing to understand what was going on, he rolled over again and started swimming for the rocks of the South Island coast. Prime Minister (later Sir) Keith Holyoake was attending a Government caucus meeting, but had left instructions that should Devenport land while caucus was still in session he was to be informed. Immediately he heard the news he sent the following telegram:

> Well done Barrie. A great swim and a wonderful achievement. Heartiest congratulations on coming back after your previous plucky effort to win honour as the first man to swim Cook Strait. It is a reward you richly deserve for your determination and an epic of sporting endeavour which all New Zealanders will admire and applaud. Warmest regards.

The strait was to wait another 11 years for a female conqueror. In February 1975 American marathon swimmer Lynne Cox completed the 22.2-kilometre course in 12 hours three minutes. Because of the swell and the rocks, her pilot, Johnny Cataldo, was unable to take his dinghy in the last few metres to pick her up after she had landed on the South Island. He yelled at her to swim over, but Lynne, who had just endured numbing cold, seasickening swells and rough waves, joked with a smile on her face, "I don't know how to swim".

Three years later 15-year-old Wellingtonian Meda McKenzie became the first New Zealand woman to swim the strait. She also broke the women's record, lowering it to 11 hours 22 minutes. Making the attempt with her was Aucklander Sandra Blewett, who had to be pulled exhausted from the water 3 kilometres from her destination and taken to hospital. It was her third failure. Two weeks later Meda McKenzie became the first person to swim the strait both ways when she crossed from south to north. Her mother, herself a former long-distance swimmer, commented: "I knew she had the ability, courage and build to make it."

One year earlier, the first south-north crossing had been done by 30-year-old Aucklander Perry Cameron in 9 hours 36 minutes, only two minutes outside the north-south record, then held by Keith Hancox. Three previous south-north attempts by Cameron had been thwarted by unpredictable tides. After his success, he was asked what he had thought during the swim:

There were three things that constantly ran through my mind. One, I am tired. Two, I am cold. Three, I am hungry. The tiredness applies from almost the first

Meda McKenzie, the Wellington girl who conquered Cook Strait on several swims. *"Evening Post"*

Sheryl McLay, who swam the strait in 1982, setting a new women's record. *Daphne McLay*

hour. You are aware that you are making a physical effort. The three kept running through my mind like a refrain.

John Coutts followed up his record-breaking 1977 swim with a phenomenal 6-hour 46-minute crossing from south to north in 1978. Early in 1980, a 17-year-old Dunedin girl, Caroline Wordsworth, produced an equally astonishing performance to lower the women's record to 7 hours 15 minutes, also swimming south-north. It was the third time

in a month the women's record had been smashed. Earlier Rhonda Smidt, a Napier school girl, had made an 8-hour 56-minute crossing, to be followed three weeks later by 18-year-old Auckland hairdresser Belinda Shields in 8 hours 32 minutes. Then came Caroline Wordsworth to beat the lot. All these women swam from south to north.

Coutts' time of 6 hours 46 minutes was well and truly broken on 1 February 1981 by veteran Australian marathon swimmer John Korrey. Korrey entered the water at 1.18

p.m. at Perano Head and had "never been so cold for the first three hours". Yet when he beat the neap tides finally to land between Ohau Point and Cape Terawhiti, it was only 6.55 p.m. — an astonishing swim of 5 hours 27 minutes, which lowered Coutts' time by over an hour. Korrey, who had turned 37 the day previous, was accompanied by Coutts for much of the way. Later, while degreasing aboard the boat after his swim, he heard of the infamous "underarm bowl" ordered that day by Australian cricket captain Greg Chappell in the match against New Zealand. Korrey took the opportunity to praise the sportsmanship of Coutts by remarking: "He's a little different to Greg Chappell in the sportsmanship stakes. He was with me all the way."

Korrey's breaking of the men's record was followed by two lowerings of the women's record in 1982. On 17 January, 21-year-old Wainuiomata swimmer Sheryl McLay swam from Perano Head to the North Island in 6 hours 59 minutes — 16 minutes under the previous record. Sheryl, an economics graduate and trainee teacher, said the hardest part of the swim came in the middle of the strait. "I wouldn't say any of it was easy, but the first bit was comfortable swimming and the first couple of hours passed really quickly. But right out in the middle it got a bit rough, with big waves. That was the hardest part. Then I started to get really tired and wondered what I was doing there."

Three weeks later, on 14 February 1982, 16-year-old Karen Bisley of Stokes Valley took the record from Sheryl McLay in an amazing swim of 6 hours 46 minutes. Her time equalled the former men's record set by

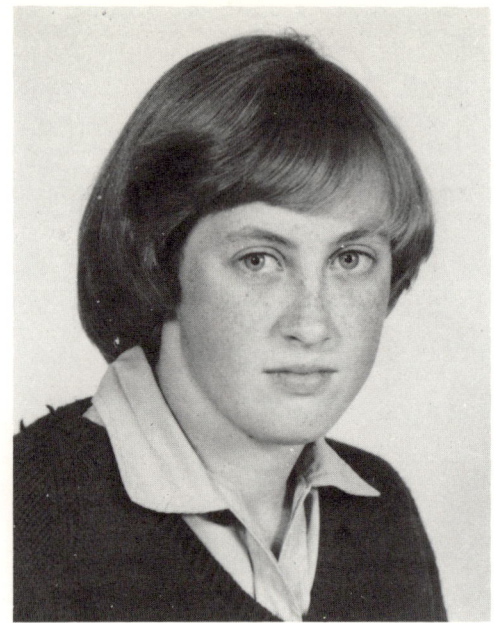

In February 1982 the women's record for crossing Cook Strait was broken yet again, this time by Karen Bisley. *Annette Bisley*

John Coutts in 1977. Conditions were fairly difficult, according to her pilot-boat skipper, with strong tides and rough seas in the middle of the strait. During the swims former Wellington breaststroke champion Alan McLay accompanied both his daughter Sheryl and Karen Bisley on a surf ski.

Skiing crossings began much earlier. Three members of the Wellington Water Ski Club were towed from Makara Beach to a spot about 3 kilometres south of The Brothers rocks on 17 January 1963. The three — 18-year-olds Wayne Davidson and Gordon Hanna and 23-year-old Michael Taylor — were each on a single ski and were towed behind two boats. The three were supposed to be four. Ski club secretary Mrs Val Hansen also made a start from Makara beach, but when the group neared The Brothers lighthouse she hit a 3-metre wave and became airborne. Val's trip ended in the safety of one of the boats.

The first surface crossings of Cook Strait were canoe trips made by Maori settlers. The first European canoeists to make the crossing were the brothers G. and J. Park, who in 1890 rowed from Mana Island to Queen Charlotte Sound, *en route* to Dunedin. They used two 4.2-metre canoes. Six years later a solo crossing was made by a 16-year-old boy, H. Shearman. He took his 3.6-metre canoe from Mana Island to Cape Koamaru on Arapawa Island. A double crossing was completed in 1953-54 by Wanganui tunneller George Hutchinson who used an auxiliary sail on his canoe to journey from Petone to Tory Channel and then back to Kapiti Island.

Mr Hutchinson took 25 hours to row his 4.1-metre canoe *Sea Fever* from the mouth of the Hutt River to a whaling station in the Tory Channel on 30-31 December. After resting and holidaying in the Marlborough Sounds he made the return crossing from Cape Jackson to Kapiti Island in 26 hours on 7-8 January. After sheltering at the island during the night he was met by the launch *Enterprise* and told that there had been some concern for his safety. He allowed the launch to throw him a line and he was towed through the Waikanae River mouth just as the Queen and Prince Philip were landing at nearby Paraparaumu.

The first skiff (a light rowing or sculling boat) crossing was done on Saturday 14 March 1981 by 27-year-old John Argue, as a sponsored effort which raised about $31,000 each for the Outward Bound organisation and the Petone Rowing Club. His route was from the Outward Bound quarters at Anakiwa, deep in the sounds, across the strait, along the coastline, through the harbour entrance to finish at Petone beach, a distance of over 90 kilometres. John took his skiff across on the ferry and he was supported by the fishing boat *Dove*, which was equipped with radio, and his father Peter in the Petone Rowing Club's runabout.

In the account of the trip written later by Mr Peter Argue, he described how the sea was particularly choppy coming through the Wellington Heads and how John stopped to change his spray-soaked shirt. The harbour pilot hove to and found it hard to believe the skiff had come from the South Island. The crew of the pilot boat gave him a big cheer, which was a boost to his morale at a time when he faced the final 15 kilometres against a strong northerly wind.

"What amazed everyone was the energy John found somewhere to really step up the pace on that final stretch," Mr Argue wrote. "There were boats circling around with big cameras and the Petone crews were really putting on a show. Then as we neared the beach there were excited women pulling up their skirts and wading out with Phyllis [John's mother] almost up to her waist in water to greet John. Yes, he had made it."

Cook Strait crossings by skiff, canoe, water ski and surf ski have aroused public interest

The Wellington yacht *Argo*, which went missing with the loss of all hands during the 1951 Wellington-to-Lyttelton yacht race. *Alexander Turnbull Library*

from time to time, but there is no doubt that yachting attracts the greatest sporting fervour. Unfortunately, the history of yacht racing across Cook Strait is marred by one of the worst yachting tragedies to occur in New Zealand.

On 23 January 1951, 20 yachts set sail from Clyde Quay in Wellington to race to Lyttelton. The race was a special event to com-memorate the Canterbury Centennial and the organisers were offering a first prize of £100. The yachts were expected to take about 36 hours to cover the course. A moderate northerly was blowing as they set off at 10 a.m., but within 40 minutes the *Restless* snapped a mast while still in the harbour. A southerly gale sprang up which battered the boats in the strait and off the Kaikoura coast.

The Nelson sloop *Tawhiri* managed to finish in 69 hours to claim first prize, which completed an amazing double. She had won the Lyttelton-Wellington race on the other occasion it was run, in 1940.

But behind *Tawhiri* was a scene of disaster. *Husky* of Nelson and *Argo* of Wellington were both lost with all hands, a total of 10 people. Pieces of wreckage were found in Cook Strait and were identified as being from *Husky*. A massive sea and air search was mounted for *Argo* and, 12 days after the start of the race, weak signals were picked up off the East Cape of the North Island, but these were never identified as coming from *Argo* and the search found nothing. Later, a lifebuoy from *Argo* was found in Palliser Bay. Another yacht, *Aurora*, was also missing for a time, but she eventually turned up safe and sound and limped into Wellington on 3 February. None of the other yachts finished the race. The six-man crew of *Astral* had a close shave when their yacht was dismasted, but they were saved by the trawler *Tawera*.

Yacht racing across the strait has been popular for decades. The Royal Port Nicholson Yacht Club, for example, celebrated its centennial in the 1982-83 sailing season. Probably the best known, and certainly the most popular, local race is the Cook Strait race. This is held on the weekend before Christmas, between Wellington and the old whaling station in Tory Channel, under the joint auspices of the R.P.N.Y.C. and Evans Bay Yacht Club. The race usually attracts between 40 to 50 boats and is often used as a means of getting across to the Marlborough Sounds for some summer-holiday fun cruising. The Cook Strait race is certainly "the" race of the year and its attraction is partly due to the fact that anyone and everyone enters. Six-metre boats with four crew can be seen tacking alongside 20-metre-plus ocean racers with a dozen crew working to tight dicipline. There is little safety hazard involved in having smaller craft in mid-strait simply because there are so many boats around to help if needed.

The race is normally held in three divisions, with the smaller and therefore slower yachts getting an earlier start. Starting times differ every year because the aim is to reach the Tory Channel entrance with a favourable tide. This can mean starting off in the early hours of the morning. It also determines finishing times (an important factor, since the time and the weather influence the partying spirit of the competitors when they reach the whaling station).

As befits a race with a long history, there are many stories to tell about the Cook Strait race. Often boats have become becalmed and hung around in the harbour for hours before making a start. On one well-remembered occasion in the late 1960s Neville Dimock in the 13-metre sloop *Caprice* had the finishing line in sight and sent a telegram home announcing that the race was in the bag. Much to his chagrin, the 11-metre *Kotuku*, under Jim Toomer, handled the tides and wind better at the entrance to Tory Channel and slipped in first. The episode provided Neville's yachtie mates with much ammunition for ribbing.

Earlier in the season there is The Brothers race, normally held in November, in which international offshore racing yachts race from Wellington, around The Brothers rocks and back. These are Southern Cross-type racers in the 10-metre-plus class with crews of between six and eight intent on serious racing. These would be mainly Wellington-based boats, but a wider entry is normally attracted to the Wellington-Nelson race, run by the Evans Bay Yacht Club on the Wellington Anniversary holiday weekend in January, in conjunction with the Nelson Yacht Club. This race was first held in 1970 with line honours going to Phil Hartley's *Camille*, but the handicap honours went to *Crescendo*, skippered by Brian Barraclough of Wellington. Four years earlier Brian had completed the Cook Strait Race in his 9-metre sloop *Charmaine*, despite having earlier broken his arm in a harbour championship race. His 15-year-old son Mark took *Charmaine's* tiller while Brian did the navigation and planning. That first Nelson race provided tight finishes, with constant sail changes and tacking duels and only seconds separating some of the leading yachts.

A number of other races are held in and around the strait each year, with most carrying points towards the yearly ocean-racing championship. Among these are the Wellington-Kapiti-Picton race, the Wellington-Ship Cove race, the Kapiti-Chetwode Islands- Ship Cove race and others from Wellington to Port Underwood, Lyttelton and Akaroa. Not all would be on the programme in a given year, but those qualifying for the championship attract a hard core of ocean racers plus one-off entrants interested in only a particular race. The championship works on the principle of adding points collected during the series, then deducting the two worst performances for each yacht.

Ocean racing has boomed only in the past 20 years and its rise has tended to take the spotlight away from the harbour racers. But it is a massive fleet of smaller craft, often trailer-sailers, that provides the bulk of club members with weekend activity around prescribed harbour racing courses. Series are held in both winter and summer.

The ocean-racing boom has sometimes rebounded on itself. The tendency has been for interest to switch from local to international events, such as the Southern Cross series in Sydney. Trials undertaken to pick a regional team for the Southern Cross series are held in Cook Strait and, consequently, the local offshore racing yachts have occasionally suffered from a clash of events.

Although Cook Strait is renowed locally as a fun venue for pleasurable sailing it has also hosted craft of sinister intent. It has provided cover for German minelayers and Japanese submarines — one of which sent a reconnaissance aircraft over the city.

Indeed one German minelayer found it so easy to manoeuvre undetected in the strait that a minefield lay undiscovered for years off the mouth of Wellington harbour. It was set down on the night of 25-26 June 1941 by the captured whale chaser *Adjutant*, which was being employed as a minelaying vessel by the German raider *Komet*. The 3,287-ton *Komet* was one of the German surface raiders which roamed the world, frequently in disguise, picking off Allied shipping. She was armed with six 10-centimetre guns, nine light anti-aircraft guns, six deck torpedo tubes and four more underwater, a seaplane

and a high-speed motor launch.

Twenty-four hours after mining the entrance to Lyttelton Harbour *Komet* sent *Adjutant* to lay a double row of 10 mines off Wellington Heads. Lieutenant Karsten, in charge of *Adjutant*, reported that the harbour was barred by two searchlights located between Palmer Head and Pencarrow Head. One acted as a constant barrier of light, while the other made irregular sweeps of the sea.

Adjutant made plans to lay the minefield at her full speed of 14 knots (26 kilometres/hour) and cover her getaway with a smoke screen. At 11.12 p.m. those at Baring Head station challenged the *Adjutant*. She did not reply. They then made a morse signal to the operator of the searchlight, which swept over *Adjutant* four times. She was laying her fourth mine when picked out by the beam. Immediately, at 11.21, she set up the smoke screen, doubled back on her course and laid the second row of mines as she prepared to run. The last mine was laid at 11.28 p.m. The smoke was quelled at 11.30 and a course was set for Baring Head. The searchlight continued to sweep the smoke screen which separated *Adjutant* from the Wellington patrol boats. Shortly after passing Baring Head *Adjutant* turned landward and was obscured from the searchlight beams.

Lieutenant Karsten described how three shore searchlights were switched on and how four patrol boats and one minesweeper began looking for the German intruder. After rounding Baring Head, he recorded:

. . . all speed is made to get away from the coast. At 0100 on 26 June, the alarm is

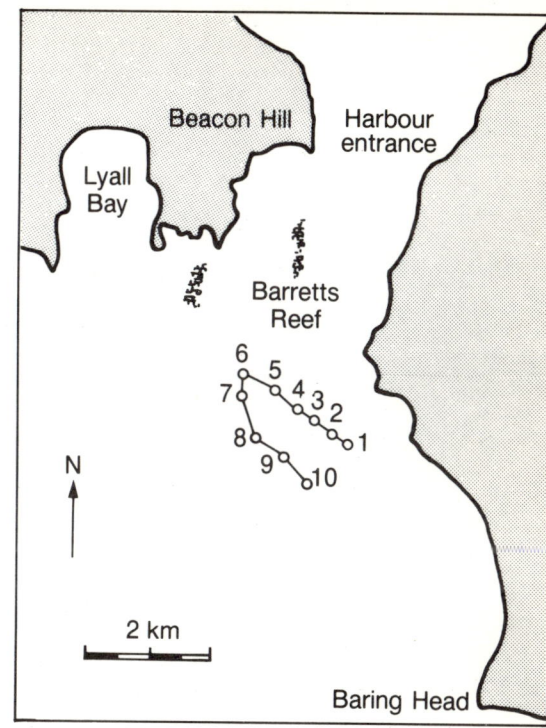

Location of minefield

over. *Adjutant* sets course 90 deg. [east] at 0130 and proceeds at 12 knots. At 0400 a halt had to be made because of engine trouble. At this stage the ship is about 70 miles from Wellington. Considerable W/T traffic can be heard between New Zealand airfields and naval bases. We can expect an organised search. During the day, the vessel proceeds with her engine knocking badly. An unsuccessful attempt is made during the night of 27 June to eliminate the trouble. The rest of the voyage has to be made under emergency sail, or using medium and low-pressure cylinders; consequently the maximum possible speed is eight to nine knots ... Ship 45 [*Komet*] comes in sight at 0730 on 1 July.

Adjutant was of no further use and was sunk by *Komet* north-east of the Chatham Islands. The mines she had laid were at depths of between 26 and 33 metres, but no shipping was lost because of them — they were of the magnetic type and were probably defective. This was undoubtedly a lucky escape because the mines were never picked up by the Wellington minesweepers and thousands of ships passed over the area before the field's presence was disclosed by captured German documents after the war.

This was not the first time a German minelayer had been in the Cook Strait area. In June 1917 the raider *Wolf* laid 25 mines off Farewell Spit. Seventeen were swept up by fishing trawlers, but on 18 September 1917 the steamer *Port Kembla* sank after being rocked by a massive explosion. The cause was thought to be a mine.

During World War II New Zealand waters were protected from mines by minesweeping flotillas. Several anti-submarine defences were based at Wellington, including anti-torpedo nets and booms. An anti-submarine training school was set up at Petone. However, Wellington was taken by surprise by the visit of the Japanese submarine *1-25* in March 1942.

The *1-25* sailed from Kwajalein in the Marshall Islands for her Pacific voyage on 8 February. She was equipped with a small

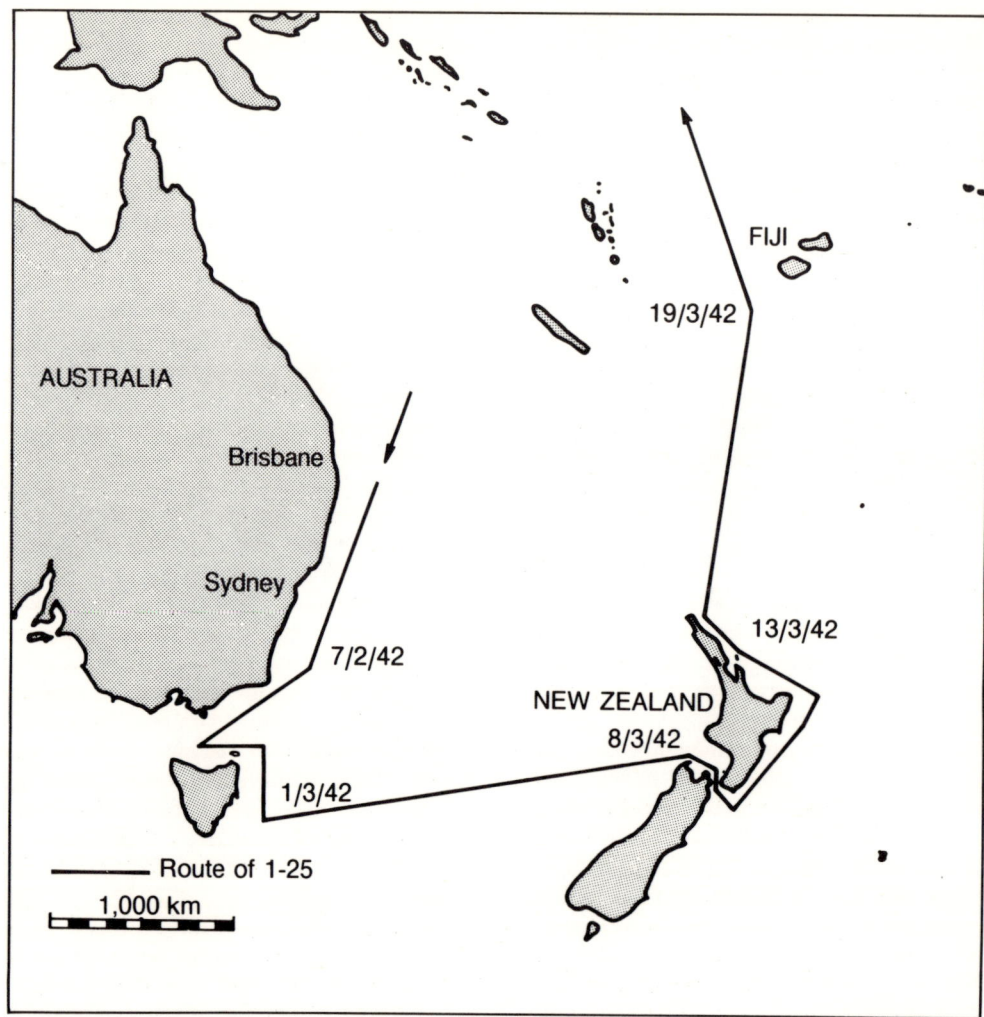

The route taken by the Japanese submarine *1-25* on its cruise into New Zealand waters in 1942
S.D. Waters, the Royal New Zealand Navy / War History Branch, Department of Internal Affairs

seaplane driven by a single pilot. The seaplane had an operating speed of 90 knots (166.5 kilometres/hour), could stay in the air for three hours and was housed in a hangar on the submarine's deck. Under Commander Masuru Obiga, the submarine cruised down the Australian coast, sending its aircraft on early morning reconnaissance flights over Sydney, Melbourne and Hobart. *I-25* then crossed the Tasman Sea and entered Cook Strait.

The seaplane made a pre-dawn flight over Wellington on 8 March. Neither the submarine nor its aircraft were spotted locally. Doubtful radio direction-finding bearings of a Japanese unit were obtained at 11 p.m. the next day, placing it some 650 kilometres west of North Cape. From Cook Strait *I-25* carried on up the east coast of the North Island and sent its seaplane over the Hauraki Gulf before heading off for Fiji and then on to its home base. No attempt was made to molest shipping in New Zealand waters.

There were other incidents which suggest that enemy submarine activity occasionally took place in New Zealand waters. On 18 June 1942 the interisland ferry *Rangatira* was making a daylight passage from Lyttelton to Wellington and reported passing an object resembling a small submarine in dense fog about 23 kilometres off Godley Head. A searching aircraft later sighted a log about 5 kilometres south of the reported position, but less than 48 hours later HMNZS *Futurist* reported sighting a suspicious object 10 kilometres off Island Bay, Wellington. All Wellington's coastal batteries were ordered to "stand to". For several nights the port was closed to traffic. Radar contacts were reported, but aircraft sweeps revealed nothing.

It appears certain that a Japanese submarine was in Cook Strait in February 1943. An unidentified radar contact was picked up in the very early hours of the morning off Cape Turakirae at the mouth of Palliser Bay. Four shore stations obtained radio direction-finding fixes. Four aircraft from Nelson made a sweep, but they found only a long streak of oil. The same afternoon a shore battery at the entrance to Pelorus Sound reported seeing a "black speck" about 25 kilometres into the strait. Another radar contact was made south of Palliser Bay. Eventually, the submarine was believed to have left the strait and headed towards Wanganui.

On 3 November the same year radar contacts were reported off Cape Campbell. The interisland steamers were warned to keep 8 kilometres outside their normal tracks and to zig-zag in the vicinity of the cape. One of the motor launches sent to investigate spotted an object and dropped depth charges, but to no avail. Then at 2 a.m. on 1 March 1944 a gun crew on the northbound ferry *Rangatira* reported seeing a torpedo pass close astern. Sailings were suspended while searches were made. About the same time an aircraft spotted what looked like a submarine off Kaikoura. On 8 March an anti-submarine trawler made an asdic contact 18 kilometres south of Pencarrow Head and dropped depth charges, again without result. It was never known whether a submarine had been prowling or whether the "sightings" were the result of jittery wartime nerves.

Besides playing host to the enemy raider, Cook Strait has been a refuge in peacetime for characters of an unsavoury nature. Chief among these was the pirate of sorts, Captain William Henry (Bully) Hayes.

Hayes, so the story goes, had only one ear. The other was cut off when fellow players caught him cheating at poker and lopped off a lobe in a case of quick Californian justice. Hayes was born in Cleveland, Ohio, in 1822 and died in 1877 at the end of a piece of iron swung brutally by an outraged seaman.

He was the son of one Henry Hayes, a liquor saloon owner, and worked for his father on the banks of Lake Erie until around the age of 18. As an adult he was over 180 centimetres tall, thickly built and had a big reddish-brown beard. It appears he left his home around the time of the California gold rush and worked as a crewman on vessels taking excited speculators from the American east coast.

By around 1855 he had command of his first ship, *Ontranto*, which he traded out of Chinese ports. He also was known to have packed Chinese "coolies" aboard and run them to Singapore. The year 1857 found him running another vessel on the Australian coast. Near Adelaide that year he met and married a widow, a woman called Amelia. By this time Hayes had shown his ability to skip paying bills, but in Adelaide creditors caught up with him and he faced bankruptcy. But despite his reputation as something of a confidence trickster, Hayes, after losing one vessel to the people who had a mortgage over it, took over as master of a ship sailing from Melbourne to Vancouver.

Once back in his old port of San Francisco

Hayes did another con-job and purchased an old rundown vessel called *Ellenita*. It sank off Samoa, and while many of the passengers were put on a life raft they were never to be seen again. Hayes and some other passengers managed to reach Samoa in the ship's boat. From there he went on to Australia and eventually ended up on the Otago goldfields as a member of the artistic troupe called "The Buckingham Family Entertainers". And in Arrowtown he opened the Prince of Wales Hotel. Oddly, he also married Rosa Buckingham — "bigamist" later came to be added to Haye's credits.

Hayes developed a scheme to take the entertainers off to China, which involved getting hold of a ship. June 1864 found him in command of the 70-ton *Black Diamond* which he bought with a mortgage from a Sydney firm. He told them he was taking his cargo of coal to Bombay, India, but instead set course for Cook Strait, hoping to reach Nelson and to elude the people who put up the money. On board with him was his wife, 20-year-old Rosa, their 13-month-old daughter Adelaida Eudora, Rosa's 23-year-old brother George Buckingham and 15-year-old maidservant Mary Cowley, in addition to the crew.

Crossing the Tasman, Hayes ran into a storm and, on 4 July, he arrived in Auckland with his ship damaged. Local businessmen extended him credit against his cargo of coal, but when the coal did not fetch nearly enough to pay back the loan, Hayes skipped town on *Black Diamond*, much to the annoyance of those who lent him money. He sailed for Cook Strait and reached Croisilles Bay, up the coast from Nelson, where he

planned to cut firewood and load it as ballast for the trip to China. While the crew worked on the wood and caulking the ship's seams, Hayes borrowed a small sailing yacht from a local settler and, with Rosa, the baby, Buckingham and the maid, he set sail into the strait, bound for Nelson.

About 2 kilometres offshore a squall suddenly came up, capsizing the vessel. The maid and Buckingham went down with the boat.

"Captain Hayes, who is a large, powerful man and a splendid swimmer," a Nelson newspaper later related, "struck out shorewards, supporting himself on two oars, and holding up his wife with one hand and his child by the other. In this way he swam for the shore, slowly and laboriously, being embarrassed by the oars, which, being under water, impeded his progress."

The baby died, but Hayes struggled on with Rosa.

"He endeavoured to support her on his shoulder, and after struggling on for some time longer he felt her lose hold, but he still held up her head by the hair, but soon after on turning round found that she too was dead."

Only the body of the baby was found.

The event brought attention to *Black Diamond* in both Auckland and Sydney. Sydney bailiffs quickly arrived in Nelson and, with the help of six whalers sworn in as special constables, they seized the ship in Croisilles Harbour.

Hayes, without a ship yet again, left Cook Strait and went on to Lyttelton and joined up with the rest of the Buckinghams. The troupe sailed out for Akaroa as passengers on a

small 10-ton cutter, *Wave*. There Hayes set his eyes on a 16-year-old Irish girl, Helen Murray, whom he attracted onto the cutter with stories of fame and fortune as a member of the acting troupe in China.

What happened next was never entirely clear, but at some stage Hayes made off with the boat, the troupe and young Helen Murray. The *Marlborough Times* claimed Hayes abducted the girl, because, after leaving Akaroa, it was clear *Wave* was sailing north and not to Lyttelton as she thought.

When Hayes made no progress with his approaches towards the girl she was left out on the deck of the cutter as it sailed north in unpleasant weather towards Cook Strait. They arrived in Tory Channel where Hayes made a great effort to get the girl to his cabin.

"That night," the newspaper report said, "Hayes lost all command of himself and determined that the girl should go below or he would put her ashore. He dragged her most violently and eventually lifted her in a boat to take her ashore after tearing off all her clothes."

Eventually young Helen Murray escaped and got to Picton where she reported the incidents to the local Justices of the Peace. Attempts were made to arrest Hayes, but he got away.

Less than a month later Hayes showed up on the other side of the strait, in Wellington, the sole owner of a 71-ton schooner, *Shamrock*. No-one knows where the money came from to buy the vessel, which he used for trading in the Pacific. In March 1866 he was off-loading passengers from the Wanganui River bar, despite a warning that the area was too rough for the small boat he was using. Four people drowned.

Hayes went on to attract the attention of the British, French and United States Governments with his personal blend of fraud, piracy, bad luck and downright crime. His name became associated with the trade of "blackbirding", the semi-slavery of Solomon Islanders taken, some times willingly, to the sugar-cane fields of Queensland. At the age of 45 he was the victim of a mutiny on board his boat *Lotus* just out of Jaluit in the Marshall Islands. He went down to his cabin to get a gun to shoot the ship's cook and when he came up, the cook, variously described as a Dutchman, a Norwegian or a Chinese, used an iron bar to crush in the skull of Bully Hayes.

Cook Strait has witnessed much violence and murder, to which Bully Hayes contributed his share. In more recent times the strait played its own unbelievable part in the discovery and solving of a tragic murder case.

On 7 May 1938 a suitcase was found on a crossbeam of Picton Wharf. Constable W.J. Harper of Picton police dragged the suitcase onto the wharf and saw a human hand protruding from it. The suitcase was taken to Picton Morgue where Detective Sergeant Bill McLennan opened it to find the trunk and arms of a man. The head and legs were missing. The trunk was clothed in two shirts, a collar and tie, a singlet, waistcoat, dark tweed jacket, woollen scarf and long underpants cut off at the thigh. Several cuts were visible in the clothing and the torso itself showed three knife wounds in the left breast and one on the right forearm. In a jacket pocket was an unemployment book in the name of E. Armstrong, 20 Hinau Road, Wellington.

Police established that the body was that of 55-year-old Edward Norman Armstrong, of Wellington's Hataitai suburb. His wife had informed the police that he was missing — he had not been home when she returned at 3 p.m. on Friday 6 May from her teaching job at Clyde Quay School. That morning he had missed an appointment with the Wellington Placement (Employment) Office, although he had still been at home when she left for work at 8.30 a.m.

The Armstrongs had two sons, Douglas, 21, a railways apprentice, and Bill, 19, a student teacher. The police learned that Douglas was also missing. When Mrs Armstrong returned home on the Friday she found a note from him mentioning a trip to Auckland and the possibility of a job for his father. Sub-Inspector John Carroll led enquiries and located a taxi driver who had picked up a young man with luggage from Hinau Road on the Friday afternoon and taken him to to the terminal of the Picton ferry, *Tamahine*.

The taxi driver recalled that the passenger had two suitcases which were too heavy for the driver to lift. He was told they contained venison meat. At *Tamahine's* gangway the bags were lifted out, leaving a trail of blood on the mat. The mat was later handed to the police. On the following Thursday, during a search of the area where the first suitcase was found, a diver located another on the seabed at a depth of about 12 metres. This contained the remainder of the body — the head and legs. Nine days after Mr Armstrong's disappearance, his remains were identified by his wife. In the meantime, Douglas, the missing son, was the subject of an intensive police search. Unknown to the police, he had already confessed to the murder in a poignant letter to his mother. He had stayed at Wellington's Hotel Waterloo under the name of J. Campbell before leaving on the Monday-night express train for Auckland.

At 9.30 a.m. on the Tuesday he was apprehended leaving the train by acting Detective E.N. Grace. Asked if he was Armstrong he said, "Yes. It's all a tragic mistake. You'll understand better when you know. I'll go with you."

Armstrong's story was particularly sad. The atmosphere in the home had never been happy, apart from a few months when his father lived in Australia. He had often quarrelled with his father, ". . . not for my own sake, but for my mother's".

On the day of the murder Douglas Armstrong had left the house at the usual time, but instead of going to work he had wandered around town until he was sure his mother had left. Then he returned to try to persuade his father to go away again. He did not know his mother had made the same appeal, unsuccessfully, the night before. Mr Armstrong lost his temper and threatened to kill his son. He raised the boot-black brush he had in his hand and at that moment Douglas went berserk, laying into his father with his fists.

He told the police he did not want to say anything more about that part of the crime, but described the necessity of getting rid of the body before his mother found it:

I cut up the body with a skinning knife I usually went out deer-stalking with, and also an ordinary tenon-saw which I got from under the house. I divided the remainder of the body into those two suitcases. I put the trunk with the decapitation of the head in one suitcase, and the head and the legs in the other. I was too upset to do anything to the clothing.

His trial lasted three days and he was found guilty of manslaughter. Armstrong was sentenced to 10 years' imprisonment and was still serving his sentence when his mother died. He was released after seven years and left New Zealand.

There was a bizarre irony to the case. Edward Armstrong died from internal haemorrhaging from stab wounds, but those wounds did more than cause his death — they also made certain his body would be found. Air escaping from his lungs filled his chest cavity which made the suitcase buoyant and it floated to the surface. Without the stab wounds, the body of Edward Armstrong may have remained hidden by the sea forever.

Another intriguing mystery about the very discovery of the strait itself remains unsolved. For many years Wellington's National Museum displayed an iron helmet thought to have been dredged off the seabed in Wellington harbour at the turn of this century. It was an unusual helmet to be found in New Zealand, and when it became known as the "Spanish helmet" all sorts of stories arose which suggested, with no supporting evidence other than the one artefact, the

Spaniards visited New Zealand before Abel Tasman arrived on the coast in 1642. Some writers claimed Spaniards visited New Zealand in the first half of the 16th Century.

The renowned international historian, Professor J.C. Beaglehole of Wellington's Victoria University, lightly dismissed the growing school of writers who saw significance in the so-called Spanish helmet: "One piece of head-gear does not make a discovery."

When we approached the National Museum about the helmet, director Dr J.C. Yaldwyn confirmed they held the item and was quite happy to have it photographed. But in a letter he made several points:

> To start with, it is not Spanish — all our identifications over the years indicate that it is a neutral type of European helmet made in the 16th Century, quite possibly in Italy. They were manufactured in large numbers for the extensive warfare going on throughout Europe in this period . . .
>
> The complete lack of records about this helmet and the stories that were building up about it led to its removal from display many years ago.

Of course, as a scientist, Dr Yaldwyn is careful not to dismiss completely the possibility that a Spanish head could have worn the helmet and that a Spaniard did make it to New Zealand. While this sounds extremely unlikely, it is not impossible.

As early as 1526 the ship *San Lesmes* under Francisco de Hozes disappeared shortly after sailing through the Straits of Magellan while with a fleet of four ships bound for Asia. Twelve vessels are known to have disap-

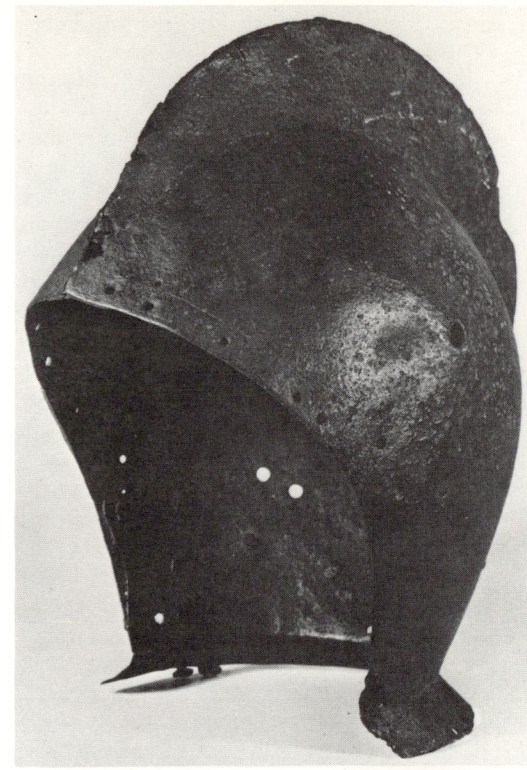

A helmet, probably of Italian origin, which was dredged up from the Wellington harbour floor. *National Museum*

peared in the Pacific and there is evidence that Spaniards settled among some Micronesian islanders. There is even some suggestion that Spaniards arrived in Hawaii before Captain Cook ever "discovered" the place. But it is *San Lesmes* that writers have constantly looked to for support of a theory of Spanish contact with New Zealand. That idea suffered somewhat with the discovery in 1929 of four Spanish cannons on the atoll of Amanu (near the French nuclear forward base Hao in the Tuamotus) believed to have come from *San Lesmes*. But all was not completely lost — the theorists came up with a new line: de Hozes and some of his men survived to sail on to some of the main islands in Polynesia, including New Zealand.

Support for Spanish contact rests on three points: the helmet, comments of early European visitors to New Zealand and the "Tamil Bell".

The bell was found in Whangarei in the 1830s, being used by Maoris as a cooking pot. They did not know where it had come from, but it was discovered to carry Tamil writing from Southern India. As no-one had seriously advanced the notion of Indian explorers, the alternative explanation offered was that it came on a Spanish ship, a number of which had called at India at various times.

The New Zealand Company scientist Dr Ernst Dieffenbach wrote last century that there can "scarcely be any doubt" that New Zealand was visited by Spaniards before Tasman. His evidence was that the Maori word for dog, *kuri*, was like the Spanish word for dog, *perro*. We feel he was barking up the wrong tree.

Yet how did the "Spanish helmet" (which we have seen is probably Italian) arrive on the floor of Wellington Harbour? We will never know, but there are certainly alternatives to the theory that a careless Spanish sailor dropped it into the water. Perhaps an excited tourist returning home to Wellington from a trip to Europe accidently let it fall into the sea.

Whatever the true nature of its discovery, Cook Strait is more than a geographical landmark — events connected with the strait have provided land marks in New Zealand's history. The strait has dominated patterns of Maori and European settlement and trade, it has provided its own playful pilot for travellers in the form of dolphin Pelorus Jack and it has seen the commercial destruction of the whales which once frequented its waters and helped to put New Zealand on the world map. The birth and decline of Cook Strait shipping services and the development of the transport links that are favoured today have provided this country with historic milestones. And the shipwrecking tragedies that have occurred are a reminder to New Zealanders that the stretch of often wild water which divides their nation is not to be taken lightly.

Appendix

Fast passages by ships in the
Wellington-Lyttelton Steamer Express Service

Date	Ship	Time
3 October 1901	*Rotomahana*	10 hours 43 minutes
15 December 1905	*Maheno*	9 hours 11 minutes
27 December 1907	*Maori*	8 hours 23 minutes
24 December 1924	*Wahine*	8 hours 21 minutes
5 September 1933	*Rangatira*	8 hours 26 minutes
23 December 1937	*Rangatira*	8 hours 22 minutes
23 December 1938	*Rangatira*	8 hours 51 minutes
6 April 1939	*Rangatira*	8 hours 8 minutes
23 December 1960	*Hinemoa*	9 hours 1 minute
20 January 1961	*Hinemoa*	8 hours 51 minutes
21 December 1962	*Hinemoa*	9 hours 3 minutes

Bibliography

Adkin, G.L., *The Great Harbour of Tara*, Whitcombe and Tombs, Wellington, 1959.

Alpers, A.A., *A Book of Dolphins*, John Murray Ltd., Wellington, 1960.

Baldwin, O., *Story of New Zealand's French Pass and D'Urville Island*, Field Publishing, Plimmerton, 1979.

Banks, J., *The "Endeavour" Journal of Joseph Banks* (ed. J.C. Beaglehole), Angus and Robertson, Sydney, 1963.

Barratt, G., *Bellingshausen, a visit to New Zealand 1820*, The Dunmore Press, Palmerston North, 1979.

Beaglehole, J.C., *The Discovery of New Zealand*, Wellington, 1939.

Beaglehole, J.C., *The Journals of Captain James Cook on his Voyages of Discovery: The Voyage of the "Endeavour"*, Hakluyt, Cambridge, 1955.

Beaglehole, J.C., *The Journals of Captain James Cook on his Voyages of Discovery: The Voyage of the "Resolution" and "Adventure"*, Hakluyt, Cambridge, 1961.

Bellwood, P., *The Polynesians*, Thames and Hudson, London, 1978.

Begg, A.C., & Begg, N.C., *James Cook in New Zealand*, Government Printer, Wellington, 1969.

Best, E., *The Land of Tara and they who settled it*, Polynesian Society, New Plymouth 1919.

Bloomfield, P., *Edward Gibbon Wakefield*, Longman, London, 1961.

Buck, P.B. *The Coming of the Maori*, Whitcombe and Tombs, Wellington, 1958.

Buick, T.L., *Old Marlborough*, Palmerston North, 1900.

Bullen, F.T., *The Cruise of the Cachalot*, London, 1906.

Burns, P., *Te Rauparaha, A new perspective*, A.H. & A.W. Reed Ltd, Wellington, 1980.

Brayshaw, N.H., *Whites Bay Telegraph Station, Marlborough Express*, Blenheim, 1966.

Clune, F., *Captain Bully Hayes, Blackbirder and Bigamist*, Angus and Robertson, Sydney, 1970.

Cook, J.H., *Pelorus Jack, A Story of French Pass, Weekly News*, Auckland, 1908.

Cowen, J., *Pelorus Jack*, Whitcombe and Tombs, Wellington, 1912.

Dieffenbach, E., *Travels in New Zealand*, London, 1843.

Earle, A., *Narrative of a Residence in New Zealand*, Oxford 1966.

Eiby, G.A., *Earthquakes*, Heineman, 1980.

Farquhar, I.J., *Union Fleet 1875-1975*, New Zealand Ship and Marine Society, Wellington, 1976.

Field, M., *Aviation Milestones*, INL Print, Taita, 1981.

Finn, G.A., *Chronology of New Zealand from the Time of the Moa*, National Printing Company, Auckland, 1931.

Fleming, C.A., *The Geological History of New Zealand and its Life*, Auckland University Press, Auckland, 1979.

Gabites, J.F., *Climate of Wellington*, New Zealand Meteorological Service, Wellington, 1960.

Gentilli, J., (ed.) *Climates of Australia and New Zealand*, Elsevier Publishing Company, New York, 1971.

Gerard, S., *Strait of Adventure*, A.H. & A.W. Reed Ltd, Wellington, 1938.

Gill, G.H., *Royal Australian Navy 1942-45*, Australian War Memorial.

Grady, D., *Guards of the Sea*, Whitcoulls, Christchurch, 1978.

Heath, R.A., *Hydrographic Aspects of Swimming Cook Strait*, New Zealand Oceanographic Institute, Wellington, 1980.

Heath, R.A., *Circulation and Hydrology off the West Coast of the North Island of New Zealand between Cape Terawhiti and Kawhia Harbour*, New Zealand Oceanographic Institute, Wellington, 1974.

Heath, R.A., *Circulation and Hydrology of Tasman Bay*, New Zealand Oceanographic Institute, Wellington, 1976.

Heath, R.A., *Resonant over-tide across and along Tasman Bay, Estuarine and Coastal Marine Science*, Academic Press Inc., London, 1979.

Heath, R.A., *Semi-diurnal tides in Cook Strait*, New Zealand Journal of Marine and Freshwater Research, Department of Scientific and Industrial Research, Wellington, 1978.

Heath, R.A., *Current measurements derived from trajectories of Cook Strait swimmers*, New Zealand Journal of Marine and Freshwater research, Department of Scientific and Industrial Research, Wellington, 1980.

Hochstetter, F. von., *Geology of New Zealand*, Government Printer, Wellington, 1959.

Kirk, A.A., *Express Steamers of Cook Strait*, A.H. & A.W. Reed Ltd, Wellington, 1967.

Kirk, A.A., *Anchor Ships and Anchor Men*, A.H. & A.W. Reed Ltd, Wellington, 1967.

Kirk, A.A., *Fair Winds and Rough Seas*, A.H. & A.W. Reed., Wellington, 1975.

Knox, J., *The Development of the Cook Strait Ferries (study paper)*, Wellington, 1977.

Lambert, M., and Hartley, J., *The Wahine Disaster*, A.H. & A.W. Reed Ltd., Wellington, 1969.

Langdon, R., *The Lost Caravel*, Pacific Publications, Sydney, 1975.

Latta, M.G., *Interconnection of the North and South Island Electric Power Systems in New Zealand*, Electric Supply Authorities Engineers' Institute, Wellington, 1961.

Lewis K.B., and Carter, L., *Sediments and Faulting on each side of the Rongotai Isthmus*, New Zealand Oceanographic Institute, Wellington, 1976.

Lewis, K.B., and Eade, J.V., *Sedimentation in the Vicinity of the Maui Gasfield*, New Zealand Oceanographic Institute, Wellington, 1974.

Lubbock, B., *Bully Hayes, South Seas Pirate*, Martin Hopkinson Ltd, London, 1931.

Lynch, P.P., *No Remedy for Death*, John Long, 1970.

MacDonald, C.A., *Pages from the Past*, Blenheim, 1933.

McDougall, J.C., *The sea floor in Oteranga Bay, Cook Strait*, New Zealand Oceanographic Institute, Wellington, 1973.

McKnight, D.G., *Benthic Faunas from the Continental Shelf, West Coast, North Island, Kawhia Harbour to Cape Terawhiti*, New Zealand Oceanographic Institute, Wellington, 1974.

McLintock, A.H., (ed.) *An Encyclopaedia of New Zealand*, Government Printer, Wellington, 1966.

McMorran, B., *In view of Kapiti*, Dunmore Press, Palmerston North, 1977.

McNab, R., *The Old Whaling Days*, Whitcombe & Tombs, Wellington, 1913.

Marine Division, *About Lighthouses*, Ministry of Transport, Wellington.

Mason, C & Mason C., *Curtain-Raiser to a Colony*, Whitcombe and Tombs, London, 1962.

Matthews, E.R., *Coastal Sediment Dynamics, Turakirae Head to Eastbourne*, New Zealand Oceanographic Institute, 1980.

Matthews, E.R., "Observations of beach gravel transport, Wellington Harbour entrance," *New Zealand Journal of Geology and Geophysics, Vol. 23, No. 2*, Wellington.

Mulgan, A., *The City of the Strait*, A.H. & A.W. Reed Ltd, Wellington, 1939.

Murray, K.W.J., & Kohorn, R.S. von., *A Cruising Man's Guide to the Marlborough Sounds and Tasman Bay*, Steven Williams Publishing, Wellington, 1979.

Nelson, A.G., *The Story of Pelorus Jack*, Wellington, 1906.

Pacific Islands Year Book, 14th Edition, Pacific Publications, Sydney, 1981.

Pickrill, R.A., *Beach and Nearshore Morphology, Lyall Bay*, New Zealand Oceanographic Institute, Wellington, 1979.

Reed, A.H., & Reed, A.W., *Captain Cook in New Zealand*, A.H. & A.W. Reed Ltd, Wellington, 1951.

Rendel, D., *Civil Aviation in New Zealand*, A.H. & A.W. Reed Ltd, Wellington, 1975.

"Report of the Commission of Inquiry into the sinking of T.E.V. Wahine", *Appendix to the Journal of the House of Representatives, Wellington, Vol IV.*, 1968.

Richard, L.S., *The Whaling Trade in New Zealand*, Minerva, Auckland, 1965.

Robinson, H., *A History of the Post Office in New Zealand*, Government Printer, Wellington, 1964.

Ross, J. O'C., *This Stern Coast*, A.H. & A.W. Reed Ltd., Wellington, 1969.

Ross, J.O'C., *The Lighthouses of New Zealand*, The Dunmore Press, Palmerston North, 1975.

Sharp, A., *The Voyages of Abel Janszoon Tasman*, Clarendon Press, Oxford, 1968,

Sinclair, K., *A History of New Zealand*, Penguin, Middlesex 1959.

Startup, W., with Illingworth, N., *The Kaikoura UFOs*, Hodder and Stoughton, Auckland, 1980.

Stevens, G.R., *New Zealand Adrift*, A.H. & A.W. Reed Ltd., Wellington, 1980.

Stevens, G.R., *Rugged Landscape*, A.H. & A.W. Reed Ltd., Wellington 1974.

Stott, B., *The Cook Strait Ferry Story*, Southern Press, Paremata, 1981.

Straubel, C.R., (ed.) *The Whaling Journal of Captain W.B. Rhodes*, Whitcombe and Tombs, Wellington, 1954.

Travers, W.T.L., *The Stirring Times of Te Rauparaha*, Whitcombe and Tombs, Auckland 1872.

Wakefield, E.J., *Adventure in New Zealand*, J. Murray, Christchurch, 1908.

Waters, S.D., *Official History of New Zealand in the Second World War, 1939-45 — The Royal New Zealand Navy*, Department of Internal Affairs, Wellington, 1956.

Waters, S.D., *German Raiders in the South Pacific*, Department of Internal Affairs, Wellington, 1949.

Westerskov, K., & Probert, K., *The Seas Around New Zealand*, A.H & A.W. Reed Ltd., Wellington, 1981.

Wilkinson, D., *Shipwreck — New Zealand Maritime Accidents, Southern Press, Paremata, 1974.*

Williams, A.L., Davey, E.L., & Gibson, J.N., *The 250 Kv d.c. Submarine Power-cable Interconnection*, New Zealand Engineers' Institute, Wellington, 1966.

Index

OTHER REED BOOKS

The Perano Whalers of Cook Strait Don Grady
This extensively illustrated book is an outstanding chronicle of a colourful era in New Zealand's history. The remarkable "inside story" of the Perano family and their whaling stations at the entrance to Tory Channel has at last been told, seventeen years after the end of whaling in New Zealand.

The Seas Around New Zealand Keith Probert and Kim Westerskov
For those who are interested in the sea and the marine life it supports, here is a volume of beauty and lasting fascination. More than 200 photographs, many of them in colour, together with a readable text by two marine biologists, look at the beaches, estuaries and harbours of the shoreline and the deeps and trenches of the open ocean around New Zealand.

A Century of Style: Great Ships of the Union Line, 1875-1976
N.H. Brewer
With contemporary accounts and more than 100 photographs, this book reconstructs the careers of thirty-six fine vessels of the Union Steam Ship Company's passenger fleet. They were the "queens of the sea" whose owners spared no expense in catering for passengers' comforts.
   A fleet list gives the vital statistics of all the passenger ships of the Union Line.

The Navy in New Zealand Grant Howard
Superbly illustrated with more than 100 photographs and peppered throughout with first hand accounts from those who have been involved in the Navy's history, this book brings to life an important part of New Zealand's seafaring heritage.

The Diver's Handbook Peter Rippon
A totally comprehensive guide to the many facets of underwater diving in New Zealand. Some of the outstanding features of this book are the detailed descriptions of more than 200 diving locations from the Three Kings Islands to Bluff and the colour and black and white photographs of many aspects of marine life and fish habitats.

COOK STRAIT
SEA FLOOR RELIEF

Scale 1:200,000   Angle from horizontal 21°
Sources: NZ62 Cape Palliser-Kaikoura, NZ01 Cook Strait Bathymetry

10
30
60
70
80
100
200
300
400
500
600
700
fathoms